Brain Matters

Translating Research
into Classroom Practice

2nd Edition

Patricia Wolfe

Brain Matters 2nd Edition

Translating Research into Classroom Practice

 ASCD   Alexandria, Virginia USA

ASCD®

1703 N. Beauregard St. • Alexandria, VA 22311-1714 USA
Phone: 800-933-2723 or 703-578-9600 • Fax: 703-575-5400
Web site: www.ascd.org • E-mail: member@ascd.org
Author guidelines: www.ascd.org/write

Gene R. Carter, *Executive Director;* Judy Zimny, *Chief Program Development Officer;* Nancy Modrak, *Publisher;* Scott Willis, *Director, Book Acquisitions & Development;* Julie Houtz, *Director, Book Editing & Production;* Jamie Greene, *Editor;* Georgia Park, *Senior Graphic Designer;* Mike Kalyan, *Production Manager;* Cynthia Stock, *Desktop Publishing Specialist*

All Web links in this book are correct as of the publication date below but may have become inactive or otherwise modified since that time. If you notice a deactivated or changed link, please e-mail books@ascd.org with the words "Link Update" in the subject line. In your message, please specify the Web link, the book title, and the page number on which the link appears.

PAPERBACK ISBN: 978-1-4166-1067-0   ASCD product #109073   n9/10
Also available as an e-book (see Books in Print for the ISBNs).

Quantity discounts for the paperback edition only: 10–49 copies, 10%; 50+ copies, 15%; for 1,000 or more copies, call 800-933-2723, ext. 5634, or 703-575-5634. For desk copies: member@ascd.org.

Library of Congress Cataloging-in-Publication Data

Wolfe, Pat.
   Brain matters : translating research into classroom practice / Patricia Wolfe.
— 2nd ed.
      p. cm.
   Includes bibliographical references and index.
   ISBN 978-1-4166-1067-0 (pbk. : alk. paper) 1. Learning, Psychology of. 2. Learning—Physiological aspects. 3. Brain. I. Title.
   LB1060.W63 2010
   370.15′23—dc22
                                                                                2010023025

20 19 18 17 16 15 14 13 12 11 10   1 2 3 4 5 6 7 8 9 10 11 12

To Alex and Kyra, my twin grandchildren,

who have provided me with a living laboratory

to view the wonders of the developing brain.

Brain Matters
Translating Research into Classroom Practice
2nd Edition

Preface and Acknowledgments

Some scientists and educators think it is too soon to apply brain research to the classroom because we don't yet have enough information. The field is so new, they say, and the discoveries in many cases are so narrow in their focus, that we run the risk of making false assumptions and perhaps even dangerous applications. Too often, the critics' caution is warranted. Educators have a history of jumping on bandwagons, and they often have accepted unproven theories as fact and applied strategies without careful analysis of their effectiveness.

We educators need to do a better job of critically analyzing the vast amount of neuroscientific information that arrives almost daily. Some of this information is reported in depth and is reliable, but other findings have been reduced to "sound bites" that invite misinterpretation. If we are to receive full benefit from this information (and be viewed as professionals), we need to develop a solid knowledge base that reflects an accurate understanding not only of the function and structure of the brain but of the procedures and protocols that were used in the research studies. We do not have to become scientific experts, but we do need to look critically at the sources of the information. Too often, the media report "facts" about brain functioning on the basis of one small study or, worse, from poorly conducted studies. The result is what we might call "neuromyths." Neuromyths are generally hypotheses that have been invalidated but nevertheless continue to leave traces. Many of these beliefs may have been disproved by science, but they continue to be stubbornly persistent and passed on into the public mind (OCED/CERI, 2007). Some common neuromyths include:

1. We only use 10 percent of our brains.

2. Listening to Mozart will make you smarter.

3. Some people are more "right brained," and others are more "left brained."

4. A young child's brain can only manage to learn one language at a time.

5. Everything important is determined by the age of three.

6. You can't change your brain.

7. The brain remembers everything it has ever experienced; forgetting is an absence of recall ability.

8. Gender differences outweigh individual differences when it comes to learning abilities.

9. There are brain differences by race.

10. Drinking plenty of water is important for brain functions.

While the skeptics' doubts are understandable, many scientists and educators are not willing to wait until all the research is in and we have absolute certainty before beginning to explore the possible educational implications and applications of research findings. In 2006, Harvard University introduced a new program in educational neuroscience, or neuroeducation, in addition to the *Mind, Brain and Education* journal to promote this new field. Many schools of higher education are offering majors and/or degrees in neuroeducation. Kurt Fischer of Harvard University and Mary Helen Immordino-Yang, assistant professor of psychology and education at the University of Southern California, are two leading scientists who believe that this new science of learning has the potential to transform educational practices (Fischer & Immordino-Yang, 2008). Science writer Sharon Begley agrees that, while the public often goes crazy "over preliminary findings that ultimately fall apart, it is naive to say that brain discoveries have no consequences for understanding how humans learn" (2008). Mary Immordino-Yang believes that there are general research principles that have implications for the way we teach math, reading, and other academic subjects (Patoine, 2007). Johns Hopkins School of Education has instituted the Neuro-education Initiative to foster dialogue among educators and brain science researchers and to develop joint research projects. It also offers K–12 teachers a 15-credit graduate Mind, Brain, and Teaching certificate. In August 2009, a Decade of the Mind symposium was held in Berlin, Germany to discuss how the latest scientific findings could be used to improve education. Scientists at the symposium were generally enthusiastic about findings that have the potential to inform teachers about the conditions in which our brains can be primed to learn best.

It is interesting to note that much of the research confirms what experienced educators have long known and used in their classrooms. What the research adds, at this point, is a partial understanding of why certain procedures or strategies work. As a result, we no longer have to operate intuitively but can begin to articulate and explain the rationale for what we do. Madeline Hunter said that the problem with teaching intuitively is that intuition is sterile; it can't be passed on (Hunter, 1991). For this reason, teachers have often had difficulty explaining their craft to others.

I am neither a neuroscientist nor a researcher in the technical sense of the words. I have spent my entire career teaching students at nearly every grade level and, for the past 20 years, working with teachers in nearly every grade level and subject area. My interest in brain research began in the early 1980s when I was a staff developer conducting workshops on effective teaching strategies. In searching for ways to understand why some strategies worked and others didn't, I began to find bits of information from sources that mentioned studies on the brain and how it acquires and stores data. This was exciting! Imagine having scientific data to back up the classroom activities we were sharing with teachers.

It wasn't quite as simple as I had imagined. First, the studies were difficult to locate, and when I found them, the language in which they were written was nearly foreign to me. I had no functional understanding of the brain, so the terms used had little meaning. Second, none of the research said anything about practical applications outside the medical field, let alone specific information about how the findings might apply to the field of education. It was several years before I found a book that discussed brain research in nonscientific terms: *The 3-Pound Universe* by Judith Hooper and Dick Teresi (1986). Today, my library contains nearly 100 books on the brain, many written for the general public by neuroscientists and some that actually discuss the learning process. There truly has been an explosion of information about the brain and a corresponding explosion of interest in it.

Although most people seem to be fascinated with information about how their brains work, teachers have probably shown the strongest interest in the research. For here, at last, may be answers to some of the problems we've struggled with for so long: Why do some students learn to read so quickly and others have such a difficult time figuring out the process? How can students sit through an excellent lesson on Monday, but on Tuesday act as if they have never heard the information before? Why are some seemingly simple concepts so difficult for some students to grasp, while others have no trouble with them?

We still don't have all the answers to these questions, but we are getting closer; and the possibility of having a better base of information about the teaching/learning process is something that educators long for. Although we are not scientists or researchers, we do work in a laboratory called the classroom, and we have a tremendous amount of knowledge and understanding of the teaching/learning process. We have gained this knowledge through experience and from research in educational psychology, cognitive psychology, and teaching methodology. It is up to us to decide how the research from all these sources (and now from neuroscience) best informs our practice.

Though I have tried to be accurate in my explanations, they are based on my own understanding of a complex subject. The implications and applications are (with a few exceptions) of my own creation, based on my own experiences and on my understanding of the research. This book does not address *all* the fascinating information about the brain; I have selected only those aspects of the research that I think have the most relevance to educators.

This book also contains more caveats than definitive answers because the field is relatively new and not all neuroscientists agree on the findings. I believe, however, that focusing staff development on the results of brain research will not only stimulate further interest and study, but it will also move us closer to a science of teaching and provide us with a more solid framework for understanding the complex and difficult job of teaching the human brain.

The book is divided into four parts. Part I is a mini-textbook on brain-imaging techniques and the anatomy and physiology of the brain. This part contains some rather technical areas, and readers may choose to skim it first and then refer back to it as needed when reading the rest of the book. (The glossary at the back of this book lists and defines terms that may be unfamiliar to some readers.) Part II (entirely new to this edition) focuses on brain development from birth through adolescence and looks at the role of exercise, sleep, nutrition, and technology on this development. Information about our increased understanding of neuroplasticity is also addressed. Part III introduces a model of how the brain processes information and explores some of the implications of this process for classroom practice. Part IV presents examples of teaching strategies that match how the brain learns best through projects, simulations, visuals, music, writing, and mnemonics.

Many people have contributed to what I know and have written in this book. Madeline Hunter was my master teacher, my friend, and my mentor; she helped me understand that there is both a science and an art to teaching. Marian Diamond shared her vast knowledge and wisdom and challenged me to read analytically and write accurately. Teachers from around the world have generously shared their practices and strategies with me. I am grateful to master teachers Marie Bañuelos, Jean Blaydes, Belinda Borgaard, Joan Carlson, Marilyn Hrycauk, Alice Jackson, James Johnson, Brian Jones, Ellen Ljung, Mary Martin, Ted Migdal, Janet Mendelsohn, Jane Politte, Bonnie Shouse, Ramona Smith, Marny Sorgen, Janet Steinman, Anne Westwater, and Alan Fisk-Williams, all of whose strategies appear in this book. Thanks also to my student Whitney Molin for sharing her very brain-compatible Civil War project. In addition, I am indebted to neuroscientist Elizabeth Jansen for taking the time to read the first edition of this book and generously offering suggestions to increase the accuracy and clarity of the content.

This new edition's accuracy and readability are due in large part to Jamie Greene, my excellent editor at ASCD. Special thanks go to Ron Brandt and Bob Sylwester, who convinced me that I could write even though I was certain I could not. I am very grateful for their encouragement, expert feedback, and support; they have been the best of coaches.

Part I

The Structure
and Function of the
Human Brain

*The more we understand the brain, the better
we'll be able to design instruction to match how
it learns best.*

The human brain is not the largest organ in the body. It
weighs only about three pounds, less than the skin covering your body. Yet this marvelous structure is the source of
all human behavior, simultaneously controlling a myriad
of unbelievably complex functions. Within a span of time
too short for humans to measure, it receives information
and relays it to the appropriate locations for processing. It
then allows you to act on these data by controlling the motor
output of your muscles. Your brain generates emotions and

lets you be aware of them. It is the source of cognition, memory, thoughts, and what we call intelligence. Your ability to speak and understand the speech of others comes from the brain. You don't have to worry about controlling your heart rate, respiration, breathing, hormone secretion, or immune system; the brain does this for you unconsciously and automatically.

In Part I of this book, we'll take a look at the major structures of the brain and the roles they play.

You may be wondering why you need all this biology. Wouldn't it be sufficient just to outline the general findings about how the brain learns without understanding the structures involved? Isn't it possible to have a general understanding of research findings and perhaps even apply the findings without really comprehending what is going on in the brain? Perhaps, but I believe that if we are to become critical consumers of neuroscience and cognitive science research, or even read reports of this research in the media with any understanding, we need to have a working knowledge of the human brain. Leslie Hart, in his book *Human Brain, Human Learning* (1983), talks about how little sense it would make to design a device to be used by human hands without being sure that you considered the nature of hands. Neither should we consider designing instruction to teach the human brain without taking into account the brain and how it functions. The more we understand the brain, the better we'll be able to design instruction to match how it learns best. Let us begin our exciting journey into the amazing universe within.

1

Opening the Black Box
of the Brain

Introduction

We've learned more about the brain and how it functions in the past three decades than in all of recorded history. What is largely responsible for this explosion of information? The answer lies primarily in improved technology. Many years ago, the only way brains could be studied was by the initially illegal method of autopsy. While studying the brain after death provided a fair amount of information—delineating the areas that allow us to produce and interpret speech, for example—it did little to increase our understanding of how information is processed and stored or why certain students have difficulty learning how to read. Today, imaging techniques allow us to look at the specific brain areas a person uses when recalling a noun versus a verb or when listening to music versus composing a song. We literally can look inside a brain and see which areas are most active while the person is engaged in various mental activities.

The chronology of brain imaging includes many methodologies that, although older and more primitive, remain viable today. As mentioned, the first method was autopsy, which has been in use since the days of Leonardo da Vinci and is still useful. Scientists have learned a great deal about what causes Alzheimer's disease,

We literally can look inside a brain and see which areas are most active while the person is engaged in various mental activities.

3

for example, by studying the brain tissue of those who died of the disease. Scientists have also learned much about the link between structure and function of the brain by studying people who have had brain injuries, strokes, or other traumas.

Animal studies have long been used to increase our understanding of how the brain works. This is possible because all mammalian brains function in a similar manner. Even though many of the methods used with animals cannot be applied to human subjects, we will see in later chapters that these studies often are useful to increase our understanding of human brain functioning.

Early Brain-Imaging Techniques

Today, the black box of the brain is beginning to share its secrets. With the advent of brain-imaging techniques, scientists no longer have to rely on autopsies or injuries to view the brain. Various new forms of technology have greatly increased scientists' ability to see—and sometimes change—what is happening inside the brain. The first of these technologies was developed in the 1800s, but the past 20 years have seen an amazing advance in the sophistication of ways to image the inner functioning of the human brain.

X-Rays

The journey to the present "electronic age" of imaging techniques began with the development of the X-ray, discovered in 1895. X-rays are high-frequency electromagnetic waves that easily penetrate nonmetallic objects. When they do, the atoms in the test object absorb some of the radiation, leaving the unabsorbed portion to strike and expose a photographic plate. The more dense objects show up lighter on the plate, while the less dense objects look darker. Although this process works well if we want to see whether a bone is broken (or what objects you are carrying in your luggage at the airport), it is of little use in depicting the brain and other parts of the body that are largely composed of soft tissue with little contrast in density between areas.

Computerized Axial Tomography (CAT) Scans

In the early 1970s, a technique was developed to increase the gradations in shades of gray from the approximately 25 of the normal X-ray to more than 200. This procedure is called computerized axial tomography (CAT) scanning. It uses X-ray technology but combines several two-dimensional images into a set of three-dimensional "slices." The images that result from a CAT scan look like a grayish X-ray but give a much clearer and more detailed picture of the brain. Neurologists and neurosurgeons routinely use these pictures to locate and determine the extent of tumors or lesions and the loss of tissue. As sophisticated and useful as they are, however, X-rays and CAT scans do not address the brain's function, which is the primary concern of those of us whose job it is to understand the learning process.

Monitoring the Brain's Energy Consumption

To understand how some of the newer imaging techniques work, we need a little background information on the brain's use of energy. Your brain is the "greediest" organ in the body; the resting brain uses oxygen and glucose at 10 times the rate of the rest of the body. Thus, even though the brain makes up less than 2.5 percent of total body weight, it is responsible for 20 percent of the body's energy consumption. The major sources of energy for the brain are oxygen and glucose, which is a simple carbohydrate. When certain areas of the brain are active, cells in those areas have a greater need for glucose and oxygen. Scientists realized that if they could trace the flow and consumption of either of these substances in the brain, they could determine which areas were working the hardest and therefore were responsible for certain actions. In the 1970s, scientists began

The resting brain uses oxygen and glucose at 10 times the rate of the rest of the body.

working to develop instruments that could construct an image of the brain by measuring the emissions given off as oxygen and glucose were consumed (Posner & Raichle, 1997). Positron emission tomography (PET) and magnetic resonance imaging (MRI) are two of the resulting brain-imaging methods.

Figure 1.1 shows a comparison of three images of a slice of brain obtained by CAT, PET, and MRI. Starting at 9 o'clock in the figure and moving clockwise are images obtained with standard photography, X-ray CAT, PET (most often created in color), and MRI.

Positron Emission Tomography (PET) Scan

PET is one of the most exciting advances in brain imaging. This technique allows scientists to picture the general anatomical areas

---

Figure 1.1
IMAGING TECHNIQUES

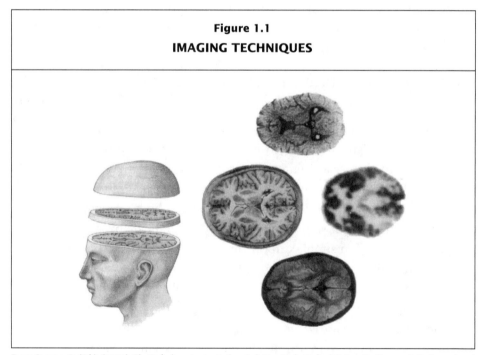

From Gregory, R. (Ed.). (1987). *The Oxford companion to the mind.* New York: Oxford University Press, p. 348. Reproduced by permission of Oxford University Press.

that become active while a person performs various mental tasks. The subject is injected with a small amount of radioactive glucose, which the blood carries to the brain. The subject is then placed in a PET scanner and asked to engage in a series of mental activities such as listening to words, saying words, or thinking about words. For example, a subject might be given a noun and asked to generate a verb that he or she associates with that noun. The brain areas responsible for these various activities will use much more of the radioactive glucose than other areas. When this happens, the radioactive material emits antimatter particles called positrons, which collide with the brain's electrons and produce gamma rays. These gamma rays travel through the skull and can be detected by sensors surrounding the head. From this information, a computer constructs colored images (tomographs). The areas of highest glucose use—and, therefore, of greatest activity—show up in white, red, and yellow, while areas of lesser use appear as green, blue, and purple (Posner & Raichle, 1997). Figure 1.2 is an example of a PET scan of a normal brain.

PET does have several drawbacks. Because it requires the injection of a radioactive tracer, PET is seldom used with children, and even an adult is generally allowed only one scanning session (usually 12 scans) a year. Another drawback is that neurons fire in milliseconds, but it requires about 40 seconds to obtain the data necessary to build an image of activity with PET. Therefore, how long an area remains active and the sequence of the activation of neural networks are not captured with this methodology. Finally, while a PET scan gives an excellent picture of overall activity in the brain, it does not show the specific area in which the activity is occurring.

Magnetic Resonance Imaging (MRI) Technology

A large part of the human body is water, which is made of magnetically polarized molecules. An MRI takes advantage of the fact that the hydrogen atoms in the body's water can be made to behave

Figure 1.2
PET SCAN

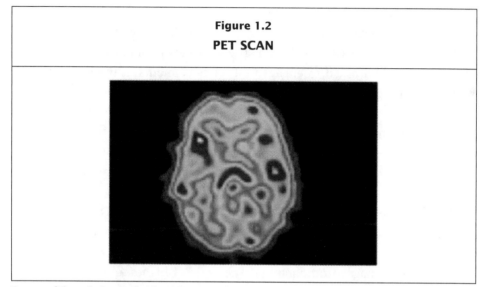

Courtesy of Phototake, Inc. Used with permission.

like tiny magnets if they are placed in a strong magnetic field. A beam of radio waves fired from an MRI scanner will make the water molecules resonate and give off radio signals of their own. These waves are detected by sensors, and the information is then assembled into an image by a computer (Greenfield, 1997). The imaging of specific organs by this technique far surpasses the detail produced by CAT because the spatial resolution is much finer. In brain research, MRI is widely used to locate tumors and lesions or to identify other areas of abnormalities. Figure 1.3 is a typical MRI scan of a normal brain.

Figure 1.4 compares MRI and PET images of the same area of the brain. The MRI is on the left, and the PET scan is on the right.

Functional Magnetic Resonance Imaging (fMRI) Technology

fMRI is one of the newest brain-imaging techniques to address some of the shortcomings of PET and MRI scans. The primary goal of fMRI is to show not only structures of the brain but also neural

---

Figure 1.3

MRI SCAN

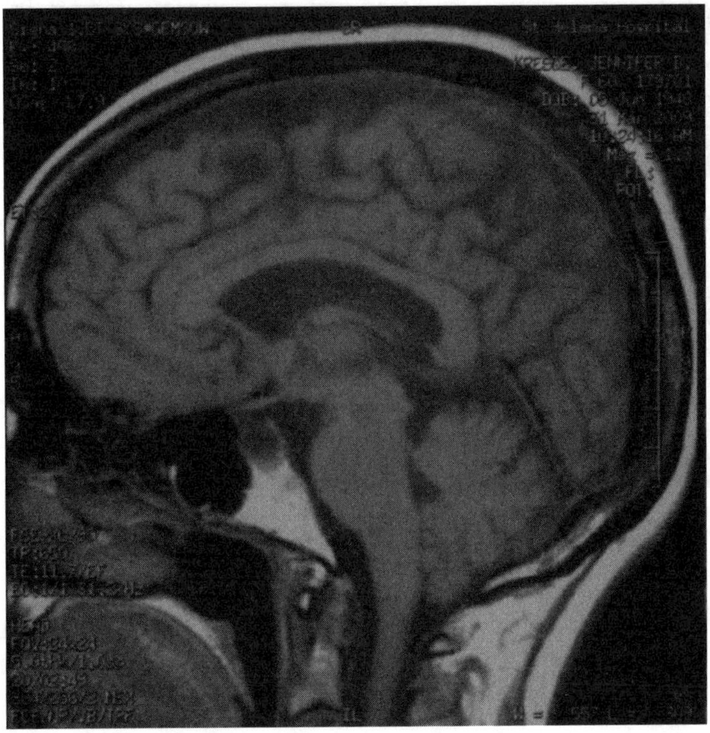

Courtesy of Jennifer Kresge. Used with permission.

activity. First used in England in 1986, fMRI scanning in the United States has expanded over the past few years, partly because MRI scanners now are widely available and partly because they are much less expensive than PET scanners.

fMRI works much like a standard MRI. The subject is asked to engage in an activity such as tapping a finger or listening to a sound. The parts of the brain that are responsible for these activities will cause certain neurons to fire. These neural impulses require energy,

Figure 1.4

COMPARISON OF MRI AND PET SCANS

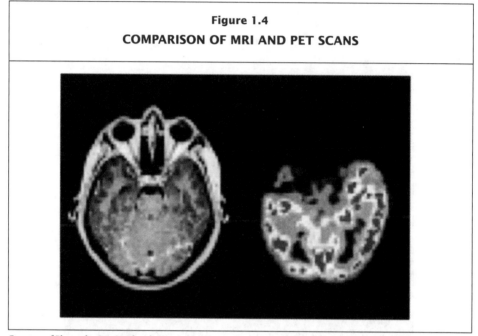

Courtesy of Phototake, Inc. Used with permission.

so more blood flows to these regions. The oxygen in the blood changes the magnetic field so that the radio signal emitted becomes more intense. The fMRI scanner detects and measures these changes in intensity and produces a computer image. By subtracting this image from an image of the brain at rest, the computer produces a detailed picture of the brain activity responsible for moving a finger or listening to a sound.

The scanner produces a rapid series of images, which results in a sort of brain activity "movie." The latest scanners can produce four images every second. The human brain reacts to a stimulus in about half a second, so the rapid scanning of fMRI can clearly show the ebb and flow of activity in various parts of the brain as it reacts to different stimuli or undertakes different tasks. A powerful fMRI can thus assemble a functional image of an entire brain in two to six seconds, compared with one minute for a PET scan. In addition, the fMRI can be repeated within seconds, while a PET takes nine minutes for the radiation to dissipate (Carter, 1998). fMRI is also less invasive than PET because it does not require the introduction of a radioactive substance into the body and can therefore be used with young children. Figure 1.5 is an fMRI scan of a normal brain showing motor activity of the left hand.

Electroencephalography (EEG)

Even though the speed of fMRI scanning is impressive, this technique cannot capture the much faster fluctuations in electrical activity that occur as neurons communicate with one another. In order to follow the moment-to-moment changes in neuronal activity, scientists must turn to other methods, such as EEG.

Figure 1.5
fMRI SCAN

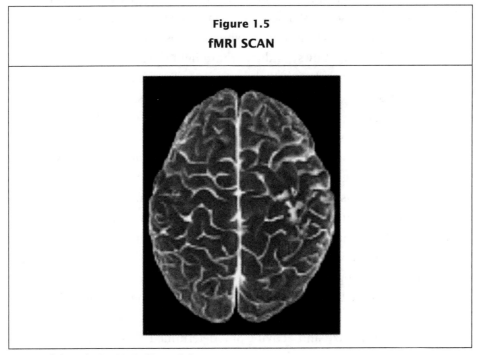

Courtesy of Phototake, Inc. Used with permission.

EEG is an imaging tool that has been in use for more than half a century. It measures electrical patterns created by the oscillations of neurons. On an ongoing basis, even during sleep, these electrical signals are constantly flashing throughout the brain. Body tissues conduct electricity well, so sensors placed on the scalp can detect impulses passing from the brain through the skull and the scalp. The electroencephalograph amplifies the signals and records them on a monitor or paper chart. You are probably familiar with the term *brain waves,* which is the name given to these various patterns of electrical activity.

Brain-wave frequency is measured by recording the number of cycles or oscillations per second. The more oscillations that occur per second, the higher the frequency of the wave. During wakefulness, the waves are small and fast and are called beta waves. Oscillations at this highest frequency occur during attention (beta I waves) and intense mental activity (beta II waves). Alpha waves oscillate a bit more slowly and occur when we close our eyes and relax. When we become drowsy and enter into light sleep, the waves slow down even more and are called theta waves. Entering into deep sleep produces large, slow waves known as delta waves.

Electroencephalography has provided a valuable tool for both researchers and clinicians, especially in the fields of epilepsy and sleep physiology, but it is also used in education-related issues such as language processing. Paula Tallal, language expert at Rutgers University, has used EEG along with MRI to determine that children with normal language skills have "lopsided" brains; that is, the left hemisphere is larger and more active than the right. This finding makes sense, as we know that in most people the left hemisphere specializes in language processing and the production of speech. Tallal has discovered, however, that children with language disorders often have balanced brains, with both left and right hemispheres nearly equal in size and activity. She determined that the underpowered left hemisphere was not fast enough to adequately process language at normal speeds (Tallal, 2000).

Magnetoencephalography (MEG)

The imaging technologies we have looked at thus far detail the structures of the brain or measure blood flow. MEG scanners work a little differently; they track the magnetic signals that neurons emit as they communicate. (Neurons produce a magnetic field every time they are active.) MEG scanners work in "real time" with no delay, contrary to PET scans, which take a second or two for blood flow to move in the brain. This type of scan allows scientists to study changes in the brain and determine which areas are active each millisecond. Since MEG scans do not show brain structures, combining them with other technologies—such as fMRI—increases their accuracy and reliability.

Event-Related Potential (ERP)

The data obtained from EEG technology are gross changes in state. For example, the data from EEG look much the same no matter what the person is doing: listening to music, reading, or watching TV. To detect more specific, fine-grained changes in mental activity, researchers sometimes use event-related potentials (ERPs). These signals are obtained by time-locking the recording of an EEG to a specific event, such as a subject reading a word, listening to a musical note, or viewing a photograph. In other words, raw EEG is made up of all brain activity recorded from the scalp at a particular point in time, while the ERP records a specific part of that activity.

Single-Photon Emission Computed Tomography (SPECT)

SPECT is a brain-imaging technique similar to a PET scan. Both use radioactive tracers; however, in a PET scan the tracer is absorbed into the tissues, while SPECT tracers stay in the blood stream, limiting the images to the areas where blood flows. SPECT scans are less expensive than PET scans, but the resolution is less refined. They are often used to view how blood flows through arteries and veins in the brain and can detect reduced blood flow to injured sites.

On the Horizon

Several newer imaging techniques promise to give us even more detailed pictures of the brain and how it functions. Among these are near infrared spectroscopy (NIRS) and Voxel-based lesion-symptom mapping (VLSM). Multimodal imaging, which combines two or more techniques, is becoming increasingly popular.

Brain-imaging techniques have already been used to delineate the neural differences that exist between dyslexics and nonimpaired readers (Shaywitz, 1999). Another area of great concern to parents and teachers, attention deficit hyperactivity disorder (ADHD), hopefully will also become better understood through brain imaging. Early studies support the idea that an underlying neurological dysfunction is linked to the behaviors of children and adults with this disorder. Attempts to understand autism, eating disorders, obsessive-compulsive disorder (OCD), and other problems that affect students' school performance are the focus of numerous current neuroscientific studies.

Interpreting Brain Imaging for Educational Purposes

Will the day come when educators have ready access to brain-imaging machines to assist them in diagnosing reading or attention problems? It may not be too far-fetched to think so; but until that happens, our best bet is to educate ourselves about how these various methodologies work and to understand what they can and cannot do for us. Rarely does neuroscience prove that a particular classroom strategy works, but the information coming from the neurosciences certainly can provide a more informed basis for the decisions we make in our schools and classrooms.

For example, PET scans of a reader show that much more frontal lobe activity occurs when the subject reads silently than when he or she is reading aloud to others. Activity in the frontal lobes often indicates higher-level thinking. On the other hand, the scan of a student reading aloud glows brightly in the motor area of the brain that governs speech but shows little activity elsewhere. One way to interpret these scans is that comprehension is greater when one reads silently. Do these scans prove that students should never read aloud? Of course they don't. Armed with this information, however, teachers are able to make more informed decisions about how to balance silent and oral reading both to obtain diagnostic information on decoding problems and to enhance comprehension of what is being read.

Synapse Strengtheners

1. Skim back over this chapter, and then close the book and see if you can explain the major differences between a PET scan and an fMRI scan.

2. If you are reading this book as part of a study group, ask each person in the group to identify one common student learning problem and speculate which brain-imaging technique might provide the most information toward understanding the problem and why.

3. Using the scans in Figure 1.1, explain to someone unfamiliar with the processes how these images were obtained and what they show.

4. Explain how new brain-imaging techniques affect our thinking about educational practice but do not necessarily prove that certain strategies work.

2

Brain Anatomy—A Short Course: Neurons and Subcortical Structures

Imagine that you are pushing a grocery cart in the produce section of your local supermarket. As you see yourself walking down the wide, well-lit aisle, visualize the neatly ordered bins, each containing a different fruit or vegetable. Can you see the vivid dark purple of the eggplant? Can you smell the ripe peaches? Imagine yourself reaching the bin containing the cabbages. Pick up a big solid head and place it in the hanging scale. You read the numbers on the scale and see that your head of cabbage weighs about three pounds.

Your ability to mentally reproduce the above scenario—complete with all the sights, tactile sensations, smells, and sounds—is the result of the interaction of millions of neurons in a brain weighing about the same as that large head of cabbage. Isn't this an amazing organ that allows you not only to experience the world outside its bony casing but also to be aware of and discuss the experiences? To start to understand it, let's begin our tour of the human brain by looking at its basic structural and functional unit, the cell.

Starting at the Beginning: The Cells

The entire body is composed of cells. The muscles, lining of the intestines, bones, skin, and brain are all made up of billions of these basic units. Each cell or group of cells has a specific job to perform.

The cells that constitute the central nervous system (CNS) compose the brain and the spinal cord; along with the endocrine system, they provide most of the control functions for the body. Two types of cells make up the CNS: neurons and glial cells. Let's look first at the basic functional unit of the CNS, the neuron.

Neurons

Neurons, found primarily in the brain and in the spinal cord (the central nervous system), number approximately 100 billion. They differ from most of the other cells in the body in two major ways. First, with some exceptions, they do not appear to regenerate on a regular, programmed basis, as do most other cells. Nearly all the cells in your body (skin cells, blood cells, the cells that form the lining of your stomach) continually renew themselves every few days or months. This is why your skin heals when you cut yourself and why when you break a leg, the fracture will usually mend if the bone is set correctly. However, if neurons are destroyed through a stroke or other trauma, they do not regenerate in the same manner.

Luckily, there's good news on this horizon. Scientists have long believed that humans are born with all the neurons they will ever have, but this long-held scientific theory has been overturned. Several studies have shown that the adult brain does generate new neurons (referred to as neurogenesis) in the hippocampal dentate gyrus (important for memory and learning) and in the olfactory system. Many of these newborn cells die shortly after their birth, but a number of them become functionally integrated into the surrounding brain tissue. The significance of the function of adult neurogenesis remains to be determined; however, it certainly lends support to the argument that the brain is able to change itself. In Chapter 7, we'll discuss the possible effects of exercise and stress on neurogenesis (Gould, Reeves, Graziano, & Gross, 1999; Kempermann & Gage, 1999).

The second major way that neurons differ from other types of cells is in their ability to transmit information. Neurons "communicate" with one another and form networks by means of electrical and chemical signals. To do this, they need a different design from other cells (which is a third way in which they are different). In Greek, the word *neuron* means "string." In Figure 2.1 you can see how this unusual-looking cell got its name.

Neurons come in several different shapes. Some are shaped like a pyramid, and others look something like a giant sea fan. Regardless of their shape, most neurons are composed of a cell body—or soma—which contains the nucleus, short projections called dendrites (derived from the Greek word for "tree," *dendra*), and a single axon, which is usually covered by a fatty substance called myelin.

Figure 2.1
THE NEURON

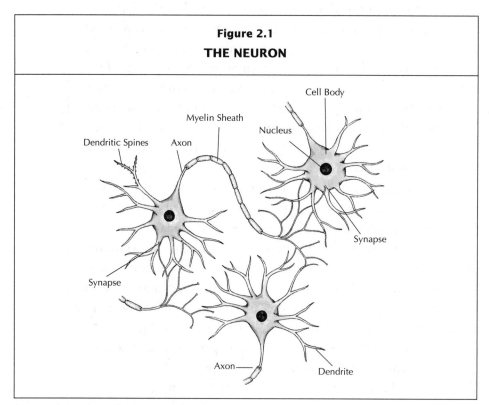

Courtesy of ArtWorks. Used with permission.

Many neurons have between 6,000 and 10,000 dendrites. In fact, dendrites are so numerous, they account for 90 percent of the cell's surface. The job of the dendrites is to *receive* information from other cells. The main job of the axon is to *send* information to other cells. The end of the axon splits into branches, each of which ends in an axon terminal or bulb. Neurons communicate electrochemically by passing messages at the junction (known as the synapse) between axon terminals and spines on dendrites or cell bodies.

Though adult neurogenesis is now accepted by most scientists, it has long been established that most new cell growth occurs from conception to birth. It is during this time that neurons (1) generate from undifferentiated stem cells, (2) migrate from the site where they were generated to their final positions, (3) aggregate into distinct brain regions, and (4) begin to make connections among one another. If a child's brain contains approximately 100 billion neurons at birth, and it already has made trillions of connections, then it stands to reason that the fetal brain has been busy producing all those cells.

In the embryonic brain, cells divide to generate new neurons at the astonishing rate of 250,000 per minute (Cowan, 1979). Hundreds of billions of neurons are created—many more, we will see, than are needed. Next, in a process known as *migration*, neurons travel to their designated places by aggregating into layers, clusters, and tracts, forming the myriad structures that make up the brain. As soon as this happens, the cells start forming random synaptic connections—again, more than are needed. If neurons fail to form enough synaptic contact points or migrate to the wrong place, they are pruned away in a process known as *apoptosis*, or programmed cell death. In her book *Magic Trees of the Mind*, researcher and neuroanatomist Marian Diamond estimates that approximately half of the neurons that have been generated are pared away before birth by this natural cell death (Diamond, Hopson, & Diamond, 1998). The purpose of apoptosis seems to be not only to eliminate neurons that

In the embryonic brain, cells divide to generate new neurons at the astonishing rate of 250,000 per minute!

don't make the right connections but also to strengthen the connections that are left and perhaps prevent the brain from becoming "overstuffed" with its own cells. Incomplete apoptosis may account for the astonishing abilities of savants, as well as being a causal factor in their deficiencies in other areas (Carter, 1998).

After brain cells have been created, migrated, and "pruned," neurons spontaneously start firing without any external stimuli, making connections and, in a sense, trying out their circuits to make certain that they work. Another pruning process will take place, although this time it is a whittling away of connections, not neurons. It isn't until the beginning of the third trimester that a fetus's sensory organs are mature enough to react to stimuli outside the womb. Susan Greenfield notes in her book *The Human Brain* that it is also around seven months in utero that convolutions begin to appear in the outer covering of the brain (1997). At this point, a fetus can respond to detectable light levels and sound. Yes, a fetus can "learn" before birth! A baby is born able to distinguish its mother's voice and odor from others, and it can even recognize music it heard before birth (Davis, 1997).

Glial Cells

As amazing as the formation of neurons and their networks is, this process could not take place without the assistance of the helper cells in the brain, the glial cells, also known as neuroglia, derived from the Greek word meaning "glue," which reflects a mistaken assumption that these cells in some way hold the neurons together. Glial cells, which outnumber neurons 10 to 1, are quite different from neurons. The major distinction is that they do not participate directly in electrical signaling as neurons do, although some of their supporting functions help in the process.

One of the primary roles that glial cells play is in the development of the fetal brain. Some of these cells, the radial glia, physically travel from their point of origin ahead of neurons and form temporary scaffolding for neurons to climb. Special adhesion molecules on the glial cells guide the neurons as they migrate to their predetermined place in one of the six layers of the cortex, the outer covering of the brain (discussed in more detail later in this chapter). According to Arnold Scheibel, former director of the Brain Research Institute at the University of California, Los Angeles, the migration process can go awry and may produce conditions that show up later in childhood development, such as certain kinds of epilepsy, dyslexia, and perhaps schizophrenia (2000).

Another type of glial cell, the macrophage, assists in removing the debris of dead cells following damage to brain areas. Still other glial cells, the oligodendrocytes, play a role in neural maturation, determining when neurons are ready to function efficiently. These cells lay down myelin, a laminated wrapping around some (but not all) axons, which speeds electrical impulses down these extensions. Myelin is light in color and accounts for what is commonly known as the "white matter" of the brain.

A fourth type of glial cell, the astrocyte, is the most abundant glial cell in the brain. Astrocytes have a star-like appearance, and their main job is to maintain an appropriate chemical environment around the neuron. They act as a sort of sponge for mopping up potentially toxic chemicals. Astrocytes also play a role in keeping certain substances away from brain tissue by helping to form and maintain the blood–brain barrier.

Central Nervous System Structures That Operate at the Unconscious Level

A simplified look at the brain would reveal two major divisions: (1) a relatively small subcortical system that operates at an unconscious level, processing basic survival tasks; and (2) a much larger cortex that processes the conscious decisions and responses we make to novel situations not covered by the subcortical systems. The structures under the cortex alert us to a danger or opportunity, while the cortex selects the most appropriate response strategy. As we look at the brain and how it functions, we will see how interconnected these two systems are. First, let's look at the individual structures that make up these two major divisions.

Early in the brain's development, neurons begin to aggregate into regions. In a four-week-old embryo, the human brain is a series of bulges at one end of a neural tube. These bulges develop into three hindbrain regions, one midbrain area, and two forebrain areas. From these six divisions will develop the 40 or so major structures of the brain, as well as all the smaller nuclei, ganglia, nerves, pathways, and canals that are essential for the CNS to function normally. (The actual number of structures depends on how you organize them. The visual system alone processes 30 tasks, and the cortex has been divided into 104 regions called Brodmann areas.) Let's look at the lowermost part of the CNS, the spinal cord. Each of the following structures is shown in Figure 2.2.

Spinal Cord

Figure 2.2 depicts an internal view of the brain. Not shown in this figure is a large bundle of nerve fibers attached to the brain-stem that runs from the base of the brain down to the middle of the back and is about 18 inches long (in an adult) and slightly thinner than an index finger: the spinal cord. Structurally, the spinal cord is an extension of the brain. During embryonic development, both develop from the same neural tube; the brain forms from the top of the tube, and the spinal cord, from the lower portion.

The chief job of the spinal cord is to carry messages between the brain and the body.

The chief job of the spinal cord is to carry messages between the brain and the body. It does this by way of two major cortico-spinal tracts, the ascending pathway and the descending pathway. The ascending pathway takes in sensory information such as pain, temperature, light, and touch from the body's sensory receptors and relays it to the specific brain regions that process these different types of sensations. This pathway also carries sensory messages about the

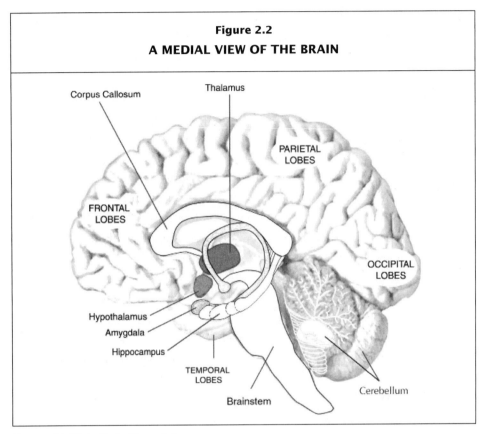

Figure 2.2

A MEDIAL VIEW OF THE BRAIN

Corpus Callosum

Thalamus

PARIETAL
LOBES

FRONTAL
LOBES

OCCIPITAL
LOBES

Hypothalamus

Amygdala

Hippocampus

TEMPORAL
LOBES

Brainstem

Cerebellum

Courtesy of ArtWorks. Used with permission.

position of joints and muscles to the brainstem for unconscious assessment of body position and posture. The descending pathway works in the opposite direction, carrying motor nerve signals from the brain to the body's muscles to cause movement.

The spinal cord is also able to carry out some reflex actions on its own, independent of the brain. Examples of reflexes are the knee jerk and pulling a hand away from a hot stove. The importance of the spinal cord is strikingly evident when damage to the cord occurs through either injury or disease. Depending on the location and severity of the damage, the effects can range from weakness in the extremities to total paralysis, loss of reflexes, and loss of sensation (Greenfield, 1996).

Brainstem

The brainstem, located at the base of the brain where the spinal cord begins, is one of the oldest parts of the brain in terms of evolution. It is made up of three main parts: the midbrain (upper end), the pons (center area), and the medulla oblongata (lower end). The brainstem is sometimes referred to as the reptilian brain, probably because its basic structure is rather like the entire brain of present-day reptiles. Given this fact, it isn't difficult to guess that its primary purpose is to ensure the body's survival. The brainstem is largely in control of autonomic functions—those functions not under our conscious control but essential for our survival. The necessity of the unconscious workings of the brainstem is obvious if you consider what your life would be like if you had to consciously control your breathing, heartbeat, and blood pressure—you would be able to do little else.

The brainstem accomplishes these feats by means of a network of neurons and fibers known as the reticular formation (RF), which occupies the core of the brainstem. The RF receives information from all over your body. Every time your body moves, some adjustment of heart rate, blood pressure, or breathing rate is needed to compensate for the changes that have occurred. The cells in the RF are in charge of regulating these basic life-support systems. In addition to controlling these vital systems, the RF contains other cells that control some eyeball movements, pupil constriction, stomach reflexes, facial expressions, salivation, and taste. The RF is fairly mature at birth; a newborn's brainstem is already able to regulate heart rate, blood pressure, and respiration (Diamond, Hopson, & Diamond, 1998).

An equally important function of the reticular system is the control of awareness levels. The RF, neurons in the thalamus, and other neurons from various sensory systems of the brain make up the

---

The necessity of the unconscious nature of the workings of the brainstem is obvious if you consider what your life would be like if you had to consciously control your breathing, heartbeat, or blood pressure; you would be able to do little else.

reticular activating system (RAS). This system receives input from the body and changes the level of cell excitation to meet the changing conditions in the environment. For example, if stimulation is decreased by cutting down sensory input, such as putting a person in a dark, quiet room, the RAS decreases the level of excitation in the cortex and the level of consciousness is changed; the person may actually go to sleep. When the body awakens from sleep, the RAS increases the level of excitation in the cortex and the person becomes aware, or conscious (Binney & Janson, 1990). Whether we are drowsy, asleep, awake, hypervigilant, or unconscious, brainstem activity continues to keep our life-support systems functioning. Severe damage to the RAS can result in a permanent coma.

The RAS also serves as an effective filter for the thousands of stimuli constantly bombarding the sensory receptors, allowing you to focus on relevant stimuli. It excludes background information and "tunes out" distractions or trivial sensory information, such as awareness of clothes on your body or the feeling of your back against a chair. It is the RAS that allows you to fall asleep on a plane but awakens you suddenly when the plane's engines change pitch.

A final, important role of the brainstem is in the production of many of the brain's chemical messengers. These chemicals come from nuclei (close-knit groups of nerve cell bodies) located in the brainstem and are projected widely to all other parts of the brain. We'll look more closely at their function in Chapter 4.

Although it might appear that the functioning of the brainstem, and especially the RAS, is rather primitive and less important than more complex structures such as the large cerebral hemispheres with their intellectual capacities, this is not true. In fact, because it is a rather small structure, damage to the brainstem is highly life threatening, whereas damage to the much larger cortex may have relatively minor consequences, depending on the location and extent of the damage (Gazzaniga, Ivry, & Mangun, 1998). You could say that this small area of the brain holds the key to life itself.

Cerebellum

Moving up in the system, we encounter the cerebellum at the back of the brain. Its name is derived from Latin and means "little brain." It is a two-lobed, deeply folded structure overlaying the top of the brain stem, just under the occipital lobes, in the posterior portion of the brain. The cerebellum, like the brainstem, is primitive in evolutionary terms and has changed little over thousands of years.

In all mammals, the cerebellum is the key to balance, maintenance of body posture, and coordination of muscle function. Because humans have an almost unlimited repertoire of movement, the cerebellum is large, accounting for 11 percent of the brain's weight. From birth to age 2, the cerebellum grows faster than does the cerebral cortex. By age 2, it has almost reached its adult size (Binney & Janson, 1990). During this early period, children learn basic movements, such as walking and grasping. The cerebellum stores these movement patterns in neural networks and then, throughout life, calls upon them whenever they are needed.

In all mammals the cerebellum is the key to coordination of balance, maintenance of body posture, and coordination of muscle actions.

Coordinated movements, such as walking, lifting a glass, or writing a word, are activities that we often take for granted. The acquisition of the skilled movements involved in these activities begins under the conscious control of the cortex. Though the cortex can plan and initiate movements, it does not have the neural circuitry needed to calculate the sequences of muscular contractions necessary for the movements. That task falls to the cerebellum. When the cerebellum receives information (in about 1/50th of a second) that the motor cortex has begun to initiate a movement, it computes the contribution that various muscles will have to make to perform that movement and sends the appropriate messages to those muscles. The action has begun.

Throughout the action, the cerebellum continuously monitors and modifies the activity in the muscles, making the changes necessary for smooth completion of the action. These complex maneuvers are also necessary when a person is sitting or standing. Information comes into the cerebellum not only from the motor cortex, spinal cord, and muscles but also from the organs of balance in the vestibular area of the brain. This allows the cerebellum to continually modify activity in the motor pathways essential for maintaining the body in an upright position.

If you ever learned to drive a car, play the piano, or touch type, you probably remember what a long, laborious process it was and how many hours of practice it took to become proficient. If you still do any one of these activities today, it is likely that you do them so unconsciously you would have difficulty explaining the processes involved to someone else. You can thank your cerebellum for this ability.

What happens over time as the movements involved in playing the piano or driving a car are repeated over and over? We all know from personal experiences that the skills become increasingly automatic and that less conscious thought is needed to accomplish the task. For example, have you ever driven your car over a familiar route, arrived at your destination, and realized that you were not aware of having driven there? The brain allows us to engage in complex motor activities with almost no conscious awareness of the task.

With proficiency, the cerebellum takes over much of the control, leaving the conscious mind free to do and think about other things. How this occurs is not totally understood, although scientists have advanced several theories. One neurobiologist, W. T. Thach, from the Washington University in St. Louis School of Medicine, suggests that the cerebellum may link a behavioral context to a motor response. He proposes that, as you repeatedly practice a motor response (such as riding a bicycle), the occurrence of the context (getting on the bicycle) triggers the occurrence of the response (riding the bicycle) (Thach, 1996). In other words, the linkages between the motor areas of the cortex and the cerebellum permit an experiential context to automatically evoke an action.

Recently, researchers have also become interested in the functions of the cerebellum that do not deal specifically with motor functions. Blood flow and anatomical studies have shown close links between the frontal cortex and the cerebellum. Perhaps we'll find that the cerebellum plays a role in cognition (such as planning or imagining movements), as well as in the movements themselves.

Thalamus

Deep within the core of the brain, just above the brainstem, are two walnut-sized, plum-shaped structures (joined by a sort of bridge) that play a critical role in regulating perception and the body's vital functions. Named for the Greek word for "chamber" or "inner room," this brain structure is in a strategic position to act as a relay station to direct the flow of information between the sense organs and the cortex. It has been called the "gateway" to the cortex, because nearly all input from the sensory organs travels first to nerve cell bodies in the thalamus, where the signals are sorted and sent to the receiving areas on the cortex. The one exception is the olfactory system, which sends its stimuli directly to the cortex.

Hypothalamus

Below the thalamus is the thumbnail-sized hypothalamus. (*Hypo* means "below," so the name *hypothalamus* tells us that this organ is below the thalamus.) It is a critical part of the autonomic system, and, along with the pituitary gland, it controls functions necessary for homeostasis, maintaining the normal state of the body. For example, when the body gets too hot, the hypothalamus increases the perspiration rate. When the body temperature falls below normal, the rate of heat loss is slowed by contraction of the capillaries and shivering ensues, which produces a small amount of heat. The hypothalamus is also the control center for the stimuli that underlie eating and drinking. For example, if you have too much salt in your blood, the hypothalamus signals you to drink water to dilute the concentration of salt; if there is too much sugar in your blood, it suppresses your appetite. The hypothalamus also plays a role in regulating sex drive, sleep, aggressive behavior, and pleasure (Binney & Janson, 1990).

The hypothalamus plays an additional role—one that is essential for survival. If you've ever been frightened by a snake or a spider (or anything else, for that matter) and found your heartbeat increase, palms get sweaty, and respiration increase, your hypothalamus is at work. It is this organ that controls the body's "fight-or-flight" response. We'll look more at this response and how it affects learning in Chapter 9.

Amygdala

Another brain structure highly involved in the fight-or-flight response, and located near the thalamus and hypothalamus, is the amygdala. If the brain could be said to have an alarm system, it would be composed of these two almond-shaped structures (*amygdala* is the Greek word for "almond") deep in the center of the brain. (It is also known as the amygdaloid complex because it is composed of three subdivisions, each connected to different brain structures or pathways.) The amygdala could also be called the psychological sentinel of the brain because it plays a major role in the control of emotions.

Various groups of cells in the amygdala are designed for different roles. One group links to the olfactory bulb and another to the cortex, especially the sensory association areas. Still another group links the amygdala to the brainstem and the hypothalamus. All incoming sensory data, except smell, travel first to the thalamus, which relays the information to the appropriate sensory-processing areas of the cortex. At the same time that the thalamus is sending information to the cortex, it sends the same information to the amygdala for evaluation. If the amygdala determines that the stimuli are potentially harmful, it triggers the hypothalamus, which in turn sends hormonal messages to the body, thus creating the physical changes that ready the body for action: heightened blood pressure, increased heart rate, and muscle contractions.

The amygdala could be called the psychological sentinel of the brain because it plays a major role in the control of emotions.

How does the amygdala "know" that a particular stimulus signals danger? There appear to be two sources of this "knowledge." One way that the amygdala assesses the emotional relevance of a stimulus is by checking with the hippocampus, the structure that allows one to store conscious memories. (See the next section for more detailed information on the hippocampus.) If, for example, the particular stimulus is a curved shape, the amygdala, in checking with the hippocampus, may receive a message back that the curved shape looks like a snake and that snakes are potentially dangerous. This lets the amygdala know that it had better trigger the physiological processes necessary to keep you from being bitten.

However, the hippocampus does not seem to be responsible for all memory acquisition. Research on conditioned fear in animals has led to the broader hypothesis that the amygdala lays down unconscious memories in much the same way that the hippocampus lays down conscious ones (LeDoux, 1996). This suggests that the amygdala forms emotional memories that can trigger responses without the corresponding conscious recollections that tie the responses to a particular event. This may be the source of panic attacks and seemingly unreasonable phobias (Carter, 1998).

Hippocampus

Although its name is derived from the Latin word for seahorse, the hippocampus looks more like two paws curving toward each other. Without it, you would not be able to remember where you parked your car, or anything else in your immediate past, as soon as you stopped giving it your attention. The hippocampus not only holds memory of your immediate past; it is also the organ that eventually dispatches the memory to the cortex, where it is stored in what is called long-term memory.

According to Joseph LeDoux, professor at New York University and author of *The Emotional Brain*, the hippocampus appears to be crucial for you to be able to remember events in your immediate past, maybe even for a few years. Gradually (over years), the hippocampus relinquishes its control over the memory to the cortex, where the memory appears to remain, perhaps for a lifetime, in long-term memory (LeDoux, 1996). In other words, once an episode is fully encoded in long-term memory, the hippocampus apparently is no longer needed for it to be retrieved. People who have suffered serious damage to the hippocampus cannot recall anything in their immediate past; neither can they encode any new memories. An example of this deficit is vividly described in a famous case study of a man known as H. M. (Hilt, 1995).

In 1953, when H. M. was 27 years old, doctors performed radical surgery on his brain in an attempt to end the convulsive epileptic attacks he had been having since he was 16. The physicians removed large regions of both temporal lobes—brain tissue containing the major sites of his disease. Medically, the surgery was successful. H. M.'s seizures could now be controlled with medication. Because the hippocampus was included in the tissue that was removed, however, H. M. essentially lost his ability to form conscious, long-term memories of episodes or factual information. (Such types of memories are called *episodic memory* and *declarative memory*. They stand in contrast to *procedural memory*, which does not require conscious recall. We'll look more closely at the various forms of memory in Part III.) H. M. died in 2009, but when he was alive, he essentially "lived" in 1953, the year of his surgery. He could remember events that occurred up to about two years before his surgery, but he had no memory of the events of the following 56 years. Brenda Milner (see Hilt, 1995), at the Montreal Neurological Institute, worked with H. M. extensively during this period, yet he had little idea of who she was.

Interestingly, H. M. was able to learn new motor-driven skills, such as mirror writing or puzzle solving, but he did not remember learning them. (These are examples of procedural memory, which does not require processing in the hippocampus.)

Once an episode is fully encoded in long-term memory, it apparently can be retrieved without the aid of the hippocampus.

Synapse Strengtheners

1. Select one of the major structures of the brain (such as the hippocampus) and, without looking back at the material, write a brief summary of where it is in the brain and what it does. Then go back and reread the information and see how well you recalled it.

2. Suppose, after reading this chapter, you are talking to a fellow educator who wants to know why one should know the names of the structures in the brain and what they do. What would you say to that person?

3. If you are reading this book as part of a study group, ask each member to select one or two major structures in the brain and prepare a presentation for the rest of the group on the location and function of the structure(s).

4. Plan one or more lessons to teach your students the parts of their brains.

3

Brain Anatomy—A Short Course: The Cortex

Thus far, all the structures we have been discussing operate at an unconscious level. Michael Gazzaniga, professor of psychology and director of the SAGE Center for the Study of the Mind at the University of California, Santa Barbara, emphasizes that most mental processes controlling and contributing to our conscious experience occur *outside* our conscious awareness (Gazzaniga, Ivry, & Mangun, 1998). We are consciously aware of only a small part of what is going on inside our brain. Such structures as the brainstem, cerebellum, amygdala, and hippocampus play critical roles in our ability to process information and form memories (and eventually to become aware of them), but we are not *consciously* aware of the activities of these structures. We now turn our attention to the part of the brain that allows us to be aware, to recognize, and to talk about how we're feeling and what we're thinking—the structures that operate at the conscious level.

We are consciously aware of only a small part of what is going on inside our brain.

The Cerebral Cortex

Covering the cerebrum (the Latin word for "brain") is a thin layer known as the cerebral cortex, or neocortex—the "new cortex." The word *cortex* is derived from the Latin word for "bark"; to a degree, the cortex resembles the bark of a tree. It is wrinkled, it is about 1/32- to

1/4-inch thick, and it is the so-called gray matter of the brain. The cerebral cortex is made up of six layers of cells, their dendrites, and some axons, and it accounts for about three-fourths of the brain's weight. If the cerebral cortex were taken off the brain and stretched flat, it would be about the size of a pillow case or the page of a newspaper. Studies of human brains by neurosurgeons, neurologists, and neuroscientists have shown that different areas (lobes) of the cerebral cortex have separate functions. Let's look at the four main lobes, which take their names from the skull bones they underlie, and at their major roles in processing information.

If the cortex were taken off the brain and stretched flat, it would be about the size of a pillow case or the page of a newspaper.

Occipital Lobes

Located at the lower central back of the brain are the occipital lobes, the primary brain centers for processing visual stimuli. (See Figure 3.1.) Covered by cortical tissue, this area of the brain is also called the visual cortex. It is split into many subdivisions, each playing a role in processing visual data coming into the brain from the outside world. (Recall that visual stimuli are first relayed through the thalamus.) When stimuli reach the visual cortex, they are first processed in the primary visual perception area, where millions of neurons are further organized into areas designed to process different aspects of vision. Through intensive work in mapping the visual cortex, scientists have discovered motion-sensitive cells, color-sensitive cells, and straight-line cells. There are also areas for general scanning, stereo vision, depth, distance, and object detection (Carter, 1998). Michael Gazzaniga, in the book *Cognitive Neuroscience*, reports that between 30 and 35 of these visual areas have been identified in the occipital lobes of monkeys (Gazzaniga et al., 1998).

Once the incoming information has been assembled in these areas (i.e., it has been perceived), it then travels to the secondary, or visual association, area, which compares the information with what you've seen before and lets you know whether you are seeing an orange or a tree.

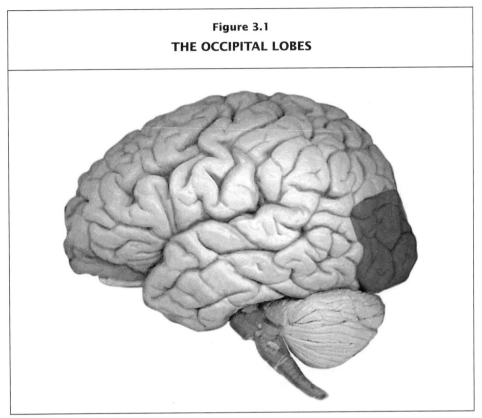

Figure 3.1
THE OCCIPITAL LOBES

Courtesy of ArtWorks. Used with permission.

Note that two people can look at the same thing and focus on something different, or "see" different things. What you attend to visually is the coordinated functioning of several brain systems. First, the visual perception area allows perception of the actual object. Your visual cortex then communicates with other brain systems to determine what visual information you have stored previously. Visual stimuli do not become meaningful until the sensory perceptions are matched with previously stored cognitive associations. In addition, we often prime our brains to pay attention to certain stimuli over others, such as looking for a friend in a crowd of

Two people can look at the same thing and focus on something different, or "see" different things.

people or finding a shape of a certain color among a large number of different-colored shapes. This is why preparing students by telling them the objective of an activity is usually desirable. It allows the brain to anticipate critical features or ideas, and it increases the likelihood that the brain will focus on essential information.

Temporal Lobes

On either side of the brain, just above the ears, are two lobes that curve forward from the occipital lobes to below the frontal lobes. These are the temporal lobes, whose main function is to process auditory stimuli. (See Figure 3.2.) The temporal lobes are composed

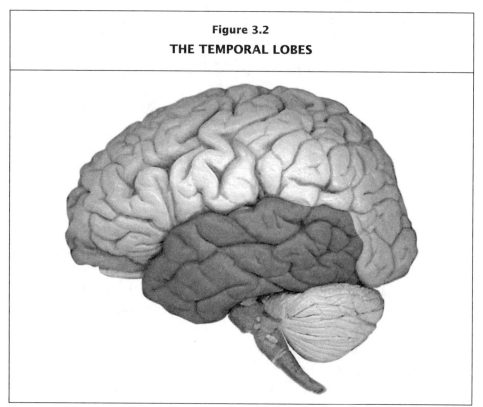

Figure 3.2
THE TEMPORAL LOBES

Courtesy of ArtWorks. Used with permission.

of several subdivisions that cope with hearing, language, and some aspects of memory, especially auditory memory. Hearing is often considered the most important sense for humans. It allows us to communicate with one another, and it gives us information vital for our survival. For example, the sound of an oncoming train tells us to move away from the track, and the sound of steps behind us tells us to check and see if we know who or what is making the sound. Deafness can be more debilitating than blindness, even though humans are highly visual creatures.

Like the occipital lobes, the temporal lobes have many subdivisions. When the primary auditory region of the temporal lobes is stimulated, sensations of sound are produced. In addition, an auditory association area has links to the primary region and other parts of the brain and aids in the perception of auditory inputs, allowing us to recognize what we are hearing. Within these two major regions, groups of neurons have specific jobs, such as registering a sound's loudness, pitch, or timbre.

At the conjunction of the left occipital, parietal, and temporal lobes (but lying mostly in the temporal lobe) is a group of cells known as Wernicke's area. This area is critical for speech. Wernicke's area—located in the left hemisphere—allows us to comprehend or interpret speech and to put words together in correct syntax when speaking. We'll see a little later in this chapter that another area (Broca's area) is necessary to produce speech.

Parietal Lobes

Sometimes, as the result of a stroke in the right hemisphere of the brain, individuals are left with a strange disorder called anosognosia, meaning "lack of knowledge of illness." These people are often paralyzed on the left side of their bodies, but they are unaware of their problem. They treat the left side of their bodies as if it weren't there, refusing to comb their hair on that side or sometimes refusing to put clothes on that half of the body. To understand how this strange disorder could occur, we need to look at the part of the cortex that handles spatial awareness and orientation.

At the top of the brain are flat, plate-like areas in each hemisphere called the parietal lobes. (See Figure 3.3.) These lobes consist of two major subdivisions—the anterior and posterior parts—that play different, but complementary, roles.

Within the anterior (front) part of the parietal lobes, immediately behind the motor cortex, lies a strip of cells called the somatosensory cortex. (See Figure 3.4.) Just as we need to send information to the muscles in our body about when and how to move, we also

Figure 3.3

THE PARIETAL LOBES

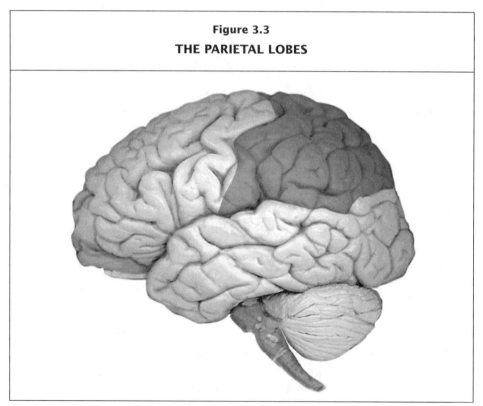

Courtesy of ArtWorks. Used with permission.

need to be able to receive information, such as touch and temperature from our environment, sensations of pain and pressure from the skin, and the positions of our limbs (proprioception). This is accomplished by the somatosensory cortex, the primary region responsible for receiving incoming sensory stimuli. Each part of the body is represented by a specific area on the surface of the somatosensory cortex. The more sensitive a part of the body, the greater the area needed to interpret its messages. For example, the lips, tongue, and throat have the largest number of receptors. Damage to this part of a parietal lobe interferes with the perception of touch and pain and with the knowledge of the body's position in space.

Figure 3.4
THE SOMATOSENSORY CORTEX

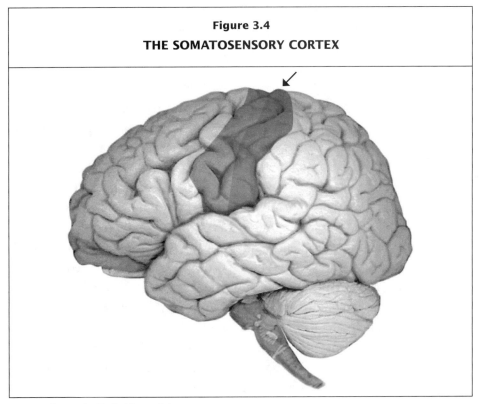

Courtesy of ArtWorks. Used with permission.

The posterior (rear) part of the parietal lobes continuously analyzes and integrates all this information to give you a sense of spatial awareness. The brain must know at all times where each part of the body is located and its relation to its surroundings. Damage to this part of the parietal lobes often results in clumsiness in manipulating objects (apraxia).

A final role of the parietal lobes is in maintaining focus or spatial attention. When one is focused on a particular stimulus, or when attention shifts from location to location, activation of the parietal lobes can be seen through brain-imaging techniques. As a stimulus becomes less meaningful, however, the attention wanes. For example, if you are wearing shoes that are tight or painful, your focus will be maintained on your feet. If you take off the tight shoes, however, the sensory receptors stop sending so much information, and your attention shifts to something else.

Frontal Lobes

The frontal lobes occupy the largest part of the cortex (28 percent) and perform the most complex functions. (See Figure 3.5.) Located in the front of the brain and extending back to the top of the head, the frontal lobe has expanded rapidly over the past 20,000 generations and is what most clearly distinguishes us from our ancestors. Our ability to move parts of our body at will, think about the past, plan for the future, focus our attention, reflect, make decisions, solve problems, and engage in conversation are all possible because of this highly developed area of the brain. Perhaps more amazing than any of these functions is the fact that the frontal lobes of the cerebral cortex allow us to be consciously aware of all these thoughts and actions.

The functions of the frontal lobes fall into two main categories: sensorimotor processing and cognition. Toward the back of the frontal lobes is a strip of cells that stretches across the top of the brain, forming a sort of band in front of the ears that resembles

The frontal lobes of the cerebral cortex allow us to be consciously aware of all these actions.

Figure 3.5

THE FRONTAL LOBES

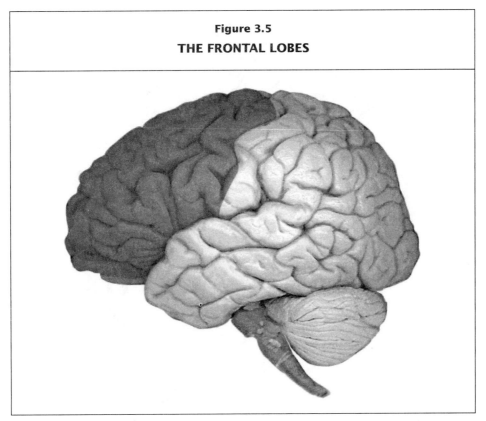

Courtesy of ArtWorks. Used with permission.

headphones. This strip is known as the motor cortex. (See Figure 3.6.) Nearly all neural activity directing muscular movement originates in the brain's motor cortex. Different areas of this strip govern the movements of specific muscles in the body. Similar to the somatosensory cortex, every part of your body, from your toes up to your lips, has a corresponding region in the motor cortex, but all parts of the body are not equally represented.

Certain muscles must carry out much more precise, fine-motor movements than others, so the areas of the motor cortex controlling these muscles are disproportionately large. For example, the areas

Nearly all neural activity directing muscular movement originates in the brain's motor cortex.

Figure 3.6

THE MOTOR CORTEX

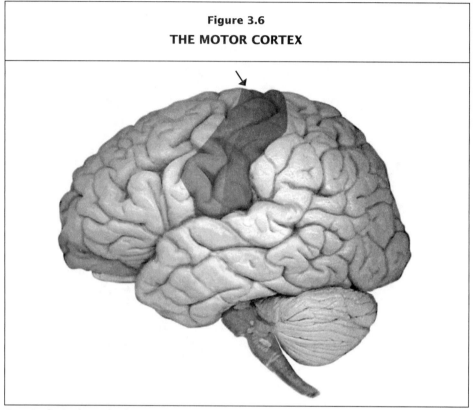

Courtesy of ArtWorks. Used with permission.

governing the fingers, lips, and tongue are much larger than the area governing the small of the back, because the small of the back doesn't have to carry out precise motions.

Immediately in front of the motor cortex is a supplemental motor area. This area contains an extremely important group of nerve cells known as Broca's area. This is the part of the cortex that allows you to speak. Broca's area is located in the left hemisphere of the supplemental motor area in about 95 percent of the population. (The other 5 percent, approximately 30 percent of left-handed persons, have the speech production area in the right hemisphere.) It probably is not surprising to find that Broca's area is connected to Wernicke's area in the temporal lobes by a bundle of nerve fibers known as the arcuate fasciculus. This linkage is important because, before any speech can be uttered, its form and the appropriate words must first be assembled in Wernicke's area and then relayed to Broca's area to be translated into the proper sounds. This information is then passed to the motor cortex for vocal production (Ackerman, 1992).

The large part of the frontal lobes situated in front of the secondary motor zones has sometimes been called the "silent" area, meaning it is free from processing sensory data and governing movement. Called the prefrontal cortex, it is proportionately much larger in humans than in other species. This may be the part of our brains that most clearly defines what it means to be human—the part that separates us from animals. As Sandra Ackerman, in her book *Discovering the Brain*, states, "Humans have the least stereotyped, most flexible lifestyle of all animal species, and it is believed that the cortex must in some way be related to liberating the individual from the fixed, predetermined patterns of behavior" (1992, p. 15).

The prefrontal cortex is sometimes referred to as the association cortex. It is here that information is synthesized from both the inner and outer sensory worlds, that associations between objects and their names are made, and that the highest forms of mental activities take place. Our human cortex allows us to build cathedrals, compose symphonies, dream and plan for a better future, love, hate, and experience emotional pain because it is in the cortex that consciousness—our ability to be aware of what we are thinking, feeling, and doing—emerges.

Research findings have implicated a part of the prefrontal cortex as critical for emotional self-regulation (Siegel, 1999). The orbitofrontal cortex (so named because of its proximity to the eye socket, or orbit) appears to be responsible for evaluating and regulating the emotional impulses emanating from the lower centers of the brain. This discovery regarding the orbitofrontal cortex deserves our attention and study. It may eventually help us understand everyday

Our human cortex allows us to build cathedrals, compose symphonies, dream and plan for a better future, love, hate, and experience emotional pain because it is in the cortex that consciousness— our ability to be aware of what we are thinking, feeling, and doing—emerges.

failures of self-regulation, such as road rage in adults or temper tantrums in children. It is possible that these inappropriate responses are the result of an injury to the brain, causing a sort of short-circuiting of the orbitofrontal cortex's wiring; genetic predisposition also may be a contributing factor. Some researchers believe, however, that the most common determiner of failure to self-regulate emotional responses is the lack of emotionally consistent parenting in the early years (Siegel, 2000).

Many parts of the brain must work together in a complex set of interactions for us to engage in a seemingly simple act.

Many parts of the brain must work together in a complex set of interactions for us to engage in a seemingly simple act. For example, Broca's area, the arcuate fasiculus, Wernicke's area, and the motor cortex all must work together in order for us to speak a coherent sentence. The same is true of walking across a room, lifting a glass, or recognizing a friend. Although the structure and function of the major structures of the brain have been addressed separately here, it is extremely important to remember that no structure works alone in this complex system.

Are We of Two Minds?

Throughout this chapter and the previous one, we noted that the various structures of the brain typically come in pairs. (The exception is the single pineal gland, which led Socrates to designate it the seat of the soul.) Looking down from the top, the whole brain appears to be composed of two seemingly identical halves. A deep groove known as the longitudinal fissure runs the length of the brain and travels nearly halfway down into its center, dividing the brain into two parts, resembling an enormous walnut.

The functions and roles of these two halves, known as the right and left hemispheres, have been debated for centuries. As early as 400 BCE, Hippocrates wrote about the possibility of the duality of the human brain. In 1874, Englishman John Hughlings Jackson introduced the idea of the brain having a "leading" hemisphere (Binney & Janson, 1990). In the 1970s and 1980s (and even today to a lesser degree), it was common to hear people described as "right brained" or "left brained," generally signifying that they were predominantly verbal and analytical (left brained) or artistic and emotional (right brained). This idea of a rigid right/left divide spawned a small industry of books and courses (with topics such as drawing on the right side of the brain or developing a right-brained management style), all designed to encourage right-brained activity and thinking. Even educators attempted to direct more of their instruction to the right side of the brain. As sometimes happens with new theories, a complex subject (though with good intentions) generated applications that were far removed from the actual scientific research. Scientists have even coined a name for the unbridled enthusiasm for our "two brains"—dichotomania.

None of these theories and ideas about the hemispheres' roles was totally accurate or inaccurate. Over the past three decades, a large body of research has emerged on the roles of the cerebral hemispheres. As often happens, the more we study any part of the brain, the more we learn just how complex it is; our hemispheres are no exception. New findings have caused some of the major researchers and writers in this field to modify their earlier views. Which of the older views still hold true, and what new information do we have about the hemispheres and their functions?

It has long been known that, for the most part, the left hemisphere of the brain governs the right side of the body and the right hemisphere governs the left. We've also known that the two hemispheres are joined by several bundles of fibers known as commissures. The largest of these is a four-inch-long bundle of fibers known as the corpus callosum. The corpus callosum is the largest fiber system in the brain. It is composed of about 300 million axons, the appendages of neurons responsible for sending messages to other cells.

This much information has been around for a long time, but the realization that each hemisphere has specialties is relatively new. In the early 1960s, several neuroscientists at the California Institute of

Scientists have coined a name for the unbridled enthusiasm for our "two brains." They call it dichotomania.

Technology were looking for ways to control epileptic seizures. Epileptic seizures, or electrical disturbances, in one hemisphere often cross over the corpus callosum and trigger a seizure in the other hemisphere. Roger Sperry, a neuroscience researcher, along with neurosurgeons Joseph Bogen and Philip Vogel, speculated that cutting through the corpus callosum might prevent the electrical activity from crossing between hemispheres and thus stop or minimize the seizures (Ornstein, 1997). They guessed right. After the surgery to sever the corpus callosum, patients' symptoms diminished considerably, and the patients appeared to function perfectly well in their daily activities.

However, studies on these "split-brain" patients revealed that something unusual had happened. If the patients held an object (such as a pencil) hidden from sight in their right hands, they could name and describe it, but when the pencil was held in the left hand out of sight, they claimed they held nothing. This finding was puzzling and led to further studies on these patients. Much of this research was conducted by Roger Sperry and his colleagues, Michael Gazzaniga and Joseph Bogen, and it led to an understanding that the two hemispheres are indeed specialized in what they do (Gazzaniga, Bogen, & Sperry, 1962). From this research, we now believe that the reason split-brain patients could not identify the pencil when it was held out of sight in the left hand is that the left hand communicates largely with the right hemisphere. This hemisphere is limited in its ability to produce speech. Therefore, when the corpus callosum is severed, and the hemispheres can't communicate with each other, the "silent" right hemisphere doesn't allow the person to name the object. (Recall that, for approximately 95 percent of the population, the left hemisphere is dominant for language and speech, while the roles are reversed in some left-handed individuals.)

Further research revealed other specializations of the hemispheres, as well. Melodies are perceived better in the left ear/right hemisphere than in the right ear/left hemisphere. Emotions appear to be lateralized, as well, with the right hemisphere processing more negative emotions and the left hemisphere processing more positive and optimistic emotions (Ornstein, 1997). People with left-hemisphere damage have difficulty recognizing faces, while damage to the right hemisphere often causes people to have difficulty finding their way around.

One of the most critical aspects of hemispheric specialization is the issue of context. Our understanding of what we read or our comprehension of what we hear depends on the context within which it occurs. For example, the comment "Oh, that's wonderful!" can be expressed with joy or with sarcasm. Unless you can compute the context through body language, the intonation of the person speaking, or the sentence that preceded it in the narrative, the sentence is virtually meaningless. Interestingly, it is the right hemisphere that decodes external information, allowing us to create an overall understanding of what we hear or read, thereby allowing us to "get" a joke or respond appropriately to a comment. This is the hemisphere that assembles the whole field of view, allowing us to see the forest as well as the individual trees. The right hemisphere gives us an overall view of the world (Ornstein, 1997).

One of the most critical aspects of hemispheric specialization is the issue of context.

The research on split-brain patients is interesting, but what about the vast majority of us who have an intact corpus callosum? Are our hemispheres lateralized in the same way? Researcher Robert Ornstein has done extensive studies of normal people using EEGs that validate the findings generated by studying split-brain patients. Ornstein and his colleagues asked people to perform simple tasks, such as writing a letter to a friend (left hemisphere) or arranging blocks into a pattern (right hemisphere), and they recorded the brain waves as the people worked. The researchers compared alpha waves (indicating an awake brain on idle) and beta waves (an awake brain actively processing information) during these two activities. When writing a letter, the left hemisphere showed more beta activity and the right more alpha. The opposite was true when the person was arranging blocks. Ornstein characterizes this phenomenon as a "turning on" of the hemisphere primarily responsible for a particular action, while the other hemisphere temporarily "turns off" (1997).

Although it now seems clear that our hemispheres each have specialties, we must remember that they work in concert at all times. In your brain right now, the information arriving in one hemisphere is immediately available to the other side. The responses of the two hemispheres are so closely coordinated that they produce a single view of the world, not two. For example, when you are engaged in conversation, it is the left hemisphere that allows you to produce speech, but it is the right hemisphere that gives the intonation to your speech. This, in turn, allows your listeners to use their right hemispheres to judge the context and fully comprehend the intended meaning of your words. The specializations of each hemisphere develop to their fullest when they are informed by the opposite hemisphere. The two halves of your brain work together in a beautifully coordinated partnership. This collaboration is described by Robert Ornstein in his book, *The Right Mind*:

> They are in the same body, after all, even though they're a couple of inches apart. They have the same cerebellum, the same brainstem, the same spinal cord. Each half of the human brain shares years of experiences with the other. They eat the same cereal in the morning and the same burger at lunch (and thus receive the same changes in their blood supply); they share the same hormones. Identical neurotransmitter cocktails mainline through each of them, they listen to the same nonsense from other people, they look at the same TV programs, and they go to the same parties. And neither hemisphere operates anything on its own, any more than we walk with one foot or the other, or whether the area of a rectangle is dependent on its length or width. *Almost nothing is regulated solely by the left or right hemisphere.* (1997, p. 68)

Although it now seems clear that our hemispheres each have their specialties, we must remember that they work in concert at all times.

Teaching to Both Halves of the Brain

Does knowledge of each hemisphere's special contributions to information processing mean much to us as educators? Does it help to know that the left hemisphere processes text while the right provides context? Maybe there are important implications that go beyond the "teaching to the right side of the brain" activities we've all heard about and perhaps tried in our classrooms. Perhaps we need to put more emphasis on teaching to *both* halves of the brain, since they work together all the time. Content (the text in which the left hemisphere excels) is important, but text without context (the specialty of the right hemisphere) is often meaningless. We need to teach content within a context that is meaningful to students and that connects to their own lives and experiences. This is teaching to both halves of the brain. Too often, the curriculum is taught in isolation, with little effort put into helping students see how the information is, or could be, used in their lives. Too many students never comprehend the "big picture" of how the content they learn fits in the larger scheme of things.

The more we understand the brain, the better we'll be able to design instruction to match how it learns best. How many of you made good grades in certain subjects but have to admit that you've never used what you learned because it was taught out of context? Does what you learned in history help you understand events occurring in the world today? Does the *A* you earned in algebra assist you in solving problems in your everyday life? If we don't connect the curriculum to the learners' experiences, much of the information gets lost, and we waste time having students engage in meaningless memorization rituals. According to David Perkins, we produce students with "fragile knowledge" that they either don't remember after the test or don't know when or how to use (1992). Perhaps an increased understanding of the cerebral hemispheres will assist us in designing curriculum and pedagogy that result not only in increased

The more we understand the brain, the better we'll be able to design instruction to match how it learns best.

student understanding of information taught but also in increased ability to use the information appropriately.

The information contained in Chapters 2 and 3 is meant to serve as a reference for the rest of this book. When various neural structures are mentioned, you can refer back to these pages to refresh your memory, thereby strengthening the neural connections that were made when you first read the information. In the next chapter, we'll look at how these neural connections are formed and their role in memory and learning.

Synapse Strengtheners

1. Without looking at the book, make a rough sketch of the brain and label the four lobes. Under each label, list the major functions of that lobe.

2. Explain to a friend why the terms "right brained" and "left brained" do not accurately explain the functions of the cerebral hemispheres.

3. If you are meeting with colleagues in a study group, devote a session to a discussion of how to teach to both halves of the brain simultaneously.

4

How Neurons Communicate

All human behavior can be traced to the communication among neurons. Every thought you think, every emotion you feel, every movement you make, your awareness of the world around you, and your ability to read these words are possible because neurons "talk" to one another. How do these cells accomplish such a variety of tasks? What does this communication look like? We once believed that transmission between neurons was simply an electrical current flowing from one neuron to the next. Today, we know that this is true for only a few of the neurons in the nervous system. Our focus in this chapter will be on the majority of neurons in the mature human brain, which do not communicate solely using electricity.

All human behavior can be traced to the communication among neurons.

The Action Potential: The Brain's Electrical Signal

Most neurons communicate with one another by means of both electrical and chemical signals. We have known for many years that the brain produces some type of electricity. As early as 1875, English physiologist Richard Caton recorded weak electrical currents in the brains of monkeys. It wasn't until 1929, however, that German psychiatrist Hans Berger first recorded electrical signals in the human brain (Greenfield, 1997). Today, the currents generated by billions of neurons in the brain are commonly measured using the electroencephalogram (EEG). What is the source of these electrical signals? How do they compare with the electricity we use to operate our computers and appliances?

Nerve impulses that travel along the axons in neurons are bio-electrical currents—not the mechanical, electrical currents that flow through the wiring in our homes. In our brains, these impulses are the result of movement of four common ions: sodium, potassium, calcium, and chloride. (Ions are atoms that have either a positive or negative electrical charge. Positive ions, like sodium, potassium, and calcium ions, are atoms that have lost one or more electrons. Negative ions, like chloride ions, are atoms that have gained one or more electrons.) Specific channels in the neuron cell membrane allow ions to move from one side of the membrane to the other. Potassium ions are distributed inside the membrane of a neuron at rest; sodium, calcium, and chloride ions are distributed along the outside of the normally impermeable membrane. The inside of the neuron has a slight excess of negatively charged ions with respect to the outside. The difference, called the resting potential, is usually expressed as a negative value, about −70 thousandths of a volt. In other words, a neuron at rest holds a slight negative charge.

When nothing much is happening, a neuron usually sends impulses down the axon at a relatively slow, irregular rate. When a neuron is stimulated (i.e., it receives excitatory signals from another neuron), however, the sodium channels in the membrane open and the positively charged sodium ions enter the cell. This makes the potential difference temporarily more positive inside than outside. As soon as this occurs, however, positively charged potassium ions leave the cell, changing the voltage to more negative than normal. This brief change in the potential difference usually lasts for about one millisecond and is known as an action potential. The action potential spreads down the axon as the sodium channels open sequentially, somewhat like falling dominoes (Restak, 1994). Each axon channel opens up the next channel, just as each domino in a line has to knock over only the next. The chain reaction that results is a great energy saver, compared to physically pushing over 50 dominoes one by one. This impulse moves in one direction until it reaches the end of the axon. Though all action potentials have the same intensity, the strength of the message can vary, depending on how frequently the action potential is generated. Some neurons can fire up to 500 action potentials per second. More normal rates, however, are 30 to 100 potentials per second. The speed of an action potential varies according to the diameter of the axon and whether or not it is insulated with myelin. Action potentials travel at speeds up to 220 miles per hour—much slower than a computer but fast by biological criteria (Greenfield, 1997).

Action potentials travel at speeds up to about 220 miles per hour!

Now that we have taken a look at the electrical component of neural transmission, we are in a better position to understand the chemical component.

The Brain's Own Pharmacy: The Chemical Signals

During the night of Easter Sunday, 1921, Austrian physiologist Otto Loewi had a dream. He awoke, jotted down some notes, and went back to sleep. In the morning he could not decipher his notes, but he knew that he had written down something important. The next night he had the same dream and immediately got up and went to his laboratory to perform the experiment suggested by his dream. It was designed around two frog hearts, which were being kept alive in special oxygenated chambers filled with a fluid similar to that normally found in the body. It was already known that if the vagus nerve (which innervates the heart) is stimulated, the heart slows down. Loewi stimulated the vagus nerve of one of the hearts, and then transferred the fluid that had surrounded it to the second heart. Even though the second heart had not been stimulated, it too slowed down. Loewi concluded that there must have been some chemical released into the fluid when the first heart was stimulated, and when that fluid was applied to the second heart, the effects were the same as on the first heart. He called this chemical *vagusstoff*, which was identified in 1933 as the transmitter acetylcholine. The discovery of the effect of acetylcholine on the heart was to have profound implications for understanding how neurons communicate with one another (Bear, Conners, & Paradiso, 1996).

Acetylcholine is one of the brain's own chemical messengers, which are generally called neurotransmitters. Many neurotransmitters today are fairly well known. You've probably heard of dopamine, serotonin, and the endorphins. Many more exist, however—perhaps as many as 100. Some of these neurotransmitters are generated within the cell bodies of neurons, and others are synthesized within the axon terminals. Regardless of their source, all neurotransmitter molecules are eventually stored in small sacs, or vesicles, in the bulb-like terminals of the axon branches, where they will be ready to go to work when needed.

Neurotransmitters are generally either excitatory or inhibitory, meaning that they either increase or decrease the probability that a neuron will fire. At first glance it might be difficult to see why there would be times when you would want neural activity inhibited, but imagine what it would be like if all the neurons in your motor cortex—or any other part of your brain for that matter—were firing all the time. Neurotransmitters are fascinating chemicals, and we'll take a closer look at them a little later in this chapter.

Imagine what it would be like if all the neurons in your motor cortex—or any other part of your brain for that matter—were firing all the time!

The Synapse

The next step in understanding neural communication is to look at how the electrical and chemical components come together to allow information to be passed from cell to cell within the central nervous system. This all-important action takes place at the junction of an axon terminal of one neuron and a dendrite on the cell body of a second neuron. This junction is known as a synapse. (See

Figure 4.1.) The axon terminal and the dendrite membrane are separated by an infinitesimal gap called the synaptic cleft. Most synapses take place on the spines of the dendrites, but 15 to 20 percent of synapses occur on the cell body itself.

When the action potential reaches the terminal of an axon, it stimulates the opening of some of the vesicles and thus triggers the release of one or more neurotransmitters into the synaptic cleft. The neurotransmitter molecules diffuse across the cleft. The more action potentials that arrive at the terminal, the more molecules are released into the gap. The electrical signal of the action potential has now been converted into a chemical signal, and the synaptic cleft is crossed within thousandths of a second. (At one point, scientists

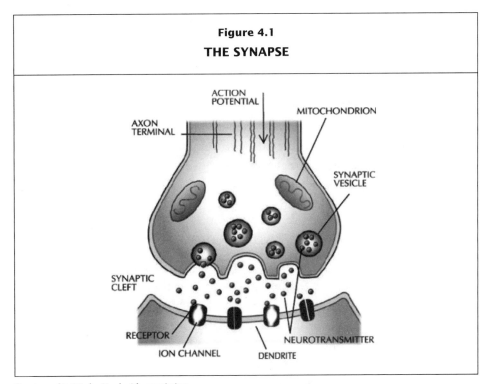

Figure 4.1

THE SYNAPSE

Courtesy of ArtWorks. Used with permission.

believed that each neuron produced only one neurotransmitter. We now know that a neuron may release two or more transmitters at a single synapse; it may even switch transmitters.)

Once the neurotransmitter molecules reach the other side of the synapse, each molecule makes contact with its target, the postsynaptic or receiving neuron. How is contact made? On the dendrite of the receiving neuron are special large protein molecules called receptors. Each neurotransmitter has a different shape, and the receptors are specifically designed for the shape of the neurotransmitter they are receiving, as precisely as a key is made for a lock. The neurotransmitter molecule fits into the receptor site, opening or closing ion channels on the membrane of the target neuron. Just as a change in the potential difference of the axon membrane generated an action potential, a change in the potential difference in the dendrite membrane causes stimulation of the target neuron (Restak, 1994).

This change then becomes one of the many electrical signals that will be conducted down the dendrites to the cell body of the postsynaptic neuron. The dendrites have now converted the chemical signal back into an electrical signal, thus, in a sense, completing the cycle. Because a neuron can have thousands of dendrites, and the dendrites are covered with tiny spines that effectively increase the surface area, this process occurs at thousands of sites. As soon as the electrical signals from all the involved dendrites arrive at the cell body, the neuron adds up all inputs to determine whether to generate an action potential. It is somewhat like a conscientious member of Congress who tallies the wishes of all his or her constituents before deciding how to vote. If the net change in voltage is sufficiently large, the ion channels will open near the cell body, the neuron will generate an action potential, and the "impulse" will begin its journey down the axon. If the voltage isn't high enough, the cell will not generate an electrical impulse, and the neuron will not fire. Remember that the neurotransmitters (being either excitatory or inhibitory) determine whether the net change in voltage is

Each neurotransmitter has a different shape, and the receptors are specifically designed for the shape of the neurotransmitter they are receiving, as precisely as a key is made for a lock.

large enough to generate an action potential (Crick, 1994; Restak, 1994; Thompson, 1985).

During this electrochemical process, the neurotransmitter involved is not "used up" in the receptor. Once the neurotransmitter has accomplished its task, it is rapidly cleared from the synapse. This can happen in three ways:

1. Through reuptake channels, the axon terminal of the cell reabsorbs many neurotransmitter molecules; the axon then "recycles" them to be used again.

2. The enzymes present in the synaptic cleft destroy some neurotransmitter molecules.

3. Still other molecules diffuse out of the cleft and are carried away as waste material by the cerebrospinal fluid.

More About Neurotransmitters

In his book *Receptors*, Richard Restak explains that no matter at what level we study the brain—behavioral, microscopic, or molecular—chemical messengers (and their receptors) underpin all behavior. Thoughts and emotions are the results of chemical processes in the brain, and so are the twitches of muscles. Restak suggests that all things mental, both normal functions and disorders of thought, originate from some corresponding order or disorder in chemical processes (1994). A basic awareness of how these chemical transmitters work is essential not only for understanding memory and learning but also for understanding the effects on the brain of drugs, medications, and foods.*

Richard Restak suggests that all things mental, both normal functions and disorders of thought, originate from some corresponding order or disorder in chemical processes.

---

*To be classified as a neurotransmitter, a chemical compound in the brain must meet six criteria. It must (1) be created in the neuron, (2) be stored in the neuron, (3) be released by the neuron in sufficient quantity to bring about some physical effect, (4) demonstrate the same effect experimentally that it does in living tissue, (5) have receptor sites on the receiving neuron specific for this compound, and (6) have means for shutting off its effect (Ackerman, 1992).

Types of Neurotransmitters

Our bodies often put common and familiar things to new uses. This is certainly true of neurotransmitters. Amino acids are the building blocks of proteins and are essential to life. With the exception of acetylcholine, all neurotransmitters are (1) amino acids, (2) derived from amino acids (amines), or (3) constructed of amino acids (peptides). Figure 4.2 shows some representatives of these three types.

Amino Acids

Amino acids are derived from protein foods and are found throughout the brain and the body. In the brain, they are involved in rapid point-to-point communication between neurons. Of the 20 common amino acids, four function as neurotransmitters: glycine, gamma-aminobutyric acid (GABA), aspartate, and glutamate.

Figure 4.2
TYPES OF NEUROTRANSMITTERS

Amino Acids	Amines	Peptides
Glutamate	Epinephrine (or adrenalin)	Endorphins
Glycine	Norepinephrine (or noradrenalin)	Substance P
Aspartate	Dopamine	Vasopressin
GABA (gamma-aminobutyric acid)	Serotonin	Cortisol (glucocorticoid)
	Acetylcholine (not truly an amine, but often included)	

Glycine and GABA (which is made from glycine) always carry inhibitory messages. The cerebellum, retina, and spinal cord, as well as many other parts of the brain, all use GABA circuits to inhibit signals. Nearly one-third of synapses in the cortex are GABA synapses.

Glutamate and aspartate always carry excitatory messages at the synapse (Crick, 1994). Pathways that carry these excitatory amino acids are widely distributed throughout the brain. Without them, brain functioning would cease. Glutamate is used extensively by the hippocampus and is a critical neurotransmitter for memory and learning (Sapolsky, 1994).

Amines

Amines (also called monoamines) are chemically modified amino acids that act more slowly than other amino acids. Rather than act directly at the synapse, they generally modulate the actions of the amino acid neurotransmitters and, for this reason, are often called neuromodulators. They bias how the target neuron responds to an incoming message, even though they do not pass it along. Produced in the brainstem or other subcortical structure, they are dispersed throughout the brain by an intricate network of axons, much as a sprinkler system disperses water to all parts of a lawn. Amine neurotransmitters are found in much lower concentrations— one one-thousandth as much as GABA and glutamate. They may be lower in concentration, but as we will see, they are important to understand because of the powerful effects they have on many parts of the brain. Some of the most noteworthy amines are described in the following sections.

Epinephrine. Our body often has a way of using the same substances and structures in different ways. A prime example is epinephrine—also known as adrenaline—which acts as both a hormone and a neurotransmitter. (Hormones are chemicals—peptides, proteins, or steroids such as estrogen, testosterone, and cortisol—that

Our body often has a way of using the same substances and structures in different ways.

are produced in one part of the body and that, when released, tell another part of the body what to do. In other words, they act at a distance from their point of origin.) As a hormone, epinephrine is synthesized in the adrenal glands that sit on top of the kidneys. It is involved in the stress response, also known as the "fight-or-flight" response. When this system is activated, epinephrine acts to speed up the heart, restrict blood vessels, relax the tubules in the lungs, and generally put the entire body in a state of alert. Scientists have also found epinephrine in the brain, where it acts as a neurotransmitter. In this case, it acts not from a distance but extremely close to its point of origin. Its structure and function are similar to norepinephrine, which is next on our list.

Norepinephrine. Also known as noradrenalin, norepinephrine is the primary neurotransmitter for the arousal mechanism of the fight-or-flight syndrome. In this role, it is responsible for dilating the pupils of the eyes, strengthening and speeding the heartbeat, and inhibiting the processes of digestion. It also stimulates the adrenal glands to release epinephrine and the liver to release large amounts of glucose, making more energy available to the muscles.

Norepinephrine has a chemical composition and function similar to epinephrine. Like epinephrine, it serves more than one purpose in the body and the brain. Norepinephrine is produced in a small structure in the brainstem (the locus coeruleus) but has pathways that project to the hypothalamus, cerebellum, and frontal cortex. These projections allow norepinephrine to control overall activity level and mood, such as increasing the level of wakefulness. Some preliminary studies have looked at the relationship between depression and norepinephrine. Though researchers have not yet found anything conclusive, there is a wide consensus that depression can be helped by two classes of drugs—one that blocks an enzyme that normally breaks down norepinephrine in the synaptic cleft and another that slows its reuptake (Ackerman, 1992).

Norepinephrine, also known as noradrenaline, is the primary neurotransmitter for the arousal mechanism of the fight-or-flight syndrome.

Dopamine. Dopamine is a neurotransmitter that plays several roles in brain functioning, but two of its major roles are to control conscious motor activity and to enhance pleasurable feelings in the brain's reward system. It is chemically similar to norepinephrine and is synthesized in several locations in the brain. Like most of the other amines, dopamine is conveyed to other parts of the brain by means of widespread pathways. Dopamine pathways lead to the frontal lobes and hypothalamus. The motor tremors and other effects of Parkinson's disease are caused when a group of cells in the brainstem (the substantia nigra) fails to produce sufficient dopamine for efficient motor functioning. Another site where dopamine is produced is in a cluster of cells deep within the middle of the brain called the ventral tegmental area. This area is known to be a mediating area for maternal behavior and for addiction. Later in this chapter, we'll look at how dopamine and other neurotransmitters are related to the reward system and to drug addiction.

Serotonin. Serotonin is, for most people, probably one of the best-known neurotransmitters. It has been called the "feel-good" transmitter. Indeed, like dopamine and norepinephrine, it is a mood enhancer. Unlike these other amines, however, serotonin appears to affect mood by calming rather than stimulating the brain. Serotonin's notoriety is the result of its relation to depression, which affects millions of people. Antidepressants such as Prozac, Zoloft, and Paxil work by inhibiting the reuptake of serotonin at the synapse, thus increasing its effect. Serotonin is also involved in memory, sleep, appetite control, and regulation of body temperature.

Like the amines norepinephrine and dopamine, serotonin is synthesized in several different locations in the brain as well as in the intestinal wall and in blood vessels. One of the major producers of this neurotransmitter is a structure in the brainstem called the raphe nucleus. Pathways from the raphe nucleus lead to such diverse structures as the cortex, hypothalamus, and hippocampus.

Serotonin is, for most people, probably one of the best-known neurotransmitters.

It is not surprising, then, to discover that serotonin appears also to be involved in (and is being used to treat) such diverse disorders as anxiety, obsessive-compulsive disorder, schizophrenia, stroke, obesity, migraine, and nausea (Borne, 1994).

Acetylcholine. Acetylcholine is the only major neurotransmitter that is not derived directly from an amino acid. Its action is generally excitatory, but it can act as an inhibitor, as was shown by Loewi's experiment in which it slowed the heart. Acetylcholine enhances rapid eye movement (REM) sleep (the phase of sleep when deepest dreaming occurs) and has been shown to be involved in our memory circuits (Hobson, 1989). The degeneration of this neurotransmitter in people with Alzheimer's disease helps explain the memory loss that usually accompanies this disease (Restak, 1994). Like the amine neurotransmitters, acetylcholine originates in subcortical structures just above the brainstem, but it is employed at many synapses throughout the brain. The cells of the motor cortex and neurons of the sympathetic nervous system both use acetylcholine to operate all voluntary and many involuntary muscles.

Peptides

We're now going to look at an entirely different group of neurotransmitters that are synthesized differently from amines and play a slightly different role at the synapse. Peptides are either digestive products or hormones. Those that are pertinent to our discussion—the peptide hormones—are composed of amino acids joined together to form a chain. Some chains are five amino acids long, while others are composed of as many as 39 amino acids. Like all hormones, they are transported from one part of the body to another in the bloodstream. For example, a peptide called angiotensin is involved in thirst. When the body becomes dehydrated, angiotensin is released into the bloodstream where it binds to a receptor in the kidney and causes the kidney to conserve water.

Many peptides have been found to operate not only in the body but also in the brain, hence the name neuropeptides. Consider our previous example of angiotensin. Acting as a hormone, it causes body tissues to conserve fluids. However, conservation isn't enough, so angiotensin acts effectively as a neurotransmitter on the brain, working at certain synapses to create the sensation of thirst. An animal injected with angiotensin will continue to drink even though it is sated with water (Moyers, 1993). Once again, we see how the human body efficiently uses the same substance for varied purposes. During the late 1970s and the 1980s, researchers found more than 50 peptides (some researchers estimate there are more than 100) that serve dual purposes in the body and the brain (Gregory, 1987). Peptide hormones function principally as modulators; rather than acting on their own to stimulate or inhibit, they facilitate this action in other neurotransmitters. A neuron may use one or more modulatory neuropeptides along with several neurotransmitters (Restak, 1994).

In 1975, neuropeptides were first discovered in Scotland by a pair of drug-addiction researchers, John Hughes and Hans Kosterlitz. They were searching for an internally produced chemical that would fit into existing opiate receptor cells. The fact that the body contains receptors for opiates was established a few years earlier by Solomon Snyder and Candace Pert, working at Johns Hopkins University. What Hughes and Kosterlitz discovered was a natural substance that acts much like morphine in blocking pain and producing euphoria. They dubbed this substance enkephalin, Greek for "in the head." Enkephalins also act in the intestines by regulating the movement of food through the digestive pathway (Pert, 1997).

Endorphins. Additional internal (or endogenous) neuropeptides similar to enkephalins are lumped together loosely under the generic name *endorphins*, a contraction of the term "endogenous morphine." When you think about it, it makes sense: Morphine

During the late 1970s and the 1980s, researchers found more than 50 peptides that serve dual purposes in the body and the brain.

Morphine could not produce the analgesic, tranquilizing, and euphoric effects it does if we didn't have a receptor site in the brain for a natural substance that deadens pain and produces euphoria.

could not produce the analgesic, tranquilizing, and euphoric effects it does if we didn't have a receptor site in the brain for a natural substance that deadens pain and produces euphoria. The brain (as far as we know) does not have receptor sites for poppy plants. The human brain, as well as the brains of all higher vertebrates, does have receptor sites for its own opiates, though, and morphine—mimicking this natural substance—slips into these sites.

Why would the brain have opiate receptors? What would be the purpose of a reward center in the brain? There must be some value for survival, or the opiate receptors (concentrated in the spinal cord, brainstem, ventral tegmental area, and nucleus accumbens) would not have been conserved across the evolutionary scale (Ackerman, 1992). Many scientists believe that the answer lies in a reward or pleasure pathway—a neural network in the middle of the brain that prompts good feelings in response to certain behaviors, such as relieving hunger, quenching thirst, engaging in sex, and escaping from a potentially dangerous situation. In other words, it appears that the brain produces opiate-type neurotransmitters to reinforce those behaviors that are essential for the survival of the individual and of the species.

It appears that the brain produces opiate-type neurotransmitters to reinforce those behaviors that are essential for the survival of the individual and of the species.

Now we can begin to understand one of the roles of endorphins (as well as of other neurotransmitters, such as dopamine, norepinephrine, and serotonin) and the reinforcing effects they have on the reward pathway. Endorphin levels rise in the brain during prolonged, sustained exercise such as running a marathon (or running away from a saber-toothed tiger). Beta-endorphin, a type of endorphin, also increases significantly during childbirth (Fajardo et al., 1994). If pain levels were not reduced, the probability of having a second child would certainly decrease. Positive social contacts, humor, and music also have been shown to increase levels of this group of opiate neuropeptides (Levinthal, 1988). It appears, then, that those behaviors that increase the likelihood of survival are chemically reinforced in the brain.

Other Neuropeptides. Numerous other neuropeptides are not as well known as enkephalins and endorphins. Substance P is a neuropeptide present in sensory neurons. When these neurons are stimulated, they transmit a message to the higher parts of the brain (those parts concerned with pain sensation and response) that painful stimulation has occurred. You've probably experienced the effects of this neuropeptide because substance P is present in tooth pulp. Endorphins are thought to block the actions of substance P at the synapse, lessening the awareness of pain. Another neuropeptide, vasopressin, regulates the motility of the intestines, but it can act as a neurotransmitter as well. Cortisol, which will be discussed in Chapter 9, is still another steroid hormone with powerful effects on the brain and body.

The Mind–Body Connection

You may have noticed that many of the same peptide modulators occur both in the brain and in the gastrointestinal tract. In *Receptors*, Richard Restak states, "Our 'gut feelings' are more than mere metaphor . . . . The mental and the physical, the mind, the brain, and the body, are intrinsically linked by means of these chemicals" (1994, p. 206). Candace Pert, in *Molecules of Emotion*, suggests that because most, if not all, neuropeptides have the ability to change our mood, we may have the capacity to alter our own physiology without drugs. She states:

> Peptides serve to weave the body's organs and systems into a single web that reacts to both internal and external environmental changes with complex, subtly orchestrated responses. Peptides are the sheet music containing the notes, phrases, and rhythms that allow the orchestra—your body—to play as an integrated entity. (1997, p. 148)

We know that the brain is not sitting in the head totally separated from the rest of the body. The two are inextricably linked in

"Our 'gut feelings' are more than mere metaphor . . . . The mental and the physical, the mind, the brain, and the body, are intrinsically linked by means of these chemicals."

many ways. The neurotransmitters that allow neurons to communicate are made up of amino acids that we obtain from the foods we eat. This fact gives new meaning to the saying "You are what you eat." We all know that we can make ourselves physically ill by worry and stress. Psychosomatic illnesses (in which mental disorders are manifested in physical symptoms) have been documented for many years. Alternative or complementary medicine is beginning to gain wider credibility and acceptance. We will see in later chapters why this is so, and how exercise, sleep, stress, and mental attitude affect the brain's ability to process information. We are just beginning to understand the mind–body connection. What implications might this fascinating new area of research have for teaching and learning?

Understanding Addiction

A chemical substance synthesized in our brain is called a neurotransmitter. One that is synthesized in a laboratory is called a drug. Often, neurotransmitters and drugs are similar in their molecular composition. We've already seen how one drug, morphine, is able to modulate pain and pleasure by mimicking (or fitting into the receptor sites for) one class of our brain's own chemical substances, the endorphins. Is the same thing true for other drugs, especially the ones frequently used for recreational purposes, such as cocaine, amphetamines, and heroin? Basically, the answer is *yes,* but with a few differences, depending on the drug we're discussing. Most drugs operate the way they do either by fitting into a natural neurotransmitter's receptor site or by modulating the effects of the neurotransmitter in some way.

Earlier, during the discussion of the effects of endorphins in the brain, we pointed out that there is a pleasure or reward pathway in the brain. It is now time to take a closer look at this circuit. Two structures appear to be heavily involved in the brain's reward system. The ventral tegmental area (VTA), as you may remember, is a group of dopamine-producing cells deep in the center of the brain. The

We know that the brain is not sitting in the head totally separated from the rest of the body. The two are inextricably linked in many ways.

If a chemical substance is synthesized in our brain, we call it a neurotransmitter. If it is synthesized in a laboratory, it's called a drug.

dopamine neurons in the VTA are connected by a bridge of fibers to the second brain structure that mediates the pleasure response, the nucleus accumbens (NA). Scientists believe that, eventually, all pleasure comes down to dopamine. This neurotransmitter has indeed been shown to bind to many receptors in the emotional center of the brain. When a drug such as cocaine, amphetamine, morphine, or heroin reaches the brain, it acts by inhibiting dopamine reuptake in the VTA, effectively causing more dopamine to remain in the synapse. The excess of dopamine overstimulates the nucleus accumbens, producing a pleasure response. The user can sustain this pleasurable feeling by taking more of the drug (Restak, 1994).

When laboratory rats are hooked to an apparatus that allows them to push a lever that will deliver cocaine or amphetamine directly to the VTA, they press the lever almost continuously, ignoring food and drink and ceasing all other normal activity. The same thing holds true for the opiates heroin and morphine. (Heroin is a derivative of morphine.) Humans appear not to behave much differently from the rats. Virtually all drugs abused by humans, including opiates, amphetamine, cocaine, alcohol, and nicotine, lead to increased levels of dopamine in the nucleus accumbens. Cocaine acts directly on the pleasure centers and produces a "high," which helps to explain why it is one of the most addictive substances known (Restak, 1994). Figure 4.3 is a list of some common drugs and the effects they have at the synapse.

Cocaine acts directly on the pleasure centers and produces a "high," which helps to explain why it is one of the most addictive substances known.

Just because a drug mimics one of the brain's own neurotransmitters, it does not necessarily have the same effect. The brain generally controls just how much of a neurotransmitter to release into the synapse, how long to leave it there, and when to dispose of it. Drugs, however, overwhelm this natural functioning and flood all the synapses, often causing effects quite different from the transmitters they mimic. Even if the drug is one that is prescribed for the treatment of a disorder, the dosage is difficult to regulate. L-dopa (which enhances dopamine development) is often administered

Just because a drug mimics one of the brain's own neurotransmitters, it does not necessarily have the same effect.

Figure 4.3

DRUGS AND WHERE THEY REACT

Drug	Where It Reacts
Alcohol	Along with barbiturates, alcohol decreases the release of GABA.
Cocaine and amphetamine	These drugs block dopamine and norepinephrine reuptake channels.
Heroin and morphine	Morphine and heroin (a derivative of morphine) mimic the natural endorphins.
Nicotine	Nicotine activates receptors on hippocampal cells that typically respond to acetylcholine.
Prozac (Paxil, Zoloft)	These antidepressant drugs block serotonin reuptake channels.

to relieve some of the effects of Parkinson's disease. Too little of this drug, however, and the symptoms remain; too much, and the patient often displays characteristics of schizophrenia, such as hallucinations and paranoia.

Why do people take illicit drugs? The reasons vary, but in some instances drug use may be the result of abnormalities in the brain's chemical balance. Studies at Harvard Medical School determined that some cases of depression are the result of low levels of dopamine in the brain. Often, afflicted individuals aren't aware of the cause of their depression; they only know that cocaine or amphetamine makes them feel better. For others, the risk for drug addiction may be caused by a lower-than-normal level of dopamine receptor sites. For these people, cocaine appears to raise dopamine levels to more natural levels.

This discussion of addiction may not appear to have much relevance for the average educator. When we consider that the reward pathway in the brain was designed for good reasons, however, and when the "natural" sources of reward (feelings of being liked, being successful or productive, and feeling attractive) are not present in students' lives, we can begin to understand why they are drawn to substances that increase pleasure. An effective classroom climate might be described as one that allows students to naturally increase the endorphin, dopamine, norepinephrine, or serotonin levels in their brains, making the students' education experiences more pleasurable and rewarding.

Synapse Strengtheners

1. In your own words, see if you can explain to a person who has not read this chapter why information processing in the brain is both electrical and chemical.

2. With the book closed, draw a diagram of a synapse between two neurons, labeling the following parts: the synaptic cleft, vesicles, molecules of a neurotransmitter, and receptors. Open the book and check your drawing for accuracy. (Artistic ability doesn't count!)

3. Design a lesson to teach your students about the chemical basis of addiction.

4. If you are reading this book as a part of a study group, discuss how the information in this chapter relates to classroom climate and what teachers can do to decrease the likelihood of students' involvement with illicit drugs.

Part II

Brain Development from Birth Through Adolescence

The brain is not only shaped by its inherited genetic code, but it is heavily influenced and shaped by its environment.

If we were born with our brains completely developed, the study of human behavior would be much simpler. The growth of the body is relatively easy to observe; the growth of the brain is not. Until recently, we could only surmise what was going on in the brain by observing behavior, which led to many misconceptions. It was once believed that a baby's brain was a blank slate, a "tabula rasa," waiting and ready for instructions to be written. We now know that the truth is much more complex. Adolescent brains were once believed to be the same as their adult counterparts. This also is not true. Adolescent brains—as we shall see—do not reach adult functioning levels until perhaps their early 20s. In order to provide the best environment for the early years and to design appropriate instruction for children and adolescents during the years of formal schooling, we need to have a better understanding of the structure and function of the brain at the various stages of development.

As we look at the developing brain, one of the most important concepts to understand is that of neuroplasticity. Simply stated, neuroplasticity means that the brain is shaped not only by its inherited genetic code but also by its environment. No other organ in the human body can boast this feat to the same degree. In his book *The Synaptic Self,* Joseph LeDoux sums this up well: "People don't come preassembled but are glued together by life. We all have a different set of genes and a different set of experiences" (2003, p. 3). For example, we know that the human brain is "programmed" at birth to hear—and eventually produce—the discrete sounds (phonemes) that constitute language. However, the sounds that children repeatedly hear reinforce the connections for their primary language, while connections for languages not heard will eventually fade away around adolescence. This is why it is relatively easy for children to learn a second language but why it is much more difficult for adults.

An amazing example of plasticity can be seen in individuals who are born blind. There are approximately 300 million neurons in the occipital lobes at birth. These neurons are activated when newborn babies first open their eyes. If the eyes open but, for some reason, the baby cannot see, this activation does not occur. It might seem evident that these unused neurons would atrophy, but not all of them do! The neurons that had been designated for sight "change their function" and assist auditory and/or tactile neurons. Norihiro Sadato at the National Institutes of Health discovered activity in the visual cortex when blind persons read Braille (Sadato et al., 1998). Helen Neville of the University of Oregon also found amazing plasticity in deaf individuals. She and her colleagues found that deaf people had more finely developed peripheral vision acuity and could detect motion better than hearing people (Neville, 2008).

Younger brains have greater malleability than older ones, but it has been shown that neuroplasticity exists from the cradle to the grave. As wonderful a feature as it is, plasticity can be a double-edged sword. We'll see that the environment can cause less-than-desirable changes in the brain as well as positive ones. In Part II, we'll take a look at the changes that occur in individuals' brains—from birth through adolescence—in varying environments. Recognizing and understanding these changes will help us gain a better understanding of what we can do to help each child or young person reach his or her full potential.

5

The Early and Middle Years

Human infants are relatively helpless and dependent on adults much longer than the offspring of most other mammals. For the first year, we can't walk, talk, or feed ourselves; and on the surface, we don't appear to do much but eat, sleep, and digest. Perhaps this is why we have historically tended to treat infants as if not much were happening in their brains. This view, however, has changed drastically over the past few decades. While it is true that we, as babies, have poorly developed brains, it appears that the reason for this is so we can learn and adapt to any environment in which we find ourselves. Studies have shown that there are significant changes taking place in young brains that are important for both parents and teachers to understand (Gopnik, Meltzoff, & Kuhl, 1999).

Brain Growth and Development: Birth to Five

The growth of the brain begins about three weeks into gestation. From that point on, neurogenesis (the growth of neurons) occurs at an astonishing rate—approximately 250,000 new cells per minute! All major structures in the brain are in place at the halfway point of fetal development. Not only is the brain growing new neurons, it

The growth of the brain begins about three weeks into gestation. From that point on, approximately 250,000 new cells develop every minute.

74

is beginning to grow new dendrites in order to make connections (synapses) between neurons (synaptogenesis).*

The explosion of new connections that begins during fetal development continues in the months following birth. Milestones in brain growth, from birth to the beginning of school, involve several processes. While a child's body grows at a steady pace, the brain develops in fits and starts through several overlapping phases. Nerve cells sprout new axons, dendrites expand their surface by growing spines, synaptogenesis continues, and glial cells increase. Synapses grow at an amazing rate during the first two years of life, and PET scans done by Dr. Harry Chugani, chief of pediatric neurology at Children's Hospital of Michigan, show a metabolic rate of glucose use in children's brains that equals that of their parents (Chugani, 1998). It is estimated that by the age of two, 40,000 new synapses form every second! This is partially due to the fact that each neuron in a child's brain contains approximately 15,000 dendrites, versus 6,000–10,000 in an adult brain (Kluger, 2008).

Not all synapses remain. At around two years, excess connections begin to be cut back in a process called pruning. During pruning, frequently used connections are strengthened and infrequently used connections are lost. This process is just as important to brain development as is the initial growth of synapses; it makes the brain more precisely organized. For example, babies are born with cells that allow them to hear and pronounce the sounds of every language in the world. During the pruning process, however, connections for the language sounds they hear every day are strengthened,

It is estimated that by the age of two, 40,000 new synapses form every second!

Babies are born with cells that allow them to hear and pronounce the sounds of every language in the world.

*Both neurogenesis and synaptogenesis are influenced by the womb environment. For example, it is well established that what a pregnant woman eats and drinks—as well as her mental state—will affect the developing brain of the fetus. Fetal Alcohol Syndrome is the leading preventable cause of mental retardation in the United States today. Maternal stress, poor diet (especially lack of protein), and ingestion of certain drugs can also have adverse effects on the developing brain (Eliot, 1999).

while those that are not heard are pruned away. This process allows children to adapt to and eventually speak the primary language of their parents or caregivers.

In the first year of life, our brain doubles its size and weight. Three factors contribute to this amazing growth: (1) new connections—the result of learning, (2) additional glial cells, and (3) myelin. Recall that myelin is a type of glial cell that wraps around individual axons, allowing the axon potential to travel at greater speeds. Before a cell is myelinated, it is immature and does not function normally. For example, horses are born with already myelinated cells that connect to leg muscles, allowing them to walk almost immediately, but these cells don't myelinate in humans for 9–18 months. Myelination appears to be largely genetically regulated and to occur in a preset pattern, yet there is some evidence that its extent and rate are affected by experience. Myelination begins to occur in the fetal spinal cord at about five months, but it does not appear in the brain until the ninth month of gestation. Other areas of the body myelinate at different speeds, generally moving from cells that regulate survival functions to those in the prefrontal cortex that are necessary for higher-level cognitive skills. We'll see that cells in this latter group don't myelinate fully until the end of adolescence, or perhaps later.

Myelination, in a sense, puts parameters around the optimal times for development of basic sensory abilities such as vision and hearing. These optimal times are often referred to as "sensitive periods," and they are shorter than periods for more complex skills. When the brain is "ready" to develop a certain area but the necessary stimulus is absent, normal development does not occur. For example, if a child is born with cataracts that are not removed very early, the opportunity to develop normal sight is significantly limited. In addition, the ability to verbally communicate through language is lost by about the age of 10 if children are deaf or lack sufficient exposure to language.

Myelination, in a sense, puts parameters around the optimal times for development of basic sensory abilities such as vision and hearing.

Emotional development also has a sensitive period. Studies have shown that infants or young children who are deprived of the opportunity to form a bond with or attach to adults usually lack the ability to form normal healthy intimate relationships later in life (Lewis, Amini, & Lannon, 2001). This stunted emotional growth has been poignantly chronicled in the studies of Romanian orphans (Nelson, 2006). These babies, reared in severely deprived conditions, were found to be delayed in nearly all their social, emotional, and cognitive skills as adults.

What is required for young children to develop and realize their fullest potential socially, emotionally, and cognitively? The concept of enriched environments has been the subject of much controversy in recent years. Part of the controversy arises from the treatment of all stimulation and environmental input as the same. Researcher William Greenough and his colleagues studied how the environment affects the brain's synapses during development (Greenough, 2002). They found that rats raised in cages with wheels, ladders, and other rats to play with developed 25 percent more synapses per neuron than rats raised in cages with no toys or playmates. This research has often been cited as evidence for the importance of early childhood enrichment. However, Greenough points out that the rats' enriched cages are very similar to the rats' normal environments. Stephen Meltzoff, coauthor of the book *The Scientist in the Crib*, states that the important question is not "What is the effect of the environment on the brain?" but, rather, "What is the effect of a deprived environment, a normal environment, and an enriched environment?" (Gopnik et al., 1999). It therefore appears to be more accurate to say that a normal environment leads to more synaptic connections than a deprived environment.

Children are innately curious and driven to master their world. Given a normal environment, barring any serious problems, this will happen without a lot of extra intervention on the part of adults. Play is incredibly important for children; it is a time when they

It appears to be more accurate to say that a normal environment leads to more synaptic connections than a deprived environment.

have ownership and are free to explore their own interests with the support of adults. Activity is critical; children do not like to learn through passive input. Flash cards, workbooks, language tapes, and "educational" computer games are not only inappropriate; they often deprive children of the natural interaction with the world that is essential to their development. What children need and enjoy is rich, varied input in natural settings. Opportunities for this type of input are everywhere, including taking a walk through the neighborhood and talking about what they see, helping to cook dinner, or sorting clothes. For example, reading to children and teaching them songs and rhymes are two of the best ways that parents can increase the probability that their children will become good readers.

What children need and enjoy is rich, varied input in natural settings.

Brain Growth and Development: Six to Twelve

Harry Chugani has been able to obtain PET scans from a representative sample of individuals of all ages. He believes that the rate of glucose shown in these scans is an excellent indicator of the growth of neural connections. What Chugani has found is a tremendous increase of synapses from birth to age four. This represents the amazing amount of learning that takes place during the first four years of life. After this period, growth plateaus and remains fairly constant for the next six years or so until age 10. At adolescence, the glucose utilization and synaptic growth values return to levels roughly equivalent to those that were present around two years of age and stay that way for the rest of a person's life. This tremendous activity results in a brain that nearly triples its birth weight in four or five years. Growth spurts during early puberty complete the weight gain, so that by age 11 or 12, an adolescent's brain is generally the size of an adult's (Diamond, Hopson, & Diamond, 1998).

What are the changes that occur in the brain during the years from 6 to around 11 or 12 (often referred to as the middle years), and what are the implications of these changes for the classroom teacher? At first glance, the changes appear much less dramatic than those that occurred during the early years; however, they are just as important. One of the most interesting changes is in the brain's cortex (i.e., the "gray matter"). More synapses are not necessarily better (thus the significance of the pruning process), and this appears to be especially true within the cortex. At around five years of age, the brain begins to prune away synapses in this outer layer, a decline associated with more streamlined and efficient communication between neurons. This decline continues until just before the onset of puberty, when it then reverses and begins to increase. This thickening, which may possibly be related to the influence of surging sex hormones, begins around 9 or 10 years old and peaks at around age 11 in girls and 12 in boys. At this point, the "gray matter" begins to thin again.

More synapses are not necessarily better—especially within the cortex.

Brain growth, it would appear, involves cycles of both subtractions and additions. While "gray matter" is in decline during the adolescent years, "white matter" (myelin) increases well into adulthood. Recall that myelin insulates axons, increases the rate at which electrical impulses (the action potential) travel, and allows neurons to communicate more effectively. Early myelination occurs on motor neurons and neurons related to basic functions. Neurons in the frontal lobes (especially in the prefrontal cortex) receive a myelin sheath later in development, as evidenced by the increased ability of children to engage in higher-level and more abstract thinking.

Throughout this period of neural sculpting, a 6- to 12-year-old could be considered to be in a state of "developmental grace." Many skills and competencies are gained more easily during these middle years—when the brain seems primed for learning—than in adulthood. The most conspicuous cognitive ability that children have during the middle years is the ability to learn languages. Striking growth spurts can be seen during this period in the temporal and parietal lobes, regions that specialize in language and understanding spatial relations. This growth drops off sharply after age 12, which is the main reason why foreign languages learned before adolescence are acquired relatively effortlessly and spoken without an accent. Languages learned after adolescence are invariably spoken with an accent, regardless of the effort given by or linguistic abilities of the student. The same is true of physical ability. During the middle years, children learn complex physical skills much more readily than they would during or after adolescence. These skills are most evident in athletics and music. If the skills of throwing a ball or playing a piano are not mastered by age 12, they may never develop to their fullest capacity. It appears that learning these skills early results in a more natural, intuitive mastery that is generally not evident in people who learn them later in life.

In addition to linguistic and physical skills, children spend much of the middle years developing reading, writing, and math skills that will form the basis of later academics. They also learn and practice social and emotional skills and behaviors for which they need effective models. It is therefore important to emphasize that, while the brain is ready and eager to learn, growth and branching of dendrites will not occur without stimulation. All children (especially those in the middle years) need exposure to a variety of rich experiences that will enable them to fully develop their mental, physical, emotional, and social capacities.

In planning instruction for these children, it's important to look at the changes that take place in the strategies naturally used by children during the middle years to remember what they are learning. We have learned that the ability of children to remember more of what they are taught increases as they get older. Why is this so? Part of the answer lies in studies that look at strategies different children use when they need to remember something. When shown a series of pictures and asked to recall what they saw, only about 10 percent of five-year-olds appear to rehearse the stimuli. By seven years of age, 60 percent show signs of rehearsal; by age 10, 80 percent seem to rehearse the information spontaneously (Flavell, Friedrichs, & Hoyt, 1970). These studies suggest that 5- and 6-year-olds seldom

If the skills of throwing a ball or playing a piano are not mastered by age 12, they may never develop to their fullest capacity.

All children need exposure to a variety of rich experiences that will enable them to fully develop their mental, physical, emotional, and social capacities.

rehearse, 7-year-olds sometimes rehearse (though not always effectively), and children older than 10 become increasingly proficient in using rehearsal strategies (Kail, 1984). However, we need not necessarily be constrained by a child's age. While children do not naturally rehearse, they can be taught strategies such as whispering the information to themselves or creating a mental image of the information. It is important to help children understand *why* and *when* a particular strategy should be used, as children do not usually transfer strategies to new situations (Kail, 1984).

Synapse Strengtheners

1. Explain to a fellow teacher how healthy brain development is dependent both on the growth and pruning of connections.

2. Design a presentation for parents that explains the function of myelination and how it helps us understand the development of various functions.

3. If you are using this book as part of a study group, allot time to discuss what you think constitutes an enriched environment in your classroom.

4. Explain why the 6- to 12-year-old student is considered to be in a state of "developmental grace," and state what you think are the implications of this period for teachers.

6

The Adolescent Brain: A Work in Progress

Consider the following child: she is cheerful, loving, and obedient; she approaches her parents or teachers for advice; she dresses in appropriate clothing; and she turns in for the night at 10:00 p.m. She completes her homework without complaint or prodding, and parent/teacher conferences to discuss her progress are a joy. Then, sometime between ages 10 and 12, a strange thing happens. Almost overnight, it appears someone has unzipped this child and put someone else inside. No longer can she be called sweet and loving; surly and antagonistic would be better descriptors. Gone are the days when she asks for advice, and if it is offered, it will almost certainly be ignored. She goes to school dressed in an outfit that no one would consider to be in good taste. She spends hours on the computer, homework doesn't get done, and parent/teacher conferences are no longer pleasant.

It doesn't take a brain scientist to tell you that adolescents can be frustrating. Most of us understand that teenagers' lives are shaped by factors such as family, friends, school, and community institutions, but there are also powerful neurological issues at play. Neuroscience has made great strides in shedding light on the changes occurring in teens' brains and why they behave the way they do. Interestingly, this new information focuses not only on the oft-blamed raging hormones but also on what's going on above the neck. Many new insights into the adolescent brain have been gained using the brain-imaging techniques discussed in Chapter 1. In addition to the teenage years being a time of great physical change, scientists have discovered compelling evidence that indicates they are also a time of significant change in the brain's anatomy and neurochemistry.

It is well understood that many factors play a role in shaping adolescent development and behavior, including family, friends, school, and the culture at large. Most people, however, would be inclined—and rightly so—to put raging hormones near the top of the list. Beginning at puberty, the testes and ovaries begin pouring the sex hormones testosterone and estrogen into the bloodstream, spurring the development of the reproductive system. Particularly active in the brain's emotional centers, sex hormones also contribute to an appetite for thrills, strong sensations, and excitement. These cravings can cause problems for adolescents because, as we will see in the following sections, their brains haven't fully developed those regions responsible for "putting the brakes" on risky behavior.

We have seen how the brain grows by expanding and pruning connections among cells—keeping the connections that are commonly used and getting rid of unused ones. We have also seen that one of the most active periods of reorganization occurs early in life (around two years of age) when there is a huge buildup of neural connections in the brain. Recall that this buildup is followed by a massive pruning, which allows the strongest and most efficient connections to function more effectively. Until recently, scientists assumed that this period of growth and reduction occurred in early childhood only and that most, if not all, of the major changes in brain organization and development occurred before adolescence. This view seemed reasonable in light of the fact that the brain reaches its full size by puberty. The conventional wisdom had been that the adolescent brain is fully developed and functions similarly

The teenage years are a time of significant change in the brain's anatomy and neurochemistry.

Particularly active in the brain's emotional centers, sex hormones contribute to an appetite for thrills, strong sensations, and excitement.

Scientists have discovered that very complex changes take place in the brain throughout adolescence.

to an adult brain. This turns out—as many middle school teachers and parents already suspected—to be untrue. Instead, scientists have discovered that very complex changes take place in the brain throughout adolescence and that the brain is not fully "installed" until 20 to 25 years of age. We now understand that the brain continues to change during the teenage years.

Changes in the Adolescent Brain

In what parts of the adolescent brain are the greatest changes occurring? A central area of focus has been the frontal lobes. A long-range study by Jay Giedd and his colleagues at the National Institute of Mental Health involved the use of functional magnetic resonance imaging (fMRI) to scan the brains of nearly 1,000 healthy children and adolescents aged 3 to 18. Giedd discovered that just prior to puberty (between ages 9 and 10), the frontal lobes undergo a second wave of reorganization and growth, representing millions of new synapses (2007). Then, around age 11, a massive pruning of these connections begins and continues into early adulthood. Recall that, although it may seem like more synapses would be beneficial, the brain actually consolidates learning by pruning away excess connections and ensuring that the most useful synapses are maintained. This, in turn, allows the brain to operate more efficiently.

The brain consolidates learning by pruning away excess connections and ensuring that the most useful synapses are maintained.

In addition to this winnowing of connections in the adolescent brain, another developmental factor is also at play. One of the final steps in developing an adult brain is myelination. Recall that myelin first develops in the more primitive areas of the brain and then gradually moves to the areas responsible for higher-level functioning. Myelin increases the speed of the axon potential up to 100 times more than in neurons without myelin. During the teenage years, then, not only does the number of connections change, but the speed of those connections becomes faster. It is not surprising, then, to find that myelination occurs in the frontal lobes last. Researchers at the University of California, Los Angeles compared scans of young adults (age 23–30) with those of teens (age 12–16), looking for signs of myelin, which would imply more mature, efficient connections. As expected, teenagers' frontal lobes showed less myelination than did those of young adults. This is the last part of the brain to mature; full myelination is probably not reached until 30 years of age, or perhaps later (Giedd, 2007).

Why are these changes in the frontal lobes significant? The frontal lobes—specifically the area right behind the forehead called the prefrontal or orbitofrontal cortex—are often referred to as the "CEO of the brain." It is in this part of the brain that executive decisions are made and where ethical/moral behavior is mediated. In fact, this part of the brain has been dubbed by Giedd as "the area of sober second thought" (2007). Individuals with damage to this part of the brain often know what they are supposed to do but are unable to do it. In these people, the damage also appears to impair their ability to imagine future consequences of their actions; they tend to be uninhibited and impulsive. Such observations suggest that teens may have difficulty inhibiting inappropriate behaviors because the circuitry necessary for this control is not fully mature.

The prefrontal cortex is responsible for many cognitive and behavioral functions, including the ability to

- Organize multiple tasks.
- Inhibit specific impulses.
- Maintain self-control.
- Set goals and priorities.
- Empathize with others.
- Initiate appropriate behavior.
- Make sound judgments.
- Form strategies.
- Plan ahead.
- Adjust behavior based on a changing situation.
- Stop an activity upon completion.

During the teenage years, not only does the number of neural connections change, but the speed of those connections becomes faster.

Observations suggest that teens may have difficulty inhibiting inappropriate behaviors because the circuitry necessary for such control is not fully mature.

These functions are practically a laundry list of characteristics that adolescents often lack. Many researchers suspect that an unfinished prefrontal cortex, with its excess of synapses and unfinished myelination, contributes to adolescents' deficits in these areas. Their brains often aren't prepared to assume the role of CEO, resulting in a lack of reasoned thinking and performance.

Scientists have discovered that, in the teen brain, the emotional center matures before the frontal lobes.

Another factor at play sheds some light on adolescents' often overemotional behavior. Scientists have discovered that, in the teen brain, the emotional center matures before the frontal lobes. Emotions, therefore, often hold sway over rational processing. Considering that the prefrontal cortex allows *reflection* and the amygdala is designed for *reaction,* we can begin to understand the often irrational and overly emotional reactions of teenagers. Our oft-asked question when teens engage in irrational behavior—"What were you thinking?"—is difficult for them to answer because, in many cases, they weren't thinking reflectively; they were reacting impulsively. This phenomenon has been further validated by a research team led by Deborah Yurgelun-Todd at Harvard Medical School's McLean Hospital. The team used functional magnetic resonance imaging to compare adolescent brain activity to activity in adult brains. They found that when identifying emotional expressions on faces, adolescents activated the amygdala more often than the frontal lobes. The opposite was seen in adults. In terms of behavior, the adults' responses were more intellectual, and the teens' responses were more reactive or "from the gut."

The neurotransmitter dopamine, a naturally produced stimulant, plays an important role in the often reckless behavior of adolescents. It is critical for focusing attention, especially when there are conflicting options. When a goal is not obvious, reflection (not impulse) is necessary to make a good decision. Early in adolescent development, dopamine levels are relatively low, which may account for teens' reactive behavior. The good news is that dopamine flows to the prefrontal cortex grow dramatically as we age, resulting in an increased capacity for more mature judgment and impulse control. Until this system is mature, though, decisions are often made by impulse.

Substance Abuse During Adolescence

Since it has become clear that, in contrast to previously held assumptions, there is a tremendous amount of change taking place in the adolescent brain, we need to consider the unique ways that alcohol and other drugs affect teen brains and behavior. The shaping and fine-tuning of the frontal lobes are, at least in part, mediated by experience. This raises the critically important possibility that drug abuse could alter normal development of the brain. Current estimates suggest that roughly 50 percent of all high school seniors consume alcohol at least once a month, nearly 50 percent have tried marijuana at least once, and 17 percent regularly smoke cigarettes (Johnston, O'Malley, & Bachman, 2001; Kann et al., 2000). The National Institute on Alcohol Abuse and Alcoholism reports that alcohol kills six and a half times more people under the age of 21 than all other drugs combined.

Much of the research on alcohol and its effects has been conducted using animal studies. Using rats, Barbara Markwiese and colleagues (Markwiese, Acheson, Levin, Wilson, & Swartzwelder, 1998) found that alcohol disrupts the activity of an area of the brain essential for memory and learning—the hippocampus—and that this area is much more vulnerable to alcohol-induced learning impairments in adolescent rats than in adult rats. There is some evidence that the human hippocampus reacts in a similar manner. A study by Michael De Bellis and colleagues (De Bellis et al., 2000) found that hippocampal volumes were smaller in individuals who abused alcohol during adolescence and that the longer one abused alcohol, the smaller the hippocampus became.

Research by Sandra Brown and colleagues at the University of California, San Diego produced the first concrete evidence that heavy, ongoing alcohol use by adolescents can impair brain functioning (Brown, Tapert, Granholm, & Delis, 2000). They found several

The shaping and fine-tuning of the frontal lobes are, at least in part, mediated by experience.

differences in memory function between alcohol-dependent and nondrinking adolescents, none of whom used any other drugs. In the study, 15- and 16-year-olds who drank heavily (i.e., more than 100 lifetime alcohol-use episodes) scored lower on verbal and nonverbal retention of information than did their peers who didn't drink.

Additional research tried to answer whether or not heavy drinking is more dangerous for the brain at 15 than at 20 (Brown et al., 2000). The researchers hypothesized that drinking may be more dangerous because the finishing touches on brain development (i.e., myelination and pruning) haven't been completed, and alcohol may interrupt or disturb these refining processes. More studies will be needed to produce a definitive answer, but this research is an important step toward confirming what many scientists have suspected for some time: teenagers who drink may be exposing their brains to the toxic effects of alcohol during a critical time in brain development.

> *Teenagers who drink may be exposing their brains to the toxic effects of alcohol during a critical time in brain development.*

Not only are the frontal lobes of adolescent brains going through major changes, but the molecular and chemical systems are also experiencing rapid change. Many substances appear to have a heightened effect on teens. Researchers at Duke University found that adolescent brains (when compared with adult brains) respond more intensely to nicotine. In other studies, dopamine receptor levels in the pleasure center of rats' brains (the nucleus accumbens) increase dramatically between 25 and 40 days after birth—the rat's adolescent phase (Spear, 2000). These receptors play a huge role in the pleasure-producing properties of drugs. It is not yet clear if the human adolescent brain evidences this same increase, but it is probable (since findings from animal studies are often later found to be true for humans).

Adolescent Sleep Patterns

A common complaint voiced by parents of teenagers is that their kids insist that they can't fall asleep until midnight, but they require shouts and coercion to get out of bed in the morning and make it to school on time. Parents aren't the only ones with complaints about adolescents' sleep habits. Teachers of early morning classes often complain that their students seem to be present in body only; students frequently nod off or, at the least, are drowsy and difficult to teach. Surprisingly, the fault may lie in biology, which is ultimately behind adolescent sleep problems. This is yet another area where adolescents' brains appear to move to the beat of a different drummer (Carskadon, 1999).

Our sleep cycles are determined by circadian rhythms, a sort of internal biological clock that determines how much sleep we need, when we become sleepy at night, and when we awaken in the morning. Sleep researcher Mary Carskadon, of Brown University's Bradley Hospital, has discovered that teenagers need more sleep than they did as children (2002).

Conventional wisdom has held that young children need 10 hours of sleep per night and that, as we become adults, this need decreases to eight hours per night. Teenagers have traditionally been included in the adult group. Carskadon, however, has shown that teens actually require more sleep than adults. In order to function well and remain alert during the day, they need nine hours and 15 minutes of sleep, possibly because the hormones critical to growth and sexual maturation are mostly released during sleep. One survey of the sleep patterns of 3,000 teenagers showed that the majority slept only about seven hours per night, with more than 25 percent averaging six and a half hours or less on school nights (Carskadon, 1999). Given that sleep is a time when brain cells replenish themselves and when connections made during the day are strengthened, sleep deprivation can have a major negative effect on learning and memory (Carskadon, 2002).

A second finding from Carskadon's research is that teenagers' biological clocks appear to be set later in the day than those of children or adults. They do not get sleepy as early as they did when they

Our sleep cycles are determined by circadian rhythms, a sort of internal biological clock that determines how much sleep we need, when we become sleepy at night, and when we awaken in the morning.

Given that sleep is a time when brain cells replenish themselves and when connections made during the day are strengthened, sleep deprivation can have a major negative effect on learning and memory.

were preadolescents, and they tend to stay up later at night and sleep later in the morning. Most teenagers' brains aren't ready to wake up until 8:00 or 9:00 in the morning, well past the time when the first bell has sounded at most high schools. Therefore, teens who must get up before their internal clock "buzzes" miss out on an important phase of REM sleep that is important for memory and learning (Carskadon, 1999).

Not all scientists agree with this research on the adolescent brain. For example, Giedd's theory that brain changes are responsible for the often erratic behavior we see in teens is speculative. The theory is somewhat controversial because the roots of behavior are complex and cannot be explained easily by relatively superficial changes in the brain. However, if the theory turns out to be true, it would underscore the importance of providing careful guidance through adolescence, which isn't a bad idea in any case. Giedd believes that, unlike infants whose brain activity is completely determined by their parents and environment, the teens may actually be able to control how their own brains are wired and sculpted (2007). Adolescents, then, are laying down neural foundations for the rest of their lives. As parents and teachers, we have an opportunity and an obligation to educate adolescents about what is going on in their brains and the role they play in determining the structure and function of their brains for the rest of their lives.

Teaching the Adolescent

Later chapters in this book will focus on brain-compatible strategies designed for various ages. However, given the unique characteristics of adolescents, it seems appropriate to take a look at some general considerations that may help teachers when they plan classroom instruction for these students.

In a sense, adolescents' brains are primed to learn, yet we often see boredom and apathy in their behavior. When we consider the hyperactivity of the amygdala and the elevated energy levels at this stage of brain development, this isn't surprising. Too much classroom instruction is classified as "sit and git"—adolescents' least favorite classroom activity! Very few teens want to sit still and listen to a teacher deliver a lecture. While this approach can sometimes be appropriate during the teen years, consider using interactive activities and exercises, such as the following:

- After hearing or reading new information, students can be asked to demonstrate their understanding of the content by various methods, such as role-play, poster demonstrations, peer teaching, or journaling.
- Most parents will attest to the fact that adolescents like to argue. This propensity can be put to good use in class debates where students discuss the pros and cons of complex ethical issues.
- Project-based activities are especially motivating to teens. In collaborative groups, they can be encouraged to seek answers to problems facing the school or community, perhaps interviewing other teachers, parents, or adults for their points of view.
- Adolescents seem to crave novelty. Teachers can use this to their advantage by changing routines or room arrangement or by giving students answers and having them determine the questions (a la *Jeopardy*).
- Going on a treasure hunt for objects in the school that exemplify a mathematical concept or grouping classmates according to likes and dislikes are other possible ways to engage teens.
- Few of us are as proficient in current technology as adolescents. They text, download music and information, and surf the Internet with ease. Teachers should consider ways to integrate teens' ability to use technology in the classroom. Given the option, students might prepare multimedia presentations

Adolescents are not adults, and they need to be taught in a manner that both enables their brains to make sense of information and helps them recognize how this new information is relevant to their lives.

rather than book reports, or use e-mail to connect with experts in biology, history, music, mathematics, neuroscience, or other fields of study. The Internet provides a speedy way to research topics for term papers and projects; however, many students will need guidance to determine the validity of information found this way.

Teens are full of promise. They are energetic, caring, and capable of making many contributions to their communities. They are also able to make remarkable leaps in intellectual development and learning. Nevertheless, we must remember: They are not adults, and they need to be taught in a manner that both enables their brains to make sense of information and helps them recognize how this new information is relevant to their lives.

Synapse Strengtheners

1. Plan a lesson for a group of adolescents to help them understand the changes that are taking place in their brains.

2. If you are using this book as part of a study group, have each member plan a brief presentation on one of the major changes that take place in the brains of adolescents.

3. Add to this chapter's list of brain-compatible strategies ones that you think would be appropriate for adolescent students.

4. Explain why neuroscientists believe the adolescent brain is particularly vulnerable to drugs and alcohol.

7

The Role of Exercise, Sleep, Nutrition, and Technology

Part II of this book began with a discussion of neuroplasticity, the brain's ability to change based on environmental factors. It seems fitting, then, to conclude this part with a look at how four specific environmental factors—exercise, sleep, nutrition, and technology—affect learning and memory.

Moving to Learn

In an effort to increase academic test scores, many schools and districts have begun focusing more of the school day on core academic subjects. At the same time, they are decreasing the amount of time spent on "peripheral" subjects such as music, art, and physical education. A look at emerging research concerning the effects of exercise on brain function would suggest that this practice may be counterproductive. It appears that exercise may play a very important role in the learning process in several ways.

The first positive physical effect of exercise is an increased oxygen flow to the bloodstream. Aerobic exercise has been shown to pump more blood throughout the body, including the brain. More blood means more oxygen, which increases capillary health and the growth and plasticity of the frontal lobes (Aamodt & Wang, 2008). In a 2007 study, Charles Hillman, associate professor of kinesiology

Exercise plays a very important role in the learning process in several ways.

93

and neuroscience at the University of Illinois, had 259 3rd and 5th graders engage in aerobic exercise routines such as push-ups and timed running. He then checked the students' physical results against their math and reading scores on a standards achievement test. The results showed that the more physical tests they passed, the higher they scored on the achievement test. The effects appeared regardless of socioeconomic and gender differences (Castelli, Hillman, Buck, & Erwin, 2007). While the results of this study do not necessarily prove that exercise improves test scores, the correlation is strong enough to warrant our consideration.

A second physical benefit comes from the release of protein IGF-1, which triggers the release of brain-derived neurotrophic factor (BDNF), which, in turn, stimulates neural growth and learning (Cozolino, 2008). John Ratey, clinical associate professor of psychiatry at Harvard Medical School and coauthor of the book *Spark: The Revolutionary New Science of Exercise and the Brain*, calls BDNF Miracle-Gro for the brain. Ratey cites studies undertaken in schools that show not only how exercise enhances student learning but how it positively affects emotional and physical well-being as well (Ratey & Hagerman, 2008).

Studies have shown that exercise enhances student learning and positively impacts students' emotional and physical well-being.

As we have seen, research shows that we continue to grow new neurons throughout our lives. Therefore, a third (and perhaps the most important) benefit of exercise is its potential impact on neurogenesis. Neurogenesis has been found in the olfactory bulb and in the dentate gyrus of the hippocampus. Knowing that the hippocampus is involved in the storage, consolidation, and retrieval of information, it is important to know if exercise plays a role in the generation of new cells in this structure. The answer appears to be that it does just that. It was previously shown that running on a treadmill generates new neurons in the dentate gyrus of the rat hippocampus (Cameron, Woolley, McEwen, & Gould, 1993). Recent research by Scott Small, a neurologist at the Columbia University Medical Center, and Fred Gage, a neurobiologist at the Salk Institute in San Diego, has shown that exercise can also induce neurogenesis in humans (Patoine, 2007).

This research may initially appear to have little significance for the classroom teacher, who typically does not control school policies regarding physical education classes or recess schedules. However, there are many classroom variables that teachers *do* control that can significantly affect their students' activity levels. For example, students can learn math facts or multiplication tables by marching to music as they count by 3s or 7s; they can act out nouns, verbs, and adjectives in a charades fashion; or they can role-play an event in history.

Some movement activities can serve as quick "brain breaks" when students have been sitting idle for a prolonged period of time. Simple movements such as jumping jacks or hopping on one foot will increase oxygen flow to the brain and release pent-up energy. Many songs also include movement, including "Head, Shoulders, Knees, and Toes" and "Hokey Pokey." Older students may enjoy dancing to familiar pop or hip-hop tunes to which they have composed new lyrics that include vocabulary words or key concepts. A very active (and very fun) activity that works particularly well in foreign language classes involves acting out fairy tales with exaggerated movements and target-language vocabulary.

Movement activities can serve as quick "brain breaks" when students have been sitting idle for a prolonged period of time.

Whatever method or activities teachers decide to use, it is important to explain to students (and perhaps the principal and parents as well) why they are being asked to get up and move around. The ability to explain the research that underlies this concept increases the teacher's professional credibility and makes it more likely that these activities will be seen as relevant to student learning.

Sleep on It

Why we sleep has long been a subject of mystery. There must be a reason why we spend one-third of our lives asleep, but it has typically been difficult to study. There has been, up until recently, little solid research and almost no consensus among experts as to the actual purpose of sleep—no one was really sure what went on in the brain during sleep. One prominent notion was that, during sleep, there was a cessation of brain activity. However, a large convergence of recent research has discovered that quite the opposite is true. In fact, there are periods during the sleep cycle when the brain is as active as when you are awake and solving a problem—which may be exactly what the brain is doing. Today, we have a much better understanding of what occurs during sleep and of the role that sleep plays in learning and memory.

There are periods during the sleep cycle when the brain is as active as when you are awake and solving a problem.

Using electroencephalographic (EEG) recordings, researchers have established that there are two distinct stages of sleep: rapid eye movement (REM) and non–rapid eye movement (non-REM). These stages cycle back and forth five or six times a night, or every 90 to 110 minutes. During non-REM sleep, brain waves are slow and have a low frequency and high amplitude. During REM sleep, though, EEGs show fast brain waves that have high frequency with low amplitudes similar to those seen during a waking state. It is during REM sleep that nearly all dreams occur, especially the vivid ones.

Consolidation is the process of stabilizing a memory trace over time, moving it from short-term to long-term memory.

So what impact does sleep have on learning? A major player in learning and memory development is consolidation (discussed in greater detail in Part IV of this book). Simply defined, consolidation is the process of stabilizing a memory trace over time, moving it from short-term to long-term memory. New information is not "fixed" the moment it is heard or read; it takes time to become gelled or consolidated. Recent research points to sleep as an important player in this process (Huber, Ghilardi, Massimini, & Tononi, 2004; Maquet, 2001; Stickgold, 2003). Sleep—a time when our brains are relieved from processing the continual input of information that occurs while we are awake—seems to be when neural connections are strengthened. It also appears to be the time when the brain's two memory structures, the hippocampus and the neocortex, communicate with each other to increase the probability that information is retained.

In his book *Searching for Memory*, Daniel Schacter relates the story of Jonathan Winson, a neuroscientist who proposed that, during sleep, the brain continues to work though the experiences of the day (1996). Winson's hypothesis has received a great deal of support from recent studies of animal and human brains. In one study, participants repeatedly typed a sequence of letters on a keyboard. They were trained in the morning and tested 12 hours later, but they showed no improvement. After a full night's sleep, however, their performance improved by almost 20 percent. Using brain imaging techniques, scientists discovered that some brain areas that were activated during the training were reactivated during sleep (Society for Neuroscience, 2003b). Another interesting study scrutinized the brain activity of rats while they ran through a maze and while they slept. Not surprisingly, the activity patterns in the rats' brains were nearly identical when they slept to when they were actually running the maze. It appears that the rats were rehearsing what they had learned as they slept (Walker, Brakefield, Morgan, Hobson, & Stickgold, 2002). Additional studies, both behavioral and molecular, suggest that the "off-line" processing of information that occurs during sleep strongly contributes to memory formation (Maquet, 2001).

Understanding that the learning process is actively taken up by the brain during sleep, the next issue explored by researchers was the connection between types of learning and types of sleep. What they discovered is that REM sleep particularly benefits consolidation of skills and habits, while non-REM sleep is more beneficial to the consolidation of facts and concepts (OCED/CERI, 2007). An additional benefit of sleep is that it appears to help store facts and make connections among them. In other words, sleep seems to support insight, sometimes called the "nocturnal *aha.*" Recall Otto Loewi (from Chapter 4), who had a dream about a problem that he had been trying to solve. After he awoke, he performed an experiment suggested by the dream, which ultimately led to the discovery of acetylcholine.

Behavioral and molecular studies suggest that the "off-line" processing of information that occurs during sleep strongly contributes to memory formation.

It should be evident at this point that sleep is more important than has been commonly believed.

It should be evident at this point that sleep is more important than has been commonly believed; it helps us learn! Two final questions that remain are: How much sleep do we need to maintain a healthy brain and improve memory? and What happens if we are deprived of sleep? The answer to the former depends largely on your age. Generally, children between 5 and 10 years old need about 12 hours of sleep each night; during adolescence, they require nine and a half hours. Unfortunately, many children in this age range do not meet this target. What are the effects of lack of sleep? Sleep deprivation has been the subject of research for many years. Overall, the result of this research indicates that brain function is visibly altered by sleep deprivation; however, the degree of alteration depends on the amount of sleep lost and on the task attempted.

At one end of the scale are people who have gone several days without sleeping. In these cases, brain function is severely affected to the point of decreased sensory acuity and motor speed, an impaired ability to memorize, and a prevalence of hallucinations (Berger, Berger, & Oswald, 1962). At the other end of the scale (and perhaps more critical for educators to understand) are people who experience only mild levels of sleep deprivation. How does this affect the brains of our students? Is a one-hour loss significant? The answer is *yes*. A study by Avi Sadeh of Tel Aviv University found that the effect of such a loss is indeed measurable. As a result of his research, Sadeh reports that a slightly sleepy 6th grader will perform in class just like a 4th grader (Sadah, Gruber, & Rav, 2003).

Sleep disturbances in children are highly prevalent, affecting nearly one-third of all school-age children (Rona, Li, Gulliford, & Chinn, 1998). Since many children have chronic sleep problems, there is naturally concern about the effects such problems have on their developing brains. Some studies suggest that lack of sleep is associated with poorer academic performance (Wolfson & Carskadon, 1998). Much more research needs to be done in this area, but even with limited knowledge it seems prudent to talk to students and their parents about establishing healthy sleep habits and ensuring a sufficient amount of sleep. Avoiding television, computer games, and other activities that "hype" the brain is helpful in achieving a restful night's sleep.

Nutrition's Role in Brain Development and Function

The importance of good nutrition for human health has long been known, but few studies considered the impact of nutrition on the brain. However, the results of several recent studies demonstrate how important nutrition is for both how the brain develops and how it functions. For example, it is now known that the brain grows rapidly between the 10th and 18th weeks of pregnancy; therefore, the food that a pregnant woman eats during this period is extremely important for the developing fetus. Babies born to mothers who maintained poor diets during pregnancy are at a higher risk for mental retardation or behavioral problems. The brain also undergoes a period of rapid growth during the first two years of life, so it is imperative that children receive adequate nutrition during this period (Chudler, 2001).

Recent studies have demonstrated the important connections between nutrition and brain development and function.

Proper nutrition is not just critical for brain development; it also plays an important role in brain function. In 1989, the results of a landmark study on the link between school breakfast and academic performance were published. The study was designed to look at how school breakfast affected the academic progress of 1,023 low-income students from 3rd through 5th grade. The students in the study who received a nutritious breakfast made significantly greater gains on standardized test scores and showed improvement in their academic scores in math, reading, and vocabulary compared to students who skipped breakfast or whose breakfast was nutritionally inadequate. In addition, their rates of absence and tardiness decreased (Meyers, Sampson, Weitzman, Rogers, & Kayne, 1989). A separate three-year study showed that a breakfast of cereal rich in

When students regularly eat a nutritious breakfast, they exhibit significant gains on standardized test scores and in their classes.

complex carbohydrates (compared to a glucose drink or no break-fast) improved attention, working memory, and episodic secondary memory (Wesnes, Pincock, Richardson, Helm, & Hails, 2003).

Another issue related to nutrition and learning deals with people who eat too much. According to the Wake Forest University Baptist Medical Center, 2.7 million children in the United States are "severely obese," a condition that affects their overall health (Bush, 2009). While there is little research that points to the impact obesity has on children's brains, it has been shown that overweight adults have 4 percent less brain tissue than average; obese adults have 8 percent less (LiveScience, 2009). Worldwide, more than 300 million people are now classified as "obese," according to the World Health Organization (LiveScience, 2009). Experts claim that the main cause of obesity is bad diet, including an increased reliance on highly processed foods (LiveScience, 2009).

According to the Society for Neuroscience, memory and learning are impaired by diets that contain high levels of saturated fats (2003a). Interestingly, recent findings have confirmed the benefits of highly unsaturated fats, commonly referred to as omega-3 fatty acids (Chudler, 2001). These fatty acids—found in coldwater fish, flax seeds, eggs, and certain meats—are crucial for hormone balance and the immune system, both of which are essential for a healthy brain. Studies in animals have shown that diets without omega-3 fatty acids lead to learning and motor problems and may affect systems that use dopamine and serotonin in the frontal cortex (Chudler, 2001).

Nearly all of the brain's neurotransmitters are composed of amino acids. We obtain amino acids from the food we eat, so it makes sense that what we eat affects the amount and efficiency of these brain chemicals. The amino acid tryptophan, synthesized from carbohydrates, is used to produce serotonin, a neurotransmitter that creates feelings of well-being and calmness. Tyrosine, an amino acid found in proteins, is used to make dopamine, a natural stimulant. Amino acids are also used to protect DNA and brain cell components

The food we eat directly affects the efficiency of neurotransmitters in our brains.

from damage. The bottom line is that the "old thinking" regarding a healthy body (i.e., what you probably learned in your elementary health studies) is still correct. Recent research has simply verified a very strong link between a healthy body and a healthy brain.

Technology and the Brain

Growing up, my parents didn't have to limit my time in front of a television or playing video games; we didn't have television, and the term *video game* was not yet in our vocabulary. When I was in high school and at university, none of my teachers told me how to use the Internet for research; we didn't have computers. For much of my life, I didn't know what a cell phone was, and the word *texting* was unheard of. Obviously, I grew up in a world that was technologically very different from the world in which today's children grow up. Whether my environment was better or worse is up for debate, but whether or not technology has an impact on brain development is not. The appropriate use of technology in schools is a hotly debated topic, and an exhaustive review of the literature in this area is beyond the scope of this book. However, given the potential effects of technology on the developing brain, a brief overview of some major research findings seems appropriate.

Few people remain neutral in the debate over how much television children should watch or which programs enhance or impede development. Jane Healy, in her book *Endangered Minds,* argues that *Sesame Street* (because of its passive nature) will be the death of reading (1990). On the other hand, the developers of the recently revived educational television show *The Electric Company* promise that their program will increase a child's ability to read (Davis, 2008). Several programs (advertised on television) promote teaching babies to read. However, leading reading researchers believe that these programs are developmentally inappropriate (Wolf, 2007).

The debate over the effects of television viewing is more complex than a simple case of "good" versus "bad"—most of the disagreement

The debate on the effects of television viewing is not a simple case of it being good or bad.

boils down to the fact that the positive and/or negative effects often depend on several factors. For example, my twin grandchildren learned to sign long before they could talk by watching an educational signing video for approximately 30 minutes each day or so. Research on teaching babies to sign (before they can talk) reveals that it increases their ability to communicate and enhances their vocabulary development (Goodwyn, Acredolo, & Brown, 2000). Conversely, recent research found that extensive exposure to *Baby Einstein* videos actually had a negative effect on the child's vocabulary development (Zimmerman, Christakis, & Meltzoff, 2007). It appears that the impact of videos and DVDs can be either positive or negative. The effect depends on many factors, including the content, age of the child, and amount of time the child spends viewing these various media.

On a positive note, perhaps it is possible that because of increasingly complex plots, storylines, and characters in modern television programs, viewers actually enhance their higher-level thinking skills. On the other hand, research has shown a link between extensive television viewing and obesity (Dietz & Gortmaker, 1985). It is fairly obvious that television, in itself, is neither a boon nor a blessing; its effects depend on the viewer's age, the content of the programs, the amount of time spent viewing, and the activities that television viewing replaces.

The same points are also true of video games and various forms of emerging technology. Writing in the *Journal of Youth and Adolescence*, Douglas Gentile argued that the influence of video games on the human brain is not an either/or proposition; games can have both positive and negative consequences (Gentile et al., 2009). While research studies often seem to produce conflicting results, these results depend on several factors: amount of time played, content of the game, structure of the game (i.e., what it requires a player to do), context (i.e., whether teamwork is required or not), and mechanics (i.e., what devices are used to play).

What are some benefits of video and computer games? Well-designed educational games can be natural teachers by focusing on critical skills, providing immediate specific feedback, adapting to individual learners, and providing opportunities to practice to the point of mastery. Games that meet these criteria not only are engaging and motivating but often produce excellent results. Another benefit may be the improvement of social skills. Studies of games that include situations where players work together in a team to help one another have shown that children are able to transfer these skills to other situations (Gentile et al., 2009).

There are two well-designed video games that serve as examples of how neuroscientific studies can be applied in the classroom to enhance student learning. The first is the result of the work of two neuroscientists, Paula Tallal and Michael Merzenich. They discovered that many reading problems stem from an auditory processing delay in the learner's brain. In response, they developed a computer game (FastForword) that has been very successful in ameliorating this problem and in increasing students' reading abilities (Miller, Merzenich, Saunders, Jenkins, & Tallal, 1997). The second is a more recent innovation that is also based on neuroscientific research. BrainWare Safari is a comprehensive video game designed to enhance cognitive skills, including visual and auditory discrimination and processing, short-term memory, long-term memory, attention, and thinking skills such as logic, reasoning, and problem solving. These skills are generally improved only by specialists working one-on-one with individuals in clinical settings. It has traditionally been nearly impossible for teachers to address these skills in the classroom. Initial research conducted on this video game, however, has shown that students can rapidly enhance their cognitive skills after 12 weeks of playing the games for 30 to 45 minutes a day, three or four times a week. The research also suggests that these skills are maintained and result in improved academic performance (Helms & Sawtelle, 2007).

Studies of video games that include situations where players work together in a team to help one another have shown that children are able to transfer these skills to other situations.

What are some negative effects of video and computer games? Many parents and educators are concerned about the violent content found in many video games. Their concern is well founded, since dozens of psychological studies indicate that playing these games increases aggressive thoughts, feelings, and behaviors (Anderson, 2004; Gentile & Gentile, 2008). In addition, some studies indicate that repeated exposure to violent episodes in a game results in players' suppressing their emotional responses (Gentile, 2009). In other words, it may be that repeated play of violent games desensitizes players to aggression and violence. Until further research is done, we will not know whether these behaviors become automatic or if they transfer to real-life settings.

As educators search for ways and means to increase student learning and positive behaviors, it has become evident that we need to look not only at what happens in the classroom but also at the impact of environmental factors outside the school. Parents, students, and teachers all need to be educated about the roles of exercise, sleep, nutrition, and technology on brain development. A partnership is necessary to educate the whole child!

Dozens of psychological studies indicate that playing violent video games increases aggressive thoughts, feelings, and behaviors.

Synapse Strengtheners

1. Prepare a lesson to teach your students about how much sleep they need and what happens in the brain as they sleep.

2. Explain to a colleague the various benefits of exercise for learning and memory.

3. If you are using this book with a study group, ask members to brainstorm ways to increase the amount of student movement in the classroom.

4. Prepare a presentation for parents about the role of movement, sleep, and nutrition on learning.

Part III

From Sensory Input to Information Storage

We now know more about why certain activities and strategies are more effective than others in increasing student understanding.

We can study the brain through many different lenses. In Part I, we looked at the anatomy (structure) and physiology (function) of the brain. Although an understanding of the parts of the brain and how they operate is important, it doesn't tell us how these parts work together to allow us to receive information; to discard what is irrelevant; or to store and recall information we've seen, heard, and thought. How does the brain create the elusive qualities we refer to as mind and memory? Studying the brain by analyzing its anatomy is a fascinating field of study, but it is limited. To further our understanding, we need another way to view the brain.

The following chapters look at the brain from the perspective of an information-processing model. This model can add to our knowledge base by helping us understand the roles that specific brain structures play in the complex acts of receiving, processing, storing, and retrieving information. Some of the theories and research discussed in this section does not come from neuroscience but, rather, from cognitive psychology and educational research. Though much of this research is not new, it takes on new meaning when viewed from a neurological perspective. For example, the concept of "transfer" has a long research history. Many classroom studies have documented the effect of prior knowledge on new learning—often called positive or negative transfer. Our comprehension of the concept is enhanced, however, when we understand its neurological underpinnings.

Information is not stored in one specific location in the brain but in various locations—visual, auditory, and motor cortices that are joined in circuits or networks of neurons. When we experience something new, the brain "looks" for an existing network into which the new information will fit. If the fit is good, the previously learned/stored memories give meaning to the new information, and we will have positive transfer. If the new information is similar in some aspects but not a complete fit, negative transfer may occur. This concept remains the same whether it is explained by an educational researcher or by a neuroscientist; however, as a teacher, I know that positive or negative transfer occurs, and I have a better understanding of *why* it occurs. This additional information increases my knowledge base and allows me to articulate to my students, their parents, and perhaps even to policymakers why certain activities and strategies are more effective than others in increasing student understanding of the concepts I teach.

8

Sensory Memory: Getting Information into the Brain

What is memory, and how does it relate to the learning process? We commonly think of memory as a "thing," and we talk about how poor our memory is or how much better someone else's memory is. In education, rote memorization of information is often viewed as poor practice. If we view memory as nothing more than simply remembering or memorizing information, it may seem to be too narrow a topic to begin a discussion of how the brain processes information. If we think about what life would be without memory, however, our perception changes somewhat. People who have lost their memories have lost much of what makes them who they are. What makes us unique—and, to a large degree, what determines who we become—is our ability to acquire and store new information. Out of that ability comes new concepts, new ideas, new feelings, and ultimately our behaviors. Memory is what enables us to learn by experience. In fact, memory is essential to survival. Without the ability to learn, store, and recall how we should respond to environmental dangers and to know when and how to run or fight, the individual has little chance of survival. Seen in this light, an understanding of memory becomes vitally important to us as parents and educators. There is only a small formal distinction between

People who have lost their memories have lost much of what makes them who they are.

107

"learning" and "memory"; the two are so inextricably linked that a study of one becomes a study of the other.

Metaphors for Memory

Memory is what enables us to learn by experience— memory is essential to survival.

Human memory is invisible and intangible; we must consider it a *process*, not a *thing*. We have historically described memory in terms of metaphors, and, over time, two major metaphors have evolved. One views memory as a kind of intellectual muscle; the more you use it, the stronger it becomes. According to this view, the hours spent memorizing lines of poetry, important dates, and Latin phrases strengthen the mind and make it better able to remember other kinds of material. This is not necessarily true; in fact, extensive memorization may even decrease the brain's ability to memorize additional information (Underwood, 1968).

Another popular metaphor for memory has its origin in the writings of Plato, who likened the human mind to a tablet of wax on which impressions are made. In this view, rehearsing experiences or information strengthens or deepens the impressions, resulting in information that is more easily remembered. While this metaphor may seem to fit with many of our own experiences (e.g., practicing the multiplication tables or rules of spelling such as "*i* before *e*"), it doesn't explain why we have vivid recollections of emotional events we experienced only once or why, when we rehearse all items in a list equally, we remember the first and last items more readily than those in the middle. It appears that the reasons for remembering and forgetting are more complex than simple repetitions of experiences.

Psychiatrist Daniel Siegel proposes the following example, which points to this complexity. Imagine that someone asks you to picture the Eiffel Tower in your "mind's eye." This person's voice creates sound waves that vibrate the tympanic membranes in your ears. Those sound waves, in turn, are transformed into electrical impulses by the organ of Corti and forwarded to your temporal lobes for decoding. Next, the information is sent to your occipital lobes for visual processing. The inputs from these two parts of the brain are integrated, and you are able to "see" the Eiffel Tower. Siegel states that, when this happens, you reactivate a neural network that was previously established when you saw the Eiffel Tower or a picture of it (2000).

While you were reading the previous paragraph, you of course did not hear the sound of my voice, but I'm relatively certain that you "saw" the Eiffel Tower. If you have been to Paris and actually viewed this landmark, in all probability you also recalled some other things related to your visit, such as the weather and the people you were with. You may even have "heard" some of the sounds you heard that day. It is interesting that when you recall a visual image of something you previously viewed, you are activating many of the same neural networks that were activated originally (Begley, 2008).

In 1949, visionary psychologist Donald Hebb proposed a similar theory in his book, *The Organization of Behavior*. He proposed that neurons that fire together simultaneously are more likely to fire together again in the future (1949). Siegel colorfully rephrases what is known as Hebb's Law when he states, "Neurons that fire together, survive together and wire together" (2000). Many neuroscientists concur that this is probably the physiological basis for memory: Experience changes the way synaptic connections are made and increases the probability of firing in a predictable association with other neurons.

An Introduction to the Model

For the past several decades, the predominant model of memory has been an information-processing model. Growing out of information-processing theory, it became popular at about the same time as, or perhaps as a result of, the invention of the computer. Many variations on this model are the result of new understanding gained from many fields, including neuroscience, cognitive psychology, and developmental psychology.

"Neurons that fire together, survive together and wire together."

The diagram in Figure 8.1, which provides an organizing framework for human memory, should be viewed as a representation of the functional (rather than structural) properties of the human memory system. In other words, this model does not imply that these three broad categories of memory are located in different areas of the brain, nor is it meant to imply that they are separate, autonomous systems. Furthermore, the three categories do not represent sharp, distinct stages in the memory process; instead, they are convenient labels to help us understand the processes by which the human mind encodes, stores, retrieves, and integrates new information with previously stored information. Our starting point in understanding learning and memory will be with *sensory* memory.

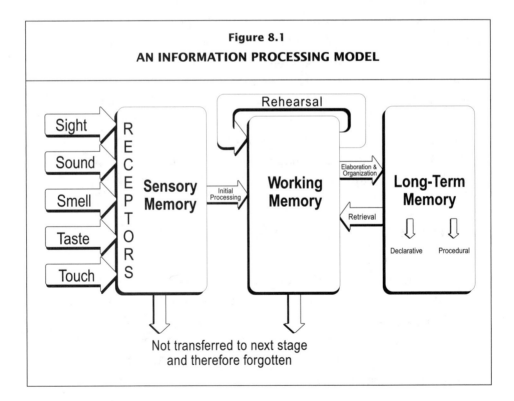

Figure 8.1
AN INFORMATION PROCESSING MODEL

Sensory Memory

Figure 8.2 illustrates the beginning part of the model, sensory memory. It might more accurately be labeled "sensory store," "sensory buffers," or even "sensory perception." Everything in our memory begins as a sensory input from the environment. The role of sensory memory is to take the information coming into the brain through sensory receptors and hold it for a fraction of a second until a decision is made about what to do with it.

This process is fairly straightforward. For example, a light ray hits the retina of the eye and forms a brief memory (an *iconic* memory), which lasts only milliseconds. It is probably best understood as a

The role of sensory memory is to take the information coming into the brain through sensory receptors and hold it for a fraction of a second until a decision is made about what to do with it.

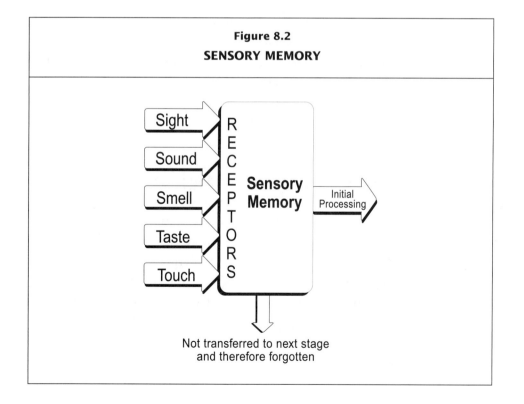

Figure 8.2
SENSORY MEMORY

prolongation of the original stimulus trace required to allow time for recognition and further processing to take place. According to Joseph Torgesen, professor at Florida State University, the same is probably true with the other senses (1996). One exception, however, may be auditory stimuli. Auditory signals are recorded briefly in what is usually referred to as *echoic* memory. There is some evidence that echoic traces may last a little longer, perhaps as long as 20 seconds (Gazzaniga, Ivry, & Mangun, 1998).

Even though the process seems relatively simple, this sensory input does not arrive one piece at a time as separate bits of information; rather, it arrives simultaneously. During any fractional moment in time, an enormous amount of sensory stimuli bombards our bodies, giving us much more information than we can possibly comprehend. If you were consciously aware of all the images, sounds, tactile sensations, tastes, and smells that simultaneously shower down upon your body, you would experience sensory overload. Without some mechanism to organize these raw sensory data into meaningful patterns, you would not be able to function. Sensory memory, then, filters the enormous amount of information we experience through our senses and discards irrelevant data.

By some estimates, 99 percent of all sensory information is discarded almost immediately upon entering the brain.

The brain is sometimes referred to as a sponge that soaks up information. A better metaphor might be a sieve; by some estimates, 99 percent of all sensory information is discarded almost immediately upon entering the brain (Gazzaniga, 1998). The reason that the brain filters out such vast amounts of information is because much of it is irrelevant. There would normally be little functional or survival value in remembering what your clothes felt like on your body a few minutes ago or how a pen felt in your hand when you were writing a week ago. The question we must consider is how the brain decides what to keep and what to discard. What factors influence the brain to pay attention to certain stimuli and not others?

From Sensory Signals to Perceptions

All information received by sensory receptors needs to be sent to the appropriate sensory cortex to be processed. As you may remember from Chapter 2, the organ that plays a major role in this transfer is the thalamus. All sensory data, except smells, travel to the thalamus first. (Smell is received and processed simultaneously by the olfactory bulb and therefore does not need to be relayed to another part of the brain for processing.) From there, the data are relayed to the specific portion of the cortex designated to process sight, sound, taste, or touch. A discussion of the complex physiology by which this happens is beyond the scope of this book, but it is important to understand that as information travels from the sensory receptors to the site where it is processed, it is, in a sense, transformed. It changes from a photon of light or a sound wave into a percept. In other words, we do not "see" the photon of light or the sound wave per se—we *perceive* a figure or a sound, and the perception is uniquely shaped by that perceiving mind at that moment.

Perception refers to the meaning we attach to information as it is received through the senses. Our eyes may capture an image in much the same way as a camera does, but what we see (or perceive) is influenced by the information we have stored in our brains. For example, look at the following: Ƀ. If you were asked what *number* this is, you would probably say "13." Yet if you were asked to name the *letter,* you might answer "B." The figure didn't change; your perception changed based on what you were asked and your existing knowledge of numbers and letters. To a young child with no stored information of either numbers or letters, these would be meaningless marks on paper. The assignment of meaning to incoming stimuli, therefore, depends on prior knowledge and on what we expect to see. In a sense, the brain checks existing neural networks of information to see if the new information is something that activates a

Our eyes may capture an image in much the same way as a camera does, but what we see (or perceive) is influenced by the information we already have stored in our brains.

The assignment of meaning to incoming stimuli depends on prior knowledge and on what we expect to see.

It is impossible to "not pay attention"; the brain is always paying attention to something.

previously stored neural network. (We'll look at the physiology of how neural networks are formed in a later chapter.) This matching of new input to stored information is called pattern recognition and is a critical aspect of attention. Pattern recognition works so well that you are able to recognize a letter whether it is printed *B*, *b*, or *B*. However, if you had never seen a *b* before and did not know what it represented, it would be meaningless no matter what it looked like because there would be no recognition or match.

From Perception to Attention

Children are often criticized for "not paying attention," but this is actually an impossible task. The brain is always paying attention to something. What we really mean when we say this is that children do not pay attention to what we think is relevant or important. Attention, as we all know, is selective.

What are the factors that influence whether a stimulus is kept or dropped? Why is it that two people can experience the same sensory input, but they each attend to totally different elements of the input? It is important to be aware that, in this initial processing stage, we're not talking about a consciously driven process. Though it is true that, with conscious effort, you are able to direct and sustain your attention on a specific stimulus, this is not the case most of the time. It would be inefficient and perhaps impossible to consciously determine what you were going to focus on at every given moment. The brain is constantly scanning the environment for stimuli, a process done largely by automatic mechanisms. As you may recall from Chapter 2, the reticular activating system (RAS) plays an important role in filtering thousands of stimuli, excluding trivial information, and focusing on relevant data. In other words, your "unconscious" brain is usually in control of the initial decision-making process for you. What factors influence the brain during this initial filtering of information? How does the brain determine what is relevant and what is not?

One key component in the filtering process is whether the incoming stimulus is different from what we are used to seeing—whether it is novel. Novelty is an innate attention-getter. To survive, our remote ancestors had to be aware of any novel or unique stimuli present in the environment. We're not much different. Our brains are still programmed to pay attention to the unusual, such as a detour sign along a familiar route we're driving. Teachers often take advantage of this phenomenon by providing information in a surprising or novel manner—they come to class dressed in the costume of a historical character or give students balloons to introduce a lesson on air pressure, for example.

However, novelty is difficult for a teacher to employ on a daily basis to obtain students' attention. The reason is something called habituation. If a sight or sound is new and unusual, we initially pay close attention to it, but if this same sight or sound occurs over and over, the brain normally becomes so accustomed to the stimulus that it ignores it. This is known as habituation. If you have ever lived near an airport, chances are you reached a point where you seldom paid attention to the planes taking off and landing. To be sure, you cannot avoid hearing a nearby jet taking off, but after the same sound is continually repeated on a daily basis, it is no longer novel and becomes filtered out by the sensory system as unimportant. This is why a device such as flicking the light switch off and on to get students' attention eventually loses its effectiveness. The students have become habituated to the flicking light and hence don't attend to it.

The intensity of stimuli is another factor that affects attention. Generally, the louder a sound or the brighter a light, the more likely each is to draw attention. When two stimuli are competing for attention, the one that is more intense will attract attention first. Advertisers take advantage of this phenomenon by increasing the volume of television commercials to get our attention.

A third factor that influences attention is movement. In general, our attention is directed toward stimuli that move. The illusion

One key component in the filtering process is whether the incoming stimulus is different from what we are used to seeing—whether it is novel.

of movement can be produced by blinking neon signs that attract attention more readily than signs that do not blink. The flashing lights on police cars are another example of movement as an attention-getting device.

At this point, we are talking about the processing that takes place during the initial presentation of stimuli to the sensory receptors. This processing is largely unconscious and, for the most part, out of our control. As we have seen, however, it is possible to influence what the brain pays attention to by using novelty, intensity, or movement. In the classroom, unfortunately, it is probable that none of these will prove useful over time because of habituation. Flicking the light switch to get students' attention may work well the first few times, but with extended use, students will fail to notice or respond to this signal. In the same vein, raising your voice level may get attention for a while, but it often results in students' raising their own voice levels to match yours. A novel event is obviously only novel for a short time. So does this mean that teachers and parents have little influence on what their students' or children's brains focus on? Are we at the mercy of a capricious brain that resists all efforts to get it to focus on a particular stimulus? No, we are not. Two factors strongly influence whether the brain initially attends to arriving information and whether this attention will be sustained. These two factors are meaning and emotion, and we do have some control over them.

Meaning and Attention

Earlier in this chapter, we discussed pattern recognition, which describes how the brain attempts to match incoming sensory stimuli with information that is already stored in circuits or networks of neurons. In other words, the neural networks "check out" sensory stimuli as soon as they enter the brain to see if they form a familiar pattern. If they do, a match occurs, and the brain determines that the new visual stimuli are familiar. In this case, the new information makes sense or has meaning. What happens if there is no

Neural networks "check out" sensory stimuli as soon as they enter the brain to see if they form a familiar pattern.

match? The brain may attend to the meaningless information for a short time because it is novel, but if it can make no sense out of the incoming stimuli, the brain will probably not process this information further.

Think about the following situation: You are sitting in a doctor's office, waiting for an appointment. You pick up a book in the waiting room and discover that the book is written in a language you don't read. What do you do? You would probably put the book down rather quickly and look around for something to read that you *can* understand. Now imagine that you are trying to read a document full of complex charts, graphs, and formulas that make no sense to you. Sustained attention to something you can't comprehend is not only boring, it's almost impossible. I'm afraid that, all too often, we expect such a feat from our children and students.

Look at the illustration in Figure 8.3. You may have some initial difficulty seeing anything but spots. With a little diligence, however, you should eventually see the image of a dog—more specifically, the image of a Dalmatian. (Hint: The Dalmatian's head is pointing down, and it is sniffing the ground or drinking from a puddle. It is moving away from you.) Once you've seen the dog, it will be difficult *not* to see it. It is almost impossible to draw an outline around the whole dog, yet you can discern it nonetheless.

Let's think about what just happened in your brain. Even though you cannot see the entire dog, your brain used the available information to allow you to recognize it. What is necessary for this to occur? Remember the example cited earlier about being able to visualize the Eiffel Tower in your "mind's eye"? You were able to "see" it because you activated a previously established circuit of neurons in which that information was stored. The same thing is true here. You would never be able to detect this dog among the spots if you had never seen a Dalmatian or a picture of one (and had that memory stored in your brain). You cannot reconstruct or reactivate a neural circuit or network if it was never activated in the first place.

Sustained attention to something you can't comprehend is not only boring, it's almost impossible.

You cannot reconstruct or reactivate a neural circuit or network if it was never activated in the first place.

Figure 8.3

ACTIVATING NEURAL NETWORKS TO CONSTRUCT MEANING

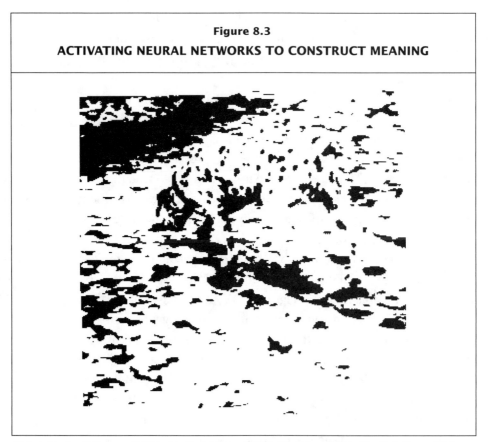

Attributed to Ronald C. James. Published in Hunt, Morton. (1982). *The Universe Within.* New York: Simon & Schuster, p. 72.

We can now begin to understand the concept of meaning and the important role it plays in attention. If the brain can find no previously activated networks into which the new information fits, it is much less likely to attend to this information. Our species has not survived by attending to and storing meaningless information.

Consider students in a classroom who are confronted with information that doesn't match anything they've previously experienced. Their brains look for an appropriate network to help them make sense of (or construct meaning from) this information. If nothing can be found, the information is discarded as meaningless. Without being facetious, is it possible that much of what we teach in schools fits this description? If so, we shouldn't be surprised when our students' brains refuse to attend to the information we teach. In later chapters, we'll discuss various strategies that can be employed to make information more meaningful; at this point, let's move on to a second factor that has an equal (if not greater) impact on attention.

Our species has not survived by attending to and storing meaningless information.

Emotion and Attention

In his talks to educators, Robert Sylwester often states, "Emotion drives attention, and attention drives learning" (1995). To a large degree, this appears to be true. Understanding why will require us to look more carefully at several subcortical structures that control emotional responses.

Recall that the brain is constantly scanning its environment, sifting and sorting through the incoming information to determine what to keep and what to ignore. Why does this occur? It occurs because it is essential for the survival of the individual and of the species. Think about it: If a dangerous animal were charging toward you, and your brain decided to focus on the animal's rate of speed or taxonomic classification, you wouldn't be around later to pass on your genes. It is imperative that we possess a system that quickly separates the essential from the frivolous, and we do. At one time, this system was called the limbic system, but this term proved to be somewhat limiting and perhaps even inaccurate. Scientists disagree about which structures compose this system, and, more importantly, they disagree over whether it is even a system. Perhaps the terminology isn't that important; what is important is that a group of structures work together to help us focus on those aspects of environmental input that are critical to our survival.

The first of these structures is the thalamus, a sort of relay station that receives incoming information and sends it on to the appropriate part of the cortex for further processing. At the same time, however, this information is also sent to the amygdala. It is as if the message is duplicated so that it can be sent to different areas of the brain simultaneously. Why are our brains designed for this type of parallel processing? As you may recall, the amygdala determines the emotional relevance of incoming stimuli. It is responsible for the immediate responses to questions such as "Is this something that could hurt me?" or "Do I run away from this or toward it?" Conversely, the cortex processes incoming stimuli rationally; it places the information in context to make sense of it and decide on a course of action.

It may not come as a surprise that the pathway between the thalamus and the amygdala is much shorter than the pathway between the thalamus and the cortex. In fact, the thalamus–amygdala pathway is one synapse long, allowing the amygdala to receive the information approximately a quarter of a second sooner than the cortex (LeDoux, 1996). The cortex provides a more accurate representation of the stimulus, but it takes much longer to do so. If there is potential danger, time is of the essence. In his book *The Emotional Brain*, Joseph LeDoux calls the thalamus–amygdala pathway the "quick and dirty route," which signifies the often less-than-rational response the brain makes in emotional situations. Understanding this unconscious emotional response system (the "quick and dirty route") also helps explain the less-than-rational reactions we sometimes observe in students who are confronted with situations that their brains perceive to be emotionally attention-getting.

The brain is biologically programmed to attend to information that has strong emotional content first.

The brain is biologically programmed to attend to information that has strong emotional content first. (It is also programmed to remember this information longer, a phenomenon we'll examine in the next chapter.) Our brains and our students' brains are designed to pay attention to not only physical dangers in the environment but facial expressions and other components of body language that contain emotional information necessary for survival.

In this chapter, we've looked at the first step in information processing or, to put it another way, the first step in memory and learning. All the stimuli that constantly bombard our senses successfully find their way into our brains, but few remain there for long. Educators need to be aware of the processes that occur in the brain during this initial "sifting and sorting" stage. Cognizance of the roles that both meaning and emotion play is critical to understanding why the brain pays attention to some stimuli and not to others. If students do not pay attention to what is being taught (or if they are paying attention to something else), there is little chance that they will learn what is being taught. Attention drives learning! In the next chapter, we'll look at how we can consciously use meaning and emotion to enhance student learning.

Educators need to be aware of the processes that occur in the brain during the initial "sifting and sorting" stage.

Synapse Strengtheners

1. Suppose a colleague of yours complains that his or her students don't pay attention. How could you help him or her understand some of the reasons this only *appears* to be the case?

2. Begin a reflection journal by writing one or two paragraphs on the role that emotion plays in attention and learning. You may want to add to your journal periodically as you reflect on your teaching, and record how you are incorporating some of what you learn about emotion.

3. If you are reading this book as a part of a study group, discuss what makes something meaningful to the brain. You might also want to discuss whether your school's present curriculum has inherent meaning or if you need to find ways to make it more meaningful.

9

Working Memory: The Conscious Processing of Information

Within the human cortex lies a critical part of the secret of human consciousness: our ability to be aware of what we are seeing and hearing, to use language to communicate with one another, to conjure up stored visual images and describe them, and other abilities considered to be the unique domain of the human brain. As you will recall from Chapter 8, not all information processing is conscious; in fact, most of it is not. The brain is constantly taking in sensory stimuli from the outside world, assembling and sorting the stimuli, discarding much of the information, and directing only some of it to our conscious attention. Although consciousness represents a small part of information processing, it is nevertheless an essential component; without it, we could not remember an unfamiliar phone number long enough to dial it or recall the first part of a sentence as we reach the end.

Although it is important, the ability to hold small amounts of information is transient and short term. We generally forget an unfamiliar phone number as soon as we dial it, and most of us would be unable to repeat the exact words of a sentence that contained more than a few words. Figure 9.1 depicts this short-term processing ability.

We should use this model with caution. As discussed in the previous chapter, we should view this diagram as a representation

Although consciousness represents a small part of information processing, it is nevertheless an essential component.

122

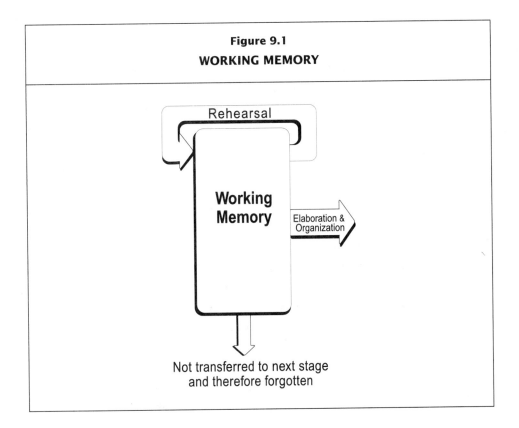

Figure 9.1
WORKING MEMORY

of the *functional*—rather than *structural*—properties of the human memory system. None of the three broad divisions of human memory is a separate, dedicated storage area in a particular region of the brain. This model summarizes the broad range of memory phenomena from the perspective of information processing. Most scientists agree that memory is a multifaceted, complex process that involves activating a large number of neural circuits in many areas of the brain. There is no uniform agreement, however, on a model that accurately represents these many facets. Some researchers view short-term memory and working memory as different processes; others consider working memory to be part of short-term memory. Some cognitive scientists do not believe that working memory and

Most scientists agree that memory is a multifaceted, complex process that involves activating a large number of neural circuits in many areas of the brain.

long-term memory are totally separate but that working memory is best conceptualized as a portion of long-term memory that is temporarily activated (Wagner, 1996). This is similar to Hebb's view that memory represents continued activity or reverberation of the neural cells involved in perception. Today, most scientists seem to prefer the term "working memory" to "short-term memory," as the former better characterizes the many complex activities that it represents. (Both sensory and working memory are of short duration, so in a sense they could both be considered "short-term.")

Working memory allows us to integrate current perceptual information with stored knowledge and to consciously manipulate the information (think about it, talk about it, and rehearse it) well enough to ensure its storage in long-term memory. We should not think of working memory solely as a conduit to long-term memory, however; much incoming sensory information is needed only temporarily and then discarded. Working memory appears to serve other purposes as well. Cognitive psychologist B. F. Pennington refers to working memory as a "computational arena," in which information relevant to a current task is both maintained in consciousness and subject to further processing (Torgesen, 1996). An example of the computational function of working memory would be what happens when you do mental arithmetic such as $24 \times 8 = 192$. Working memory is also involved in higher cognitive "executive functions," such as planning, organizing, and rehearsing. Think of working memory as the CEO of a company, responsible for keeping track of who does what and for making sure everything gets done.

Although working memory appears to reside in multiple locations in the brain (depending on the task it is given), many scientists believe that the frontal lobe (specifically the prefrontal cortex) is the primary location of this activity (Bear, Conners, & Paradiso, 1996; Gazzaniga, Ivry, & Mangun, 1998). Researchers with the National Institute of Mental Health used fMRI technology to scan the brains of subjects as they were exposed to an unfamiliar face or a series

Working memory allows us to integrate current perceptual information with stored knowledge and to consciously manipulate the information (think about it, talk about it, and rehearse it) well enough to ensure its storage in long-term memory.

Think of working memory as the CEO of a company, responsible for keeping track of who does what and for making sure everything gets done.

of letters, processed the information briefly, and then recalled it. The imaging revealed increased activity in the prefrontal cortex. When the investigators gave the subjects increasingly longer strings of numbers to remember, the prefrontal brain areas distinguished themselves by working harder as the load became more complex (Callicott et al., 1999).

Studies of patients with lesions in their frontal lobes have highlighted another function of this area: the shaping of behavior and the ability to carry out plans. Antonio Damasio, in his book *Descartes' Error* (1994), extensively examined one of the most famous cases of frontal lobe damage: Phineas Gage, a railroad crew foreman. One day in 1848, Gage was tamping explosive powder into a hole in preparation for blasting when the tamping iron he was holding contacted a rock, and the powder exploded. When the charge went off, it sent the rod into Gage's head just below his left eye. After passing through his left frontal lobe, it exited the top of his head. Amazingly, Gage survived, but his personality was drastically and permanently altered. Before the accident, he was responsible, respected, and known as a shrewd businessperson. Following the accident, he behaved erratically, had difficulty making decisions or planning ahead, and became much like a recalcitrant child in his social interactions. Damasio proposed that the neural connections between the unconscious body states we call emotion and the conscious processing structures in the frontal lobes (which were severely damaged in Gage's brain) are what allow us to function rationally, plan for the future, and make appropriate cognitive and emotional decisions. Without the circuits and structures that make up working memory, we would be unable to access the emotional connections so critical for rational thought and planning.

Characteristics of Working Memory

We might think of working memory as a "scratch pad" that doesn't hold much information and is more easily lost than a notebook or larger volume. Indeed, its abilities are limited. Let's look first at its limitations and then focus on methods for overcoming some of them.

The 18-Second Holding Pattern

The first limitation of working memory deals with its ability to hold on to information. Without rehearsal or constant attention, information remains in working memory for only about 15–20 seconds (McGee & Wilson, 1984). Peterson and Peterson carried out the first systematic study of this phenomenon in 1959 (Gazzaniga, Ivry, & Mangun, 1998). They gave subjects the task of remembering a set of three consonants, such as *SVL* or *XCJ*, that flashed on a screen for a fraction of a second. The subjects were immediately instructed to count backward by threes in time with a metronome. The researchers assumed that this interference task would prevent the subjects from remembering and correctly repeating the letters, thus providing an accurate measure of how long unrehearsed information remains in working memory. On different trials, they asked subjects to stop counting and name the consonants after 3, 6, 9, 12, or 18 seconds. At 3 seconds, approximately 20 percent of the subjects had forgotten the consonants, and at 18 seconds, no one could remember them.

Eighteen seconds may seem to be so brief a memory span as to be almost useless, but a closer look suggests that this is actually efficient. If you could not remember information for at least 18 seconds without rehearsal, you would have already forgotten the words that made up the first part of this sentence, and comprehension would be impossible. On the other hand, it would be a disadvantage to remember permanently every word in every sentence you have ever read. A memory system that provides temporary storage of just the right amount of information without overloading itself is indeed efficient. Fortunately, as we will see later in this chapter, strategies exist for retaining information much longer than 18 seconds.

The Cocktail Party Effect

A second limitation of working memory is its inability to process two conscious trains of thought at the same time. In the noisy, confusing environment of a cocktail party, where many conversations are taking place, you are able to focus on a single conversation. The brain accomplishes this using selective auditory attention, often referred to as the "cocktail party effect." This allows you to filter out other, often louder conversations and pay attention to the one that is most relevant. However, if you wanted to listen to two conversations simultaneously or wanted your students to pay attention to what you were saying and what they were reading at the same time, you would have difficulty. As nice as it would be to focus on both tasks at the same time, it's not possible in most circumstances.

British psychologist E. C. Cherry first studied the cocktail party effect in the early 1950s. He analyzed the effect by providing competing speech inputs into each ear with headphones (dichotic listening). He sometimes asked subjects to repeat or "shadow" the train of thought coming into one ear while ignoring a similar input into the other ear. Under these conditions, the subjects could remember little of the un-shadowed message (Cherry, 1953). Although the cocktail party effect refers to auditory processing, a similar effect can be observed in visual processing.

The following experiment will allow you to experience this. Look at the group of words in Figure 9.2. Some of the words are written in bold type and some in light. As quickly as you can, read *only* the words in bold type.

Once you have finished, recall all you can about the message in bold without looking back. Now try to recall the words written in light type. Like the subjects in the shadowing experiment, you probably did not recall many of the latter. Even if you recall a word or two, did you notice that the words in light type are the same seven words repeated over and over?

Figure 9.2

A COCKTAIL PARTY EXPERIMENT

In performing an experiment like this one on man **attention** car **it** house **is** boy **critically** hat **important** shoe **that** candy **the** man **material** car **that** house **is** boy **being** hat **read** shoe **by** candy **the** man **subject** car **for** house **the** boy **relevant** hat **task** shoe **be** candy **cohesive** man **and** car **grammatically** house **correct** boy **but** hat **without** shoe **either** candy **being** man **so** car **easy** house **that** boy **full** hat **attention** shoe **is** candy **not** man **required** car **in** house **order** boy **to** hat **read** shoe **nor too** **difficult.**

It is nearly impossible to consciously process two trains of thought at the same time, especially if they involve the same sensory modality.

As a parent or teacher, you have no doubt witnessed the cocktail party effect in your child or student, or perhaps in yourself as well. It is nearly impossible to consciously process two trains of thought at the same time, especially if they involve the same sensory modality. (When you are talking on the phone and someone in the room wants to give you a message, it is far easier to process the message if it is written rather than spoken.) Consider the typical class lecture for which students are required to take notes. Trying to take coherent notes is a difficult task. As a student, if you begin to think about what the teacher just said, you may miss the next input. Students often write words on paper but have little conceptual understanding of what they just wrote. If students don't comprehend what is being said, don't see the relevance, or begin to daydream, none of the lecture is processed. Every teacher has had the experience of saying something one day and finding that his or her students act as if they've never heard it the very next day. Now we can begin to understand why this might happen.

Note that *doing* two things at the same time is different from consciously *processing* two inputs at the same time. It is certainly possible to *do* two things at the same time if one of them is automatic. Recall from Chapter 2 that motor neurons (with assistance from the cerebellum) may become so used to being activated in a particular sequence that they fire automatically with little or no conscious processing. When writing becomes automatic, it is no longer necessary to consciously determine when to dot an *i* or cross a *t*, allowing us to pay attention to the content of our writing. Most of the time, we are able to comprehend what we read because the decoding process is automatic. However, 1st grade students who still phonetically sound out most of the words in a sentence—and for whom decoding is not automatic—typically have a difficult time comprehending what they read.

The Magical Number Seven (Plus or Minus Two)

A third limitation of working memory is not being able to work with too much information at one time. In the 1950s, cognitive scientist George Miller conducted studies to determine how much information individuals can process consciously. Miller presented subjects with various numbers of items. Regardless of type—words, objects, or numerals—the number of items that subjects retained typically proved to be around seven. Miller described this phenomenon in a paper about "the magical number seven" (1956). His research validated something we've long known intuitively. Think about it: How many digits are there in a phone number? How many notes are in a scale? How many days are in a week? Miller referred to this characteristic of human memory as the span of immediate memory.

To test this for yourself, try the following test. Spend about seven seconds memorizing the following list of seven digits:

7 4 3 8 5 9 2

Students who phonetically sound out most of the words in a sentence—and for whom decoding is not automatic—typically have a difficult time comprehending what they read.

When you finish, look away and try repeating them in order. If you have an average memory span, you probably had no difficulty recalling all of them. Now spend 10 seconds trying to memorize the following list of 10 digits:

6 7 9 4 5 8 1 3 2 9

Unless you have an unusual memory span, you probably did not do as well on the second list.

Studies have shown that the number of items that can be held in working memory varies with age (Pascual-Leone, 1970). If a test requires a subject to recall strings of digits, such as the one in the previous paragraph, the typical five-year-old child can recall only two digits, plus or minus two. At 7, children can recall an average of three digits; and at 11, the average recall is five digits. The number of digits children can accurately recall increases by one every two years until a mental age of 15. At this point, the normal adult capacity of seven (plus or minus two) is reached (Pascual-Leone, 1970).

We should be cautious, however, in our attempts to determine the capacity of working memory from tests of digits or words alone. Working memory is more than a passive storehouse for discrete bits of information. In most learning situations, we are required to hold some bits of information in our consciousness while we manipulate other bits of information that are relevant to the task. Whether we are reading a passage in a text or solving a mathematical problem, the cognitive activity includes interplay of processing and storage. Tests of working memory that measure our ability to retain some information (while simultaneously carrying out ongoing processing activities) appear to be more accurate measures of the capacity of working memory in real-life tasks. When these more complex measures are used, we find that age does not predict capacity as reliably as do the difficulty and duration of the task (Towse, Hitch, & Hutton, 1998).

Overcoming the Limits of Working Memory

Working memory is indeed limited. Still, before we become too discouraged with its space limitations, we need to realize that these limitations can be circumvented somewhat. Understanding and using the methods for overcoming the shortcomings of working memory can greatly increase student learning.

Chunking

The first method for overcoming the limits of working memory is to "chunk" information. In discussing the number of items that can be held in immediate memory, Miller noted that the information did not have to be single, discrete bits of data but could be "chunks" of information. A chunk is defined as any meaningful unit of information. For example, take about 14 seconds to memorize the following sequence of 14 individual letters:

IB MJ FKFB IUS ACD

This is difficult to do because 14 bits exceeds the capacity of your working memory. However, if you rearranged the same letters into meaningful units, the letters form five chunks that are easy to remember:

IBM JFK FBI USA CD

This second arrangement is easier to remember because we recognize certain strings of letters, such as IBM and USA, as a single unit. It is this phenomenon that would make Social Security numbers much more difficult to remember without the hyphens that group them into three memory-manageable chunks. Phone numbers are not remembered as a list of ten numbers but as two chunks of three numbers and one chunk of four. Grouping information together in classes or categories is another method of chunking.

The limitations of working memory can be circumvented somewhat by the ability to "chunk" information.

The difference between novices and experts (in any field) appears to be that experts tend to organize information into very large chunks, while novices work with isolated bits of information. Experienced chess players can reproduce the exact configuration of all 16 chess pieces on a board after examining it for only five seconds. How is this possible? Researchers at the University of Pittsburgh's Learning Research and Development Center estimate that a chess master has stored roughly 100,000 possible patterns of pieces in long-term memory (Chase & Simon, 1973). By using this information, the player can code the position of all 16 pieces in just two or three chunks of information—an amount easily handled by working memory. The manner in which a chess master chunks information together gives us an important clue for "improving" our own working memory. Although we cannot increase the number of chunks we can store, we can (by reorganizing or recoding) increase the amount of information that can be stored in each chunk.

Being able to see how information fits together in chunks is, therefore, a hallmark of learning; it is a way of working with increasingly larger amounts of information. One of the inherent problems associated with teaching occurs when we attempt to teach something to another person who cannot yet see connections that we can. We may be tempted to "give" our students the benefit of our experience and tell them what the connections are or how the information fits together. This seldom works; students need to make the connections themselves.

Mark Twain is credited with saying, "If teaching were the same as telling, we'd all be so smart we could hardly stand it." He was right, unfortunately; teaching *isn't* the same as telling. Teaching is the process of guiding and facilitating the formation of neural connections in students' brains. Chess players don't become experts by simply listening to someone else tell them how to play. They have to do the work themselves, play thousands of games, become familiar

Being able to see how information fits together in chunks is, therefore, a hallmark of learning; it is a way of working with increasingly larger amounts of information.

"If teaching were the same as telling, we'd all be so smart we could hardly stand it."

with the patterns, and reorganize the information to be able to "see" the chunks. Our students are no different. We provide the experience and the guidance, but they must ultimately do the work. What does the work look like? Just as working memory's capacity can be increased by chunking, the amount of information stored in long-term memory can be increased by repeated exposure to that information. This process is called rehearsal or practice.

Rote Rehearsal

There are many ways to rehearse information or a skill. Rote rehearsal consists of repeating the information or action over and over. It's what we generally use when we need to remember a phone number, from the time we look it up until we dial the phone. It's also what we use to learn to ride a bicycle or type on a keyboard. Rote rehearsal, however, is much more effective for learning a procedure (a skill or habit) than it is for remembering a phone number. (If someone says something to you as you are repeating the phone number, it's quickly lost.) It is easy to see why rote rehearsal is essential for forming the strong neural connections necessary to get a skill or habit to the automatic level. Driving a car without paying conscious attention, or decoding text so automatically that you are able to concentrate on the meaning of what you are reading, requires that you practice or rehearse these skills repeatedly. You don't learn to swim or play the piano by reading a book about it. Although the information in a book may be helpful, it is still necessary to practice the skill repeatedly to develop it to the point where it works well without conscious attention. Benjamin Bloom labeled this "automaticity" and described it as the ability to perform a skill unconsciously with speed and accuracy while consciously carrying out other brain functions (1986). He interviewed numerous experts in a variety of fields and reported that they all devoted a great amount of time to practice and training—up to 50 hours per week.

You don't learn to swim or play the piano by reading a book about it.

Elaborative Rehearsal

Some of the information we teach in school requires students to engage in hours, if not years, of rote rehearsal. Examples include reading (decoding), writing, classroom procedures, and basic arithmetic. Much of the standard curriculum, however, falls into the semantic memory category, where rote rehearsal is not an effective method of practice. Repeatedly rehearsing a dictionary definition (commonly called memorizing) may allow students to write the definition correctly on a test (if no one talks to them just before the test), but as every teacher knows, it may not have any meaning and is seldom remembered a week later. The same is true for *comprehending* an event in history, an algorithm in mathematics, or a formula in chemistry. For these types of learning, elaborative rehearsal strategies are much more effective.

Elaborative strategies increase memory by making information more meaningful or relevant to learners.

Elaborative rehearsal is a broad category encompassing a variety of strategies. These strategies encourage learners to elaborate on information in a manner that enhances understanding and retention of that information. Usually, elaborative strategies increase memory by making the information more meaningful or relevant to learners. Why does elaborative rehearsal work more effectively than rote rehearsal for these types of data? A look at some of the research on forgetting, and a review of the things we've learned about how the brain processes information, will help us understand.

Meaning and Retention

The human brain is continuously scanning the world to make sense of the stimuli that constantly bombard the body.

The human brain is continuously scanning the world to make sense of the stimuli that constantly bombard the body. This overarching characteristic of brain functioning is understandable when we recall that the main purpose of a brain is the survival of the individual and of the species. If the brain deemed every stimulus to be important, we would be overloaded to the point of a complete inability to make decisions essential for our survival. Fortunately, the brain sifts through all incoming sensory stimuli and selects those that are the most relevant or meaningful. The brain's determination of what is meaningful and what is not is reflected in the initial perceptual processes and in the conscious processing of information. Recall that the information-storage mechanisms of the brain can be best described as networks of associations. These networks are formed over our lifetimes by the experiences we've had. Information that fits into or adds to an existing network has a much better chance of storage than information that doesn't.

What happens when information has no meaning? Hermann Ebbinghaus conducted one of the first research studies on memory in 1885. He composed long lists of nonsense syllables (*zek, dof, fok,* and so forth), which he then memorized. His purpose in using nonsense syllables was to eliminate any effects personal experience might have on his ability to recall the syllables. He memorized a list of syllables well enough that he could recite it twice in a row. He then tested his recall over several days. His measurement of forgetting was the time he needed to relearn the list until he could recall it with no errors. This method produced a predictable curve, which is shown in Figure 9.3. Ebbinghaus's curve shows what happens to retention of material when there are no previous associations or meaning (Ornstein, 1998).

In our attempts to help learners store information and improve their ability to recall it, we need to make certain that what we are teaching is not "nonsense" to their brains. It is essential that we take advantage of the brain's natural proclivity to attend to what is meaningful.

One of the most effective ways to make information meaningful is to associate or compare the new concept with a known concept—to hook the unfamiliar with something familiar. This is often accomplished with analogies, similes, or metaphors. In attempting to explain the concept of parallel lines, for example, a teacher might point out that such lines appear everywhere, such as railroad tracks, the sides of a sheet of paper, and door and window frames. In doing this, the teacher is forming an association in students' minds between

Information that fits into or adds to an existing network has a much better chance of storage than information that doesn't.

One of the most effective ways to make information meaningful is to associate or compare the new concept with a known concept—to hook the unfamiliar with something familiar.

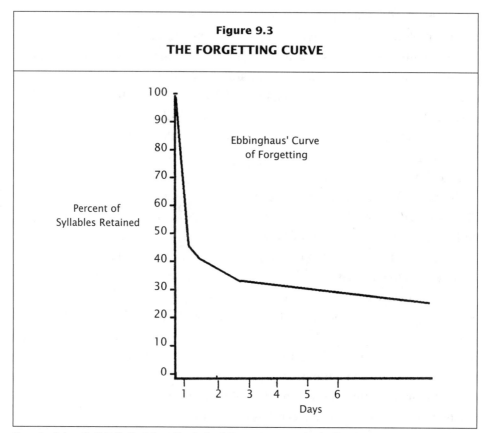

Figure 9.3
THE FORGETTING CURVE

Ornstein, Robert E. (1998). *Psychology: The Study of Human Experience* (2nd ed.). San Diego, CA: Harcourt Brace Jovanovich, p. 332. Reproduced with permission.

a "foreign" mathematical concept and something they already understand. In the same manner, you could explain how chunking increases the capacity of working memory by using an analogy of a purse that can hold seven pennies, seven dimes, or seven quarters.

If you want learners to understand why the brain organizes information into networks, you might ask them to think about the process of looking for a book in a library where the volumes are randomly arranged on shelves. How long would it take to locate a specific book? Then draw the comparison to the human brain, where, if information were not stored in networks or categories, retrieval of information would take much longer. The most effective associations link new learning to something that is personally relevant to students. This is why teachers sometimes use sports results to teach students how to calculate percentages or why they introduce the concept of "math families" to younger learners.

Some things that students need to have "at their fingertips," however, have little inherent meaning. When meaning or relevance is difficult to establish (such as remembering the letters of the alphabet or the stages of mitotic cell division), using a mnemonic device is another effective elaborative technique. Acronyms and acrostics associate a list of items in order with a known word or sentence, thereby making them much easier to remember. For example, anyone who has ever studied music knows that the spaces between the lines on the treble clef spell FACE. We'll look at other examples of mnemonics in Part IV.

Emotion and Retention

In Chapter 8, we saw that emotion strongly influences whether or not the brain initially pays attention to information. The short pathway between the thalamus and the amygdala ensures that we react quickly to emotionally relevant information. This is not the only result of facing emotional or potentially dangerous situations. In addition to a behavioral reaction, the event is nearly always stamped with extra vividness, which results in enhanced memories. Our own experiences—and a lot of research (LeDoux, 1996)—validate this. We remember events that elicit emotional reactions for a longer time than those that don't. To understand why, we need to look at the neurochemical nature of the stress response.

We remember events that elicit emotional reactions for a longer time than those that don't.

The Stress ("Fight or Flight") Response

The chemical chain of events involved in the stress response begins with the perception of an emotionally relevant event. The psychological sentinel of the brain, the amygdala, sends a message via the hypothalamus that engages the entire body and readies it to meet the demands of the situation. Many hormones are involved in carrying out these bodily responses, commonly called the stress response, but three play a major role. Epinephrine and norepineph-rine (also known as adrenalin and noradrenalin) sometimes act as neurotransmitters in the brain, but they also circulate as hormones in the bloodstream, where they act in seconds to set the stress response in motion, affecting the endocrine, circulatory, muscular, and digestive systems.

During the stress response, heart rate increases, blood pressure goes up, senses become more alert, muscles tense, palms become sweaty, blood-clotting elements increase in the bloodstream, and all movement centers become mobilized. Simultaneously, cortical memory systems retrieve any knowledge relevant to the emergency at hand and take precedence over other strands of thought. Stress does not heighten or increase all systems, however; some actually are curbed. The digestive and immune systems are suppressed dur-ing the stress response because they are not immediately essential. Whereas epinephrine and norepinephrine act in seconds, a third hormone, cortisol, is secreted by the adrenal glands and backs up the activity of the stress response for minutes or hours. Cortisol, as we will see later, can have negative effects, but let's first look at the positive effects of these hormones.

The Stress Response and Memory

This response system obviously is critical for survival; it can save your life. What does it have to do with memory though? The neurochemical system that primes the body for an emergency also stamps that moment in memory with extra vividness. Epinephrine and norepinephrine, which are secreted by the adrenal medulla to activate the automatic responses we have been discussing, find their

The neurochemical system that primes the body for an emergency also stamps that moment in memory with extra vividness.

way back to the temporal lobe of the brain. The action of these hormones in this area enhances memory for the event that activated the stress response. Studies by James McGaugh and his colleagues at the University of California, Irvine showed that injecting rats with epinephrine right after they learned something enhanced their memory of the learning situation (LeDoux, 1996). Another researcher, Larry Cahill, demonstrated the same effect in humans, using epinephrine a little differently but producing a similar result. Under normal circumstances, subjects show enhanced memory for emotional pictures over neutral ones. When Cahill gave his subjects an epinephrine-blocking drug soon after viewing an emotionally laden picture, their recall of the emotional pictures decreased, and they did not remember them with any more frequency than neutral pictures (2000). LeDoux says the following about this type of research:

> This suggests that if adrenaline [epinephrine] is released naturally (from the adrenal gland) in some situation, that experience will be remembered especially well. Since emotional arousal usually results in the release of adrenaline, it might be expected . . . that explicit conscious memory of emotional situations would be stronger than the explicit memory of non-emotional situations. (1996, p. 206)

Cahill proposed that anything you do that engages students' emotional and motivational interest will quite naturally involve this system and result in stronger memories of whatever engaged their attention (2000). Although investigators conducted most of the research in the area of fear, it also holds true for even mildly emotional or positive events. For example, this mechanism should be just as involved whether you experience something positive (such as winning the lottery) or something negative (such as hearing about a terrible tragedy). However, the more intense the arousal, the stronger the imprint. It is almost as if the brain has two memory systems: one for ordinary facts and one for those that are emotionally charged.

Adding an Emotional Hook to Learning

Educators need to recognize the power that emotion has to increase retention and plan their classroom instruction accordingly. Simulations and role-plays often are highly engaging and enhance not only the meaning of the material but the emotional connections as well. Teachers who have students act out a particular event from history or actively form a mathematical equation using fellow students are increasing those students' chances of retention. Simply setting up a grocery store in the classroom, to teach students about the value of money and how to figure change, is certainly more likely to hook into the emotional/motivational network than is completing a worksheet on the same subject.

Solving real-life problems is another way to raise the emotional and motivational stakes. For example, students can identify a particular issue, such as water conservation, and then work together to design potential solutions. They can interview local experts about the issue, brainstorm solutions that would work in their local communities, contact state legislators to help them draft a bill, and then lobby for passage of the bill in the state capital. Regardless of whether or not their solutions are implemented, I doubt that the students will ever forget the experience.

Effective teachers, perhaps without knowing the neurological basis for the effect emotion has on learning, intuitively design ways to make the information that students study more meaningful and emotional. They do this by bringing in parents as guest speakers, taking students on field trips, holding mock trials or debates on historical or current events, designing experiments so students "discover" the process, having students build models or take notes by "mind mapping," and countless other activities. Think back on your own experiences as a student, and recall which ones stand out. Chances are you'll be able to recall the emotional component of those experiences that caused you to remember them over all others.

Educators need to recognize the power that emotion has to increase retention and plan their classroom instruction accordingly.

Effective teachers, perhaps without knowing the neurological basis for the effect emotion has on learning, intuitively design ways to make the information that students study more meaningful and emotional.

The Flip Side of Emotion

If you have no stress in your life, then you probably won't get out of bed in the morning; if you have too much stress in your life, then chances are you won't get out of bed in the morning. As with many things, more is not necessarily better, especially when it comes to the stress response. The ability to experience and talk about our emotions is a singularly wonderful human quality, but it has its downside. The stress response was designed for life in caves, but the situation has obviously changed. The contemporary human brain does not distinguish between physical and psychological danger; in either case, it sets the same physiological chain of events in motion. If you are faced with a bear in nature, an increase in blood pressure, a release of blood-clotting elements into the bloodstream, and a suppression of the immune system make for a fine reaction. However, this may not be particularly helpful when someone pulls into a parking space you thought was yours.

The stress response, with its release of cortisol and epinephrine, was designed to last a relatively short time—until you outran the bear or became its dinner. In contemporary life, however, we often extend the response by talking about the stressful event, reliving it, or worrying that it will happen again. We have a tendency to keep ourselves in a chronic, prolonged state of "fight or flight," with potentially negative consequences. High concentrations of cortisol over a long period can provoke hippocampal deterioration and cognitive decline. With prolonged stress, the immune system is compromised, increasing the risk of illness, acceleration of disease, and retardation of growth (Sapolsky, 1994).

Obviously, students can and do suffer the same stress-related disorders as adults. In the classroom, a student can perceive even a mild stressor to be threatening, initiating the stress response and lessening his or her ability to perform. You probably have no difficulty thinking of circumstances during which this can happen: being bullied or laughed at, taking part in timed testing, or being called on when not

The ability to experience and talk about our emotions is a singularly wonderful human quality, but it has its downside.

We have a tendency to keep ourselves in a chronic, prolonged state of "fight or flight," with potentially negative consequences.

prepared, to name a few. Under these conditions, emotion is dominant over cognition; the rational/thinking cortex is less efficient. (Have you ever received an insult and not been able to think of a retort until the next day?) Why does the stress response impede rational thinking and learning? The answer can be found at the cellular level.

In the next chapter, we will see that in order for a connection to be made at the synapse, proteins need to be synthesized in the cell. Stress-released cortisol makes energy available for emergency situations, and it also results in a shutdown of protein synthesis (Cozolino, 2008). In addition, the hippocampus appears to be especially vulnerable to the destructive effects of cortisol, which may result in deficits to learning new information (Bremner, 2002).

Emotion is a double-edged sword with the ability to either enhance or impede learning.

Emotion is a double-edged sword with the ability to either enhance or impede learning. Understanding the biological underpinnings of emotion helps educators see why we need to provide emotionally healthy and exciting school environments to promote optimal learning.

Synapse Strengtheners

1. Using the full information-processing model diagram shown in the preceding chapter, explain to a colleague the major differences between sensory memory and working memory.

2. Without looking back at the book, write a paragraph about the difference between rote rehearsal and elaborative rehearsal, giving examples of appropriate classroom uses for each.

3. If you are reading this book as part of a study group, ask members of the group to select a topic or unit that they normally teach in a traditional, didactic manner. Design a way to make it more meaningful to the students. Share these plans with the group.

4. Design a lesson to teach your students about the emotional nature of their brains and why emotion can be a double-edged sword.

10

Long-Term Memory:
The Brain's Storage System

You smell a particular antiseptic, and the memory of a hospital stay comes flooding into your consciousness, even though you haven't thought about that event for years. At a high school reunion, the sight of a former classmate who was in your chemistry class brings back a memory that you didn't know was there. At a party, people start singing songs from the 1970s, and you remember most of the words to songs you haven't sung for 30 years. You haven't ridden a bicycle for years, but when your nephew asks if you can ride, you climb on his new bicycle and show him how to perform a "wheelie." How did each of these things happen? You can thank your long-term memory for its ability to hold onto memories for decades in some cases. Without it, you would be unable to learn or profit from experience. Life would be a moment-to-moment occurrence, similar to that experienced by H. M., as described in Chapter 2.

Long-term memory, the last part of our information-processing model, is truly remarkable in what it allows us to recall. When we compare long-term memory to sensory or working memory (both of which are relatively short term), we find that the name is indeed appropriate. Information stored in long-term memory is relatively permanent but not always accurate. The capacity of our long-term memory is unknown, but it is considered to be extremely

Some estimates suggest that our long-term memory contains a million billion connections.

large—some estimates suggest that it contains a million billion connections. In this chapter, we will look at the processes that allow our brain to store and retrieve information over time and the factors that influence the strength of these memories. It is a fascinating journey into the unconscious depths of human memory and one that has powerful implications for teaching and learning.

Types of Memory Storage

Figure 10.1 shows several subheadings in the "long-term memory" box. Although we often think of memory as a single process, memory storage is actually more than one type of process. As early as 1911, the French philosopher Henri Bergson stated that our past survives

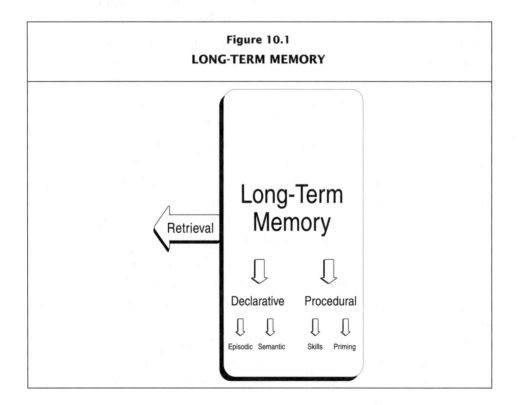

Figure 10.1
LONG-TERM MEMORY

in two fundamentally different forms, conscious and unconscious memories (Schacter, 1996). Scientists usually use the words *declarative* and *procedural* to describe conscious memory and unconscious memory, respectively. (Other scientists use the terms *explicit memory* and *implicit memory* for declarative and procedural memory, respectively.) In this book, the words *declarative* and *procedural* will be used. As we will see, these two forms of memory are localized in different neural systems.

Declarative Memory

Declarative memory is our ability to store and recall information that we can declare (speak or write). Unlike procedural memory, declarative memory requires conscious processing; it is *reflective* rather than *reflexive*. Instead of the automatic, unconscious recall of how to do something, declarative memory permits us to consciously recall and discuss what something is or recall and describe an event that occurred in the past. This dual function has led to the subdivision of declarative memory into two categories, episodic and semantic memory.

Episodic memory is sometimes called source memory because it involves remembering where and when information was acquired. It allows you to recall a hike you once took, how much you loved your 1st grade teacher, or a surprise party on your 16th birthday. It is your record of faces, music, facts, and individual experiences—a sort of "autobiographical reference" (Squire & Kandel, 2000). As critical as episodic memory is (e.g., it's important to remember where you parked your car), it can also be problematic. The brain does not store memories in a linear manner, like a video camera records images; it stores memories in neural circuits or networks. When we recall an event, we are actually reconstructing it. Even though many events are important or emotional enough to be remembered, the details often escape us. In these cases, the brain "fills in" the details by a process known as refabrication. This process can be defined

The brain does not store memories in a linear manner, like a video camera records images; it stores memories in neural circuits or networks.

as the reconstruction of a memory from bits and pieces of truth. As we tell stories over and over, we embellish them, add to them, and make them a bit more elaborate. Eventually, the refabrication becomes the memory, and it is virtually impossible to distinguish it from what actually happened. Even though the memory of the event is quite vivid, the details may actually be inaccurate.

Semantic memory, on the other hand, is generally fairly accurate. Semantic memory includes words, their associated symbols, rules for manipulating those words, and the relevant definitions. It also consists of rules of grammar, chemical formulas, mathematical rules, and your general knowledge about the world. These facts are normally independent of a particular time or place. Knowing that $6 \times 7 = 42$ is an example of semantic memory; remembering what grade you were in when you first learned the multiplication tables is an illustration of episodic memory.

Procedural Memory

Procedural memory is best described as knowing *how* versus knowing *what*. It is sometimes called nondeclarative; in other words, you do not need to "declare" anything—and you may not be able to say much about what you are doing—for the information to be stored.

The first type of procedural memory is your ability to store automatic processes for routine actions. You can think of these processes as skills, the "how" to do things. They may be simple procedures, such as walking, brushing your teeth, or tying your shoes, or they may be more complex, such as driving a car or decoding words. These procedures have in common their automatic nature. After a good deal of repetition and practice, we perform them without conscious thought. Cognitive psychologist Jerome Bruner called procedural memory a "memory without record" (Squire & Kandel, 2000). The automatic procedures form a sort of unconscious stimulus–response bond. Once we have a skill or habit at this level, however, it becomes difficult to access it in any way except by performing it. Imagine trying to teach someone to tie a shoe, swing a golf club, or write a word without physically demonstrating it. We no longer know *how* we accomplish the procedure; its separate parts or rules of operation are virtually inaccessible to our consciousness.

Most of the skills mentioned above involve motor activity, but some types of skillful behavior are not based on learned movements. An example of such a nonmotor skill is reading. When you first learn to read, your eyes move slowly from word to word; but with a great deal of practice, you move through the words much more quickly. Skilled readers move their eyes about four times a second, taking in the meaning of more than 300 words per minute (Squire & Kandel, 2000).

A second type of procedural memory is known as priming. Priming involves the influence of a past experience without any awareness or conscious memories of that experience. In a sense, priming is similar to skill learning; in neither case are you consciously aware of what you are doing—which is why both skills and priming are sometimes called *implicit* memory, in contrast to conscious recollection, or *explicit* memory (Schacter, 1996). In priming experiments, researchers show subjects lists of words and then, hours or days later, show them another list and ask whether they have seen any of the words before. Subjects are also given the beginning of a word from the lists (e.g., abs____ for "absent," inc____ for "income") and asked to complete the word. Subjects perform much better on the fragment completion task (nondeclarative/implicit memory) than on the task in which they have to identify whether or not they have seen the word before (declarative/explicit memory). It may be that, for a period after seeing a word, less neural activity is required to process that word again on the fragment completion task (Squire & Kandel, 2000). This phenomenon has been seen in amnesiacs who are able to learn new procedural skills but have no memory of learning them. This is why H. M. was able to improve his performance of new motor skills (such as mirror writing) but did not remember ever doing them before (Amaral, 2000). This type of experiment indicates that human memory can be influenced by experiences that we fail to recollect consciously; seeing or experiencing something previously seems to prime our ability to recall it later. Procedural memory, whether skill learning or priming, provides dramatic evidence that unconscious mental activities do exist.

The Cellular Basis of Memory

So far, we have been looking at the "big picture" of memory and its various types. It is important to remember, however, that underlying our memory (regardless of type) are neural changes that form the physiological basis of information storage and retrieval. What are the cellular mechanisms that allow information to make the crucial leap from working memory to long-term memory? Endel Tulving, considered by some to be the world's foremost authority on cognitive theories of memory, states,

> As a scientist I am compelled to the conclusion—not postulation, not assumption, but conclusion—that there must exist certain physical-chemical changes in the nervous tissue that correspond to the storage of information, or to the engram, changes that constitute the necessary conditions of remembering. (Gazzaniga, 1997, p. 97)

The study of the molecular events underlying memory formation is one of the most exciting fields of neuroscientific study. In the 1940s, Canadian neuroscientist Donald Hebb proposed that a synapse between two neurons is strengthened if the neurons are active or firing at the same time (Hebb's Law). His theory is generally accepted in the field of neuroscience today; however, *how* this occurs is still open to some debate (Squire & Kandel, 2000). One current hypothesis is that the synapses among neurons that represent experiences

Seeing or experiencing something previously seems to prime our ability to recall it later.

Long-term potentiation occurs when synapses between neurons that represent experiences become strengthened over time.

become strengthened over time. This is referred to as long-term potentiation (LTP). LTP has been scientifically demonstrated with animals and has been the predominant model of the cellular basis of memory for more than three decades. Not all neuroscientists agree that these experiments necessarily reflect what happens during memory storage in humans, but most agree that it is at least one of the important mechanisms involved in changing the synaptic strength among neurons in neural networks (Squire & Kandel, 2000).

Long-Term Potentiation (LTP)

How might LTP result in a memory? First, let's review what we understand about how neurons allow us to see or hear. We know that the experience of seeing a yellow rose or a blue ball is the result of the activation of a particular group of neurons in the visual cortex. Likewise, a group of neurons firing together in the auditory cortex will result in the experience of a certain tone or note of music. A memory appears to entail a similar firing of neurons, but the pattern of firing remains encoded in a neural circuit or network after the stimulation that originally caused the neurons to fire has ceased. You can therefore remember the image of the rose or the ball, and you can hear the melody of a song in your head. It appears that this is possible because when two or more neurons are active at the same time, they become more sensitive and are more likely to fire a second time. The more often a pattern of neurons is activated, the more efficient the associated synapse becomes.

The more often a pattern of neurons is activated, the more efficient the associated synapse becomes.

This increased efficacy of the synapses is what many scientists refer to as LTP. Researchers have demonstrated LTP in several parts of the hippocampus and surrounding structures in the medial temporal lobe, which we will see are critical to the formation and storage of memories. There is some evidence that the chemicals released at the synapse that lead to LTP may result in the modification of proteins, synthesis of new proteins (implicated in memory), and changes in gene transcription (Amaral & Soltesz, 1997).

Growth of Synapses

In the 1960s, Marian Diamond, Mark Rosenzweig, and their colleagues at the University of California, Berkeley, demonstrated that substantial changes in the brain's architecture can be influenced by environment (Diamond, 1988). Somewhat later, William Greenough at the University of Illinois extended the research on "enriched" environments (2002). Enrichment for rats in both studies was provided by placing a colony of rats together in a large cage with toys that were changed every few days. The rats raised in this enriched environment showed growth in the thickness and weight of their cortices, due to larger cortical neurons, heavier branching of dendrites, and larger synapses. Increases of up to 20 percent more synapses per neuron were found in the visual cortex of some of the animals. These structural changes in the rats' brains resulted in enhanced abilities to solve complex maze problems (Diamond, 1988). Interestingly, Diamond also reported that wild rats obtained from their natural environment had even more dendritic growth—and heavier cortices—than those in enriched environments (Diamond, personal communication). The reason for this is speculative, but perhaps being in an environment where survival is an issue results in a more efficient brain.

Truly amazing changes take place in the neural connections in our brains, and the methods we use to structure learning experiences for our students affect the strength and duration of those changes.

There is still much to be understood before the mystery of how experiences are stored at a cellular level comes close to being solved. Whatever the process or processes may turn out to be, the fact remains that when we learn, truly amazing changes take place in the neural connections in our brains, and the methods we use to structure learning experiences for our students affect the strength and duration of those changes.

Memory Storage and Retrieval

Suppose you were asked to recall an event in your life, perhaps a graduation celebration or a surprise birthday party. In all probability you would be able to describe many aspects of that experience: the people who were there, the food that was served, the room you were in, the sound of people singing, and perhaps some of the gifts you received. The memory probably came to you in a fairly complete form, so that it seems that this particular memory must be stored in a special place in your brain, ready to be recalled in its entirety whenever you wish. In actuality, no complete scenarios or pictures are stored anywhere in the brain; you have to reconstruct these memories every time. While this may seem inefficient and even counterintuitive, the process by which we encode experiences and later recall them really makes a lot of sense.

In his book *Inside the Brain*, science writer Ronald Kotulak uses the metaphor of eating a meal to represent the encoding and storing of information.

> The brain gobbles up its external environment in bites and chunks through its sensory system: vision, hearing, smell, touch, and taste. Then the digested world is reassembled in the form of trillions of connections between brain cells that are constantly growing or dying, or becoming stronger or weaker, depending upon the richness of the banquet. (1996, p. 4)

When you think carefully about it, this process is quite efficient. Our experiences are disassembled into parts and stored in specialized networks of cells, meaning that the same brain cells can be used many times to recall similar colors or smells. For example, the cells in the visual cortex that allow us to perceive the color red can be used to see a red rose, a red heart, the red in a sunset, or a red tie. The same is true in the auditory cortex and other sensory areas. In a sense, many parts of the brain each contribute something different to the memory of a single event. Our knowledge is built on bits and pieces of many aspects of a given thing—shape, color, taste, or movement—but these aspects are not laid down in a single place; there is no memory center in the brain that represents an entire event at a single location.

The same brain cells can be used many times to recall similar experiences.

If memories are not stored in specific locations in the brain, then how do we retrieve them? Our ability to remember is essentially a process of reconstruction or reactivation. As we have seen, the various elements of past experience reside all over the brain—in the visual cortex, auditory cortex, and other areas. Antonio Damasio describes *recall* as an activation of all these separate sites in unison, creating an integrated experience (1994). You don't even need all the pieces to reconstruct the total; you only need the definitive elements. Recall the picture of the Dalmatian in Chapter 8. The dog is not clearly defined, but you don't need all the components to reconstruct the total picture, just the definitive elements. When a critical mass of sensory neurons is activated, the brain fills in the missing pieces to complete the picture. Keep in mind, though, that the image of the Dalmatian must have been previously stored in order to be retrieved; that is, if you had never before seen a Dalmatian, your brain probably wouldn't be able to fill in the blanks.

The same is true when you remember an event. Depending on the cue or reminder, only certain fragments of the total memory may be activated. If the cue is weak or unclear, what is reactivated may differ from the original memory or even belong to another episode. This is why episodic memory details are often fuzzy or even completely inaccurate and why "eyewitnesses" to events are generally unreliable. Memory researchers Elizabeth and Geoffrey Loftus are well known for their studies of how memories can be modified or distorted by the type of questions asked in a memory retrieval test. They have also demonstrated that false memories can be planted if the memories contain some aspect that reasonably could have occurred (1975).

Pathways to Long-Term Storage

Declarative and procedural memory, though they share many of the same cellular mechanisms, do not employ the same brain structures for processing. The two major structures involved in memory processing are the cortex and the medial temporal lobe. It appears that the brain stores memories in the same structures that are engaged in initially perceiving and processing stimuli. However, these structures differ, depending on whether the memory is procedural or declarative. Understanding the anatomy involved in these two types of memory will further clarify the types of activities and practice best suited to each one.

The Procedural Pathway

Do any of the following scenarios sound familiar? You drive your car along a familiar route, arrive at your destination, and then realize that you were not aware of driving there. You meet someone new, and you automatically extend your hand in greeting. You read a page of text, get to the bottom of the page, and realize that you do not remember what you just read. These motor skills, habits, and perceptual skills are all examples of procedural or nondeclarative memory, and all are accomplished without conscious awareness. Trying to consciously express any of these skills while performing them impairs your performance, but if you think back to when you first learned to drive or read, none of these skills or habits was automatic. They required a great deal of conscious attention and practice.

In the early stage of skill learning, three major brain areas are involved in laying down new pathways: the prefrontal cortex, parietal cortex, and cerebellum. Their combined activity allows you to pay necessary conscious attention to the task and ensures that the appropriate movements are assembled correctly. With practice, however, these areas show less activity, and other structures, including the motor cortex and cerebellum, become more engaged (Squire & Kandel, 2000). Recall from Chapter 2 that, with repeated rehearsal of a skill, the cerebellum and motor cortex assume control of the movements needed to accomplish the skill, and that skill becomes automatic and unconscious.

In nonmotor procedural learning, such as word decoding, the brain area that appears to be most heavily involved is the visual cortex. With extended practice, we improve our ability to discriminate between different line orientations and letter configurations. The ultimate long-term effect is to change the actual neural structure of the visual cortex, which alters the machinery of perception. Remember that these changes do not involve understanding word meanings, for example, but only the ability to quickly recognize letter configurations. All this occurs outside awareness, as has been demonstrated by amnesiac patients who are able, with practice, to improve their speed in reading a selection of prose but do not remember the text in any ordinary sense (Squire & Kandel, 2000).

The Declarative Pathway

The journey from perception to storage of both semantic and episodic memory begins when sensory receptors receive stimuli. The stimuli register in the appropriate areas of the cortex (visual, auditory, etc.) and then travel to the hippocampus and an adjacent cluster of structures within the medial temporal lobe. These structures register the stimuli as neural patterns in much the same way as they were registered in the cortex. Note that the hippocampus is not the ultimate storage repository of memory; rather, it acts as an intermediate storage site for cortical representations on their way to long-term memory (Squire & Kandel, 2000). These representations can be reactivated during recall, when the messages return to the cortex where the stimuli originally registered. This reactivation of the original neural patterns strengthens them and makes them less likely to fade. With repeated activation, the memories form neural links that become more or less permanently embedded in the frontal and temporal cortices. These links remain in long-term memory long after the hippocampal representations have faded. We can therefore see why the hippocampus is essential for forming new memories, but it becomes less essential over time as these memories are eventually

The ultimate long-term effect is to change the actual neural structure of the visual cortex, which alters the machinery of perception.

stored in the cortex. This provides an explanation of why amnesiacs with damage to the hippocampus can no longer lay down new permanent memories but often are able to remember events that occurred before the brain damage.

Consolidation

Patients who receive electroconvulsive therapy (a controlled series of electric shocks to the brain) often forget experiences and learning that occurred just before the treatment. This condition is called retrograde amnesia. However, if the treatment is delayed for a while after the acquisition of new information, the shock is less likely to disrupt recall. The reason for this appears to be that after an event has been placed into memory, some time must pass for the memory trace to become fully established or organized in the brain.

In the late 19th century, German psychologists Georg Müller and Alfons Pilzecher conducted studies using the nonsense syllables of Ebbinghaus's experiments and found that learning a second list of syllables immediately after learning a first list interfered with later recall of the first list. Without disruption, though, the newly formed memories gradually became more stable. The researchers labeled this time the consolidation period (Squire & Kandel, 2000). We now know that memory is not formed at the moment information is acquired; it is not a simple fixation process. Rather, it is dynamic, with unconscious processes that continue to strengthen and stabilize the connections over days, weeks, months, and years (Gazzaniga, Ivry, & Mangun, 1998). Consolidation is undoubtedly enhanced by rehearsal. When we "replay" our experiences (i.e., when we talk and think about them), we provide more opportunities for consolidation. Perhaps this is why instruction that allows students to connect new information to previous experiences increases the strength and complexity of their neural connections and, therefore, their retention of the information.

Scientists have studied the consolidation process extensively in rats, mice, and fruit flies. These experiments have shown that

Instruction that allows students to connect new information to previous experiences increases the strength and complexity of their neural connections and, therefore, their retention of the information.

consolidation requires new protein synthesis. At the cellular level, specific genes that produce proteins are turned on. The synthesis of these proteins is essential for memories to become stable—to move from short-term to long-term memory. In other words, long-term memory is formed by stabilizing the memory trace established immediately after an experience. The difference between short-term and long-term memory can be understood as the strength of the memory trace (McGaugh, 2003). When mice receive an injection of a substance that inhibits protein synthesis (e.g., anisomycin) just before training, they have a profound loss of long-term memory when tested three or more hours later. Mice given a saline injection, however, show no long-term memory loss.

Consolidation seems to be the result of biological changes underlying the retention of learned information.

Consolidation, therefore, seems to be the result of biological changes underlying the retention of learned information. Given what we know about the importance of the hippocampus in the formation of long-term memory, it is not surprising that the function of the hippocampus and of nearby structures in the medial temporal lobe is integral to consolidation. Without the mediating effects of the hippocampus, consolidation could not take place. As we practice or repeat experiences, however, the associated memories consolidate, and the hippocampal structures are no longer needed. In other words, long-term memories are formed in a two-way conversation between the hippocampus and the cortex until the hippocampus "breaks" the connection and the memory is fixed or consolidated. This process can take years to complete.

Learning a motor skill sets in motion neural processes that continue to evolve after practice has ended.

Researchers most frequently discuss the concept of consolidation in terms of declarative memory, which relies on brain structures in the medial temporal lobe. Recent research indicates that learning motor skills (a procedural memory) also involves consolidation. Researchers at the Massachusetts Institute of Technology's Department of Brain and Cognitive Sciences discovered that learning a motor skill sets in motion various neural processes that continue to evolve after practice has ended (Brashers-Krug, Shadmehr, & Bizzi,

1996). When subjects learned a second motor task immediately after a first skill was learned, the consolidation of the first motor skill was disrupted. This disruption did not occur if four hours elapsed between learning the first and second skills, though. The researchers proposed that motor skill consolidation relies on the same structures in the medial temporal lobe that are necessary for the consolidation of explicit (declarative) memory tasks.

Educational Implications

It is tempting to want to apply consolidation research very specifically to the classroom. Obviously, it would be helpful for teachers to know just how long students' brains need to consolidate a particular skill before moving on to another. Unfortunately, the available research doesn't give us this kind of detailed information. We do know, however, that consolidation occurs and that it takes time. We also know that teaching something new too soon disrupts consolidation of previous learning. What we don't know is how *much* time is needed for consolidation; therefore, we should be wary of specifying time lengths between the introduction of new concepts or skills. Neuroscience seldom provides information that can be applied directly to classroom practice, but we need to take what we know about consolidation into account when we design instruction. For example, building elaborative rehearsal strategies into our instruction—allowing students time to process information in depth—will likely increase the strength of students' learning because these strategies allow consolidation to take place. Another way to increase the possibility of consolidation is to incorporate new information gradually and repeat it in timed intervals. Seldom is information stored reliably after being introduced once. Most memories disappear within minutes, but those that survive the fragile period strengthen with rehearsal spaced out over time (Medina, 2008).

Most learning in life is incidental. In everyday life, we generally make no particular effort to record our experiences for later. Our interests, preferences, and survival needs direct our attention and determine how well information is encoded. Although incidental learning has value, we cannot trust that everything we need to remember will be "incidentally" encoded. More often than not, we have to expend some effort to make certain that we'll be able to recall the information when we need it. No one knows more about how difficult this can be than teachers. Students often memorize information for a test and then promptly forget it. This problem is exacerbated by the demands to cover more information—and *covering* is often all that happens. Coverage (going over information superficially) does not build strong neural connections and is seldom remembered, or it is remembered incorrectly. This problem is difficult to solve, but perhaps the information in this chapter will help educators understand what is necessary to produce long-term retention of information.

We are now in a better position to understand why elaborative rehearsal (rather than rote rehearsal) is a more effective process for producing long-term declarative memory. The more fully we process information over time, the more connections we make, the more consolidation takes place, and the better the memory will be. In the remaining chapters, we will discuss a number of elaborative rehearsal strategies. Most of them require students to reflect on the information being taught, relate it to something they already know, form meaningful mental associations, or employ some other effective elaborative encoding strategy.

The more fully we process information over time, the more connections we make, the more consolidation takes place, and the better the memory will be.

Synapse Strengtheners

1. Based on what you know about long-term memory storage, explain why many educators say, "We need to teach a lot less a lot better."

2. Without looking back at the text, create a diagram of long-term memory and its subdivisions. Under each subdivision, include at least one relevant example.

3. If you are reading this book as part of a study group, devote one session to discussing what constitutes an enriched environment for students. You might also want to describe the elements of an enriched environment for teachers.

4. Explain to a fellow educator what is meant by consolidation and what the implications of consolidation are for teaching.

Part IV

Matching Instruction to How the Brain Learns Best

The most powerful strategies increase retention, understanding, and students' abilities to apply the concepts they are learning.

In this final section of the book, we move from looking at the structure and function of the brain—and its memory processes—to a discussion of how this knowledge might be applied to educational settings. Some material comes from studies conducted by educational researchers and cognitive psychologists, but I have selected many of the strategies and activities because I believe they take advantage of what we're learning about how the brain processes and stores information.

In this respect, much of Part IV has its basis in the wisdom of practice more than in research. I believe that one of the best "laboratories" for educational research is the classroom, where creative teachers work to make the curriculum meaningful, try new methods, monitor and adjust their instruction, and share what they have found to be effective. This section of the book includes strategies that I directly observed or that teachers of all grade levels and subject areas shared with me. I have attempted to provide a "brain-based" rationale for why these strategies work, but I want to make it clear that the rationale is mostly my own and not that of any specific researchers.

This book addresses curriculum primarily in terms of its relevance or meaning to students. Not addressed, but vitally important, is how schools and teachers select and structure curriculum. Of course, we need to be aware of existing research on brain structure and function, and we need to try to use this information to teach in meaningful ways so that students truly understand the content, but all this new knowledge will be to no avail if the curriculum is either irrelevant or taught out of context. Pedagogy does not stand alone; it goes hand in hand with intelligently selected content that is structured within meaningful contexts. We need to ask ourselves questions such as *What are the big ideas or concepts of this lesson? What is the lifelong benefit of what I'm teaching? How will students be able to use what they are learning today in their adult lives?*

Too often, classroom instruction and activities focus solely on facts and details. It is true that specific pieces of information are important, but they have limited usefulness by themselves. More important are what I like to call "enduring knowledge" concepts. Such concepts are broad truths that are almost universally valid, even as times and cultures change. They have direct applications to students' lives, both inside and outside of the classroom. Examples include change, patterns, interdependence, systems, and power. An excellent resource for understanding and teaching concepts is H. Lynn Erickson's book *Concept-Based Curriculum and Instruction* (2002).

Another problem is that historically, we have taught subject matter in separate modules—in time blocks at the elementary level or in specialized classes at the secondary level. In recent years, educators have tried to integrate various aspects of the curriculum into more meaningful units. Thematic teaching has become popular in many schools; however, in many instances the thematic units, such as "dinosaurs" or "the rain forest" appear to have been designed with no apparent underlying concepts in mind. It is often difficult to determine why the theme was chosen, let alone answer questions concerning its relevance or potential applications.

> From brain research, we . . . have come to understand that the brain is a pattern-seeking device in search of meaning and that learning is the acquisition of mental programs for using what we understand. Thus, the most usable and useful curriculum for classroom teachers would be one that made clear for teacher and student what the patterns are (The Concepts to Be Learned) and how those understandings would be used in the real world (Expected Student Performances). (Olsen, 1995, p. 5)

Part IV, then, provides examples of activities that match how the brain learns best. Teachers need to consciously select strategies that assist students in learning broad concepts that are embedded within rigorous, relevant content. The strategies and activities in this section serve several different purposes.

First, some strategies assist students in recalling important information. For example, how do we remember how many days are in each month? We use a rhyming strategy ("30 days hath September"), or we count the peaks and valleys of our knuckles. There's nothing particularly emotional or meaningful in either of these strategies, but they are certainly useful. Mnemonic strategies have sometimes been denigrated as nothing more than memorization. At times, however, we need to have relatively meaningless information (e.g., spelling, punctuation) at our fingertips, and mnemonic strategies work very well for this purpose. Therefore, they do indeed have a place in the teacher's repertoire. Research on mnemonic strategies used with special education students has shown that students may become very proficient in using the mnemonic as taught, but they seldom transfer the strategy to another area unless taught to do so (Pressley & Levin, 1978).

A second group of strategies helps students remember both facts and their understanding of concepts. When students use manipulatives in math or science (or any other curricular area), they are much more likely to understand the concepts than if they merely read about them. Simulations that take advantage of the mind–body connection are powerful tools for retention and understanding. For example, the concept of a food chain or web may be difficult for students to comprehend. However, if the teacher engages students in a simulation where some students "become" different parts of the web and others "become" factors that influence the web, retention of individual facts and understanding of the overall concept will both increase.

Finally, the most powerful strategies increase retention, understanding, and students' abilities to apply the concepts they learn. Nearly any strategy in the second group can also fit into this category if the teacher includes explicit examples of application and then has students generate examples of when and how a concept might be used or applied in another area. For example, a teacher who asks students to engage in a simulation of food availability in developed and developing countries could easily follow the exercise with a discussion of how this also applies to students' own lives and of possible solutions to the problem of world hunger.

As you begin the strategies section of this book, keep in mind some of the tenets of effective rehearsal. To summarize, remember the following:

1. The more elaboratively information is rehearsed at the moment of learning, the stronger the memory becomes.

2. The more modalities used to rehearse, the more paths that are established for retrieval.

3. The more real-world examples given for a concept, the more likely it is that the concept will be understood and remembered.

4. The more information that is linked to previous learning, the stronger the memory will become.

11

Making Curriculum Meaningful Through Problems, Projects, and Simulations

Learning is a process of building neural networks. Over a lifetime, you have constructed networks in your brain's cortex that contain information about an unbelievable variety of concepts. For example, imagine a network that contains information about animals. If you were asked to list everything you know about animals, you would discover you have a tremendous amount of stored knowledge: the difference between a mammal and a reptile, where animals live and what they eat, which animals are kept as pets and which ones are raised primarily for food, which animals are extinct, and even perhaps some information about the cloning of animals. Throughout your lifetime, your networks expand or are pruned depending on your experiences.

Three Levels of Learning

Our networks are originally formed through our experiences. However, all experiences are not the same. We learn some things by experiencing them concretely, others symbolically, and still others in abstract terms. Let's take a look at each of these three levels of learning.

Concrete Experience

Imagine that you are a young child going for a walk with your father. Suddenly, a small, furry, four-legged creature that you have never seen before sits on the sidewalk in front of you. After telling you not to be afraid, your father labels this creature for you. He tells you that this is an *animal* and it is called a *dog*. If he decides that it is a friendly dog, your father may even let you touch it. This experience will be stored in your brain as an actual physiological connection between neurons. If, on subsequent walks, you encounter this same dog again, the connection will be strengthened, and you will learn what this animal is.

Learning isn't this simple, because there is not just one dog but many dogs in your neighborhood. It won't take long for you to realize that dogs come in many shapes, sizes, and colors. All this information will be incorporated into your "dog network." Some dogs you encounter will be friendly, others will not, and you will add emotional associations to the existing information. This network is well under way to becoming complex when something puzzling occurs. You are again out for a walk with your father when you encounter another small, furry, four-legged creature. This time you don't need anyone to label it for you. You point to the animal and say, "dog." Your father laughs and tells you that this animal is not a dog, it's a *cat*. Your brain now has to begin forming a new network containing information about cats. In the course of time, this new web will be part of a larger "animal network."

With repeated experiences, your animal network becomes stronger, even though it is limited to only two types of animals. Then your parents decide to take you to the zoo. You are now exposed to a large number of creatures you haven't seen before. Some have long necks, others have horns on the ends of their noses, and still others look like cats but are much, much larger. Your parents tell you that they are all animals. Amazingly, your brain takes all this information and begins to fit it into the previously established animal network. Because connections in the brain become stronger the more they are activated, your dog and cat connections are probably more easily accessed than those for a giraffe or tiger. Is there any way these connections can become stronger without daily trips to the zoo?

Symbolic or Representational Learning

Although our brains make some of our strongest links through concrete experience, we are fortunately not limited to this one way of learning. Continuing with the animal example, children enhance their ability to recognize and label zoo animals by looking at pictures in a book or playing with toy replicas. Children quickly learn to match the name of an animal to its picture. Repeated exposure to these pictures can make the more exotic animals as familiar as domestic pets, but the initial concrete experience (seeing the animals in a zoo) will make the exotic animals much more meaningful than if the children had never had that experience.

Using symbols or representations of real objects is a second level of learning that is directly related to concrete experiences. In other words, their effectiveness is dependent on the degree of exposure to the real entity. At the zoo, you looked at the animals while your brain also took in the entire environment. All these sensory data become part of the animal memory and are activated when it is remembered. When you look at a picture of an elephant, the neural network you activate allows you to recall where you were when you saw one, how it smelled, the trumpeting sound it made, and perhaps the feel of the water the elephant sprayed on you. Without a concrete experience, the representation or symbol may have little meaning, no matter how much someone explains it to you. This is certainly true in schools, where students often are exposed to representational information that has no concrete antecedent. Textbooks are crammed with pictures of science experiments, photographs of people in other communities, diagrams of digestive systems, and other such symbols or representations of real things. Though they may be visually appealing, they do not bring to students' minds the rich sensory information contained in a concrete experience, and therefore they have less meaning.

Without a concrete experience, a representation or symbol may have little meaning no matter how much someone explains it to you.

Abstract Learning

A third level of learning uses only abstract information, primarily words and numbers. Let's say you are now older, and your parents no longer take you to the zoo or buy you picture books about animals. Is there any way you can expand your neural network of animals? It is probable that you can now discuss animals you've never seen, both real and imaginary. How are you able to do this? You do it by reading about them or having someone give you a description. With a strong neural network formed by concrete experience and representations of animals, it is possible to read or hear about an animal and see it in your "mind's eye."

Many abstract concepts, such as democracy or culture, have no visible concrete counterpart. An understanding of these terms will depend on the student's developmental age and on the teacher's ability to make abstract concepts understandable with sufficient examples that relate to the student's experiences.

An understanding of abstract concepts depends on the student's developmental age and on the teacher's ability to make those concepts understandable with sufficient examples that relate to the student's experiences.

Involving Students in Real-Life Problem Solving

Many of our strongest neural networks are formed by actual experience. It is often possible to take advantage of this natural proclivity by involving students in solving authentic problems in their school or community. John Dewey contended that school should be less about preparation for life and more like life itself (1937). Most school goals contain references to developing critical-thinking and problem-solving skills, but they are often not addressed in the classroom. In my experience, too many classrooms (especially at the secondary level) still rely on lecture and recitation as the primary mode of instruction. Even when teachers give students the opportunity to solve problems, these "problems" are seldom more than hypothetical case studies with neat, convergent outcomes. With a little research and creative thinking, teachers can find actual problems in their own schools and communities for students to solve.

School should be less about preparation for life and more like life itself.

These real problems may not be easy to solve because of time constraints or insufficient information, but it is through struggling with these issues that students learn both content and critical thinking. Following are several examples of methods teachers have used in an attempt to increase authentic problem solving.

Lower Elementary School

A 3rd grade class was brainstorming what they needed to do to prepare for an upcoming field trip. When the issue of transportation was raised, one student suggested that several parents could drive and save the school the cost of buses. The teacher challenged the class to determine whether this would indeed be true. The students were divided into two groups, and each group set out to determine the costs involved in each mode of transportation. Students made calculations regarding the number of vehicles needed to transport the students, insurance costs for private cars versus school buses, and fuel costs per mile for each type of vehicle. Another problem-solving opportunity arose when one student questioned whether there would be enough parents available to drive on the day of the field trip. The problem was solved when the children determined that there were not enough parents who would be able to drive; the real benefit to students was not the solution but the data collection, analysis, and problem-solving skills they gained.

Upper Elementary School

Students in a 5th grade class were challenged by their teacher to determine whether public opinion in their city matched that of the nation in a public poll regarding the selection of a presidential candidate. The students researched how polls are conducted, studied data collection, and learned how to form appropriate polling questions. After conducting a mini-poll at the local shopping mall, students tabulated the results, compared them to the national results, and discussed the reasons for any differences.

Middle School

A California teacher read a news story to his students that noted that human consumption accounted for a small percentage of the state's water usage, while landscaping and agriculture used much more. He challenged his students to find a way to conserve the limited water supply. After doing some research, the students discovered that some species of plants use much less water than others. They eventually drafted a water conservation bill requiring all new state buildings to be landscaped with drought-resistant plants. They convinced their local state senator to sponsor the bill, which they calculated would save taxpayers millions of dollars and millions of gallons of water. They wrote letters to newspapers, prepared press kits, made all the arrangements for a press conference, and went to the state capital to testify in support of their bill.

Secondary School

In a school-to-career program, teachers contact local businesses and ask them to identify problems they need to have solved. They then challenge students to find possible solutions to these problems. The students determine what information they need and set up interviews with the business owners to gain a better understanding of the relevant issues. After analyzing their data, the students brainstorm solutions and select those they consider the most feasible. As a final step, they present their solution to the business owners. The teachers reported that, in the first year of the program, most of the students' solutions were implemented. In addition to the obvious benefits of engaging in authentic problem solving, teachers report that it also immeasurably enhanced the students' motivation, sense of efficacy, and self-esteem.

Authentic problem solving has been shown to immeasurably enhance students' motivation, sense of efficacy, and self-esteem.

All Levels

Creative teachers have reported numerous other examples of problem solving using community and school resources to help

students connect to the meaning of what they are teaching. Many problems facing our communities (and the world) can be used to involve students in critical thinking and problem solving. Examples include natural habitat preservation, homeless issues, the spread of infectious diseases, anti-smoking campaigns, quality of cafeteria food, effects of global warming, and freeway congestion.

Problem solving can be an effective way to address behavioral and academic issues at the same time. One teacher challenged her 6th grade students to find a way to improve their own math scores. A band director asked his students to find a way to purchase new band uniforms. In response to students' questions about when they would ever need the information they were learning, an algebra teacher suggested they research which professions require a knowledge of algebra and how it is used.

An excellent source of authentic problems is a curriculum development and delivery system called problem-based learning. Numerous books and Web sites outline the program and suggested curricula for all grade levels and subject areas (e.g., Azer, 2008; Center for Problem-Based Learning, 2001; Kain, 2003).

Using Projects to Increase Meaning and Motivation

Busy students engaged in an activity is always a rewarding sight. When compared to the passive activity of sitting and listening to the teacher talk, student involvement in a project or experiment appears to be a much better way to learn. Indeed, projects and activities have rich potential as a means of engaging students and increasing understanding. However, caution is warranted when deciding when and how to use them. Too often, we select activities that look like a lot of fun without considering what it is we want our students to gain from doing them. For example, in a study of early missions in California, a teacher instructed students to construct missions with sugar cubes. The students enjoyed this project and may have learned something

about using sugar cubes as a building material; however, I wonder what this project taught the students about the effects of missions on American Indians, the contributions of these settlements, or the role they played in California history.

Projects and activities should be a means to enhance learning, not an end in themselves. An activity should relate directly to a clearly defined objective or standard, not just superficially relate to it. Students need help to understand the purpose of a project or activity, which can be done with an introductory discussion or during the processing and debriefing at the end of the activity or completion of the project. Given these caveats, let's look at some examples of carefully planned and executed projects.

Lower Elementary School

There is no reason why younger children cannot become meaningfully involved in projects. A teacher in Oregon decided to tackle the issue of violence with her 2nd graders. After students had brainstormed examples of violence, they watched several children's television programs and tallied the acts of violence, which included threats and threatening behavior, hitting, kicking, and the presence of various weapons. Every student in the class was involved in some aspect of the project. They then reported their findings to their schoolmates in other classes. A reporter heard about the project and recommended that the students contact a member of the County Board of Commissioners, which had declared the reduction of youth violence to be a priority. The reporter visited the classroom and brainstormed with the children how they could communicate their research results to others. As a result of this meeting, the children wrote a "Declaration of Independence from Violence," which included a pledge to boycott products advertised by shows that contained excessive violence. They contacted radio and other media, wrote letters to U.S. senators and representatives, and eventually were featured on *ABC World News Tonight* (Evans, 1996).

Upper Elementary School

Sometimes the impetus for a project arises from students' questions about or interest in a topic they are studying. A 4th grade class was studying the American Indians who introduced corn to the Pilgrims. During their study of corn and its importance to the early colonists, the students determined that a corn muffin would be an excellent choice for state muffin. They researched the workings of government, wrote letters, and eventually lobbied the Massachusetts State House and testified before a legislative committee. The entire class was present to watch their bill signed into law by the governor of their state.

An Arizona teacher developed a unique project to teach about the native Hohokam culture. His 5th grade students built a simulated archaeological site on their school grounds, and after researching their topic, they proceeded to build a full-size housing site out of adobe bricks. In the following years, other students were involved in an archaeological dig at the site. Students learned proper methods of excavation and used written logs to enter all the data on each artifact they found. At the conclusion of the dig, students created a book with information on each artifact and their conclusions about what the Hohokam people were like. They also made more artifacts and reburied the ones they had already found, so the site could be used by the next class. The teacher reported that this project was unparalleled in teaching about the local American Indian culture in their community.

Middle School

A special education class studying the Great Depression found it difficult to obtain firsthand information about what it was like to live during that time. The teacher contacted local senior citizens and asked if they would be willing to be interviewed. Upon receiving a positive response, she had the students determine what they

Though they are not necessarily based on problem solving, projects offer many of the same benefits in making the curriculum more meaningful to students.

wanted to know, write and edit questions, and set a convenient time for the seniors to be interviewed. Later in the year, during a discussion about living on a fixed income, the students asked to interview the seniors a second time. The teacher reported that an unexpected side benefit of this project was a bonding between the seniors and the students. The students prepared and served a potluck dinner for their new friends, and the seniors began a volunteer program to assist the students in the classroom.

Secondary School

A team of students in an advanced English course decided to raise awareness and eliminate misconceptions about the homeless in their community, a suburb of Chicago. They surveyed 100 business owners and employees and found that 54 percent of the respondents thought there was a real homelessness problem and 20 percent thought it affected their business. The team devised a brochure presenting the survey results along with facts about homeless people in the community and information about relevant local resources. Other students in the program have tackled school issues such as crowded hallways and the attendance policy. Their teacher believes that they are getting a true sense of how to define and deal with real-world issues.

Authentic problems and projects can be powerful learning experiences, but the lessons learned do not necessarily transfer to new problems or settings. In other words, students who solve a problem in one context often fail to transfer what they've learned to a different context. One way to deal with this issue is to provide students with an additional, similar case and help them recognize similarities. In this way, students can learn to identify general principles or "big ideas" that are transferable. Another method to increase the probability of transfer is to engage students in a "what if" scenario: "What if this part of the problem was changed or the variables were different?" (National Research Council, 1999).

All Levels

Projects or problem-based learning activities can be designed for almost any area of the curriculum. Whenever students ask why something is so or why one method works better than another, it is an opportunity to assist them in finding the answer themselves. Though science may seem to lend itself more easily to experimentation and problem solving, these methods are equally effective in mathematics, social studies, language arts, and other areas of the curriculum. Students at any grade level can be presented with a challenge to solve a problem or create a project that answers the challenge. Examples of challenges include: "How could we get more students involved in recycling?" "Are there other ways we can learn the multiplication tables (or vocabulary words or spelling words) instead of flash cards?" and "What are the different methods we can employ to make sure homework gets turned in on time?"

Using Simulations and Role-Plays to Make Meaning

It is unrealistic to expect that all curriculum topics can be addressed through authentic problem solving and projects.

It is unrealistic to expect that all curriculum topics can be addressed through authentic problem solving and projects. At times, such activities are neither desirable nor feasible. In these situations, simulations become useful teaching strategies. Simulations are not real events, and they need to be carefully planned and processed for the full benefits to be realized. To gain the most benefit from simulations, I suggest two basic rules or considerations. First, make certain that you have a specific object or concept in mind to be addressed by the activity. Second, spend sufficient time debriefing the simulation with students. They often need guidance to compare and contrast a simulation with an actual event so they can abstract the relevant general principles. Remember that it is always best when students can tell the teacher what they have learned rather than having the teacher tell them! Some simulations are highly emotional, and though this can be an added benefit for retention, there is a potential danger if students aren't able to separate the simulation from reality and become upset or angry. In some cases, such as simulating the spread of HIV, parents should be made aware of the planned activity. Teachers also need to know when to stop an activity if students become too emotionally involved.

Lower Elementary School

Punctuation is often meaningless to young children. One 2nd grade teacher helps students understand the purpose of the various punctuation marks by having them "walk the punctuation" as they read silently. They pause when they reach a comma, stop for a period, shrug their shoulders for a question mark, and jump if the sentence ends in an exclamation mark. A 3rd grade teacher gives her students opportunities to demonstrate how apostrophes are used in contractions by acting them out. Students stand in a line and hold separate letter cards that form the two words to be contracted, such as *is* and *not.* One student, acting as the apostrophe, moves to the letter *o* and asks it to leave as he is its replacement. The *o* moves out, the apostrophe moves into its place, the letters move together, and the contraction *isn't* is formed. The same teacher makes learning punctuation fun by asking students to generate sounds to represent different punctuation marks, which they can sound out as they read sentences and dialogue.

Upper Elementary School

Students in a 4th grade classroom in Alberta, Canada decided to simulate an oil spill to determine which substances did the best job of removing oil from the water and from the birds that may have been contaminated. They filled bowls with oil-covered water and dipped cotton balls (representing the birds) into the water. The students noted that the oil clung to the ball, leaving no part of it untouched. After testing several substances, they found that peat moss absorbed most of the oil when sprinkled on the surface of the water. After using the peat moss to absorb the oil, they dipped the cotton ball "bird" again and found that it came out of the water with only a few bits of peat moss and almost no oil. The teacher asked the students who they thought needed to know this information; they determined that the prime minister of Canada was the most likely person, and they set out to design a packet of materials to send to him. It included a videotape of students conducting and explaining their experiment, a formal write-up of the experiment, close-up photographs of the "bird" before and after cleanup, and a cover letter explaining why they were sending this packet to him.

To help students understand the counterintuitive fact that sound travels faster through a solid than through a gas, one 5th grade teacher had several students "become" molecules by first distributing themselves far apart, as in a gas, and then close together, as in a solid. One student represented a sound, touched the first molecule, and said, "Beep." This molecule then touched the next, and so on, until the sound traveled through all the molecules. The students quickly saw how much faster sound traveled through the closely spaced molecules of a solid.

Middle School

Students in a certain middle school pre-algebra class I observed spent little time at their desks solving equations with pencil and paper. Instead, they engaged in an exercise in "human graphing," finding their places as coordinates on x- and y-axes marked on the floor with masking tape. Students observing the activity sketched and described the shape they saw. On another day, they walked a large number line painted on the floor to simulate the addition and subtraction of integers.

In a social studies classroom, students draw pictures of workers in a simulation of an assembly line. In the debriefing following the simulation, the students eagerly discuss the pros and cons of assembly line work (Teachers' Curriculum Institute, 1999). In still another classroom, middle school students simulate the process of photosynthesis while it is videotaped to show parents at an open house.

Our brains have difficulty comprehending large numbers because we have nothing in our experience to "hook" them to. Helping students comprehend the distribution of Earth's population and resources often is an exercise in memorizing meaningless statistics, but in one 8th grade classroom, students are involved in a simulation that brings these data to life. The teacher divides the classroom into six major political/geographic regions and assigns students to "populate" each region in the same proportion as in the world today. The teacher then distributes matchbooks to represent energy consumption, peanuts for protein, and small chocolates for wealth. Students can easily identify with the "haves" and "have-nots" of the world when they see people in the North America region with a highly disproportionate amount of wealth, energy, and food.

An 8th grade student in Iowa designed a simulation to help her classmates comprehend the large number of people killed in the Battle of Antietam during the Civil War. She used corn kernels to represent individual people. She emptied a small bag of corn on a tarp to represent the 168 people who lost their lives in the Oklahoma City bombing, a larger bag for the more than 1,800 who perished as a result of Hurricane Katrina, and an even larger bag for the nearly 3,000 people who perished on September 11th, 2001. She then poured out a very large bucket full of kernels to represent those who died during the Battle of Antietam: roughly 12,400 from the North and 10,300 from the South.

Secondary School

An English literature teacher who was beginning a study of *Robin Hood* wanted her students to understand the historical context of the story, so she designed a simulation to accomplish this goal. She divided the class into two groups, representing the Saxons and the

Our brains have difficulty comprehending very large numbers because we have nothing in our experience to "hook" them to.

Normans. She assigned four students the role of historian to objectively record the events. The Saxons were each given a small package of candy; the Normans received no candy. The teacher informed them that she was going to ask questions alternately of the two groups to determine a winner. If the Saxons answered the questions correctly they could keep the candy, and if the Normans were correct, they could take candy from the Saxons. The questions, however, were rigged so that only the Normans were successful.

At the end of the simulation (when the Normans had all the candy), the teacher asked the historians to read their observations. They reported that the Saxons had tried to hide their candy, ruined the candy before giving it to the enemy, and angrily threw their candy at the Normans. The Normans had gloated, taunted, and tried to take two pieces of candy at a time. After all students wrote their reflections in their journals, the teacher debriefed the activity with them. Students reported that they now understood why the Saxon thanes had burned their homes rather than let the Normans take them and how conflicts often are unfair, with one side having more resources than the other. The teacher reported that *Robin Hood* was much more meaningful to these students than it had been to students in previous classes.

To make the composition of an element more meaningful, a science teacher took his class out to the football field and divided them into three groups, representing protons, neutrons, and electrons. The students who were neutrons stood up and made a big O with their hands; this represented a neutral charge. The students representing protons became positive by making crosses with their arms, and those representing electrons stood with their arms pointed front and back to represent a negative charge. As the teacher called out the name of an element, the students ran to the appropriate positions to simulate its composition.

All Levels

Setting up a business in which students produce a product is a simulation that provides experience with planning, marketing, accounting, production scheduling, and banking. Some school districts, with help from local attorneys and judges, have implemented peer courts where students learn about the judicial system in an authentic setting. Simulating a grocery store in the classroom (where shelves are stocked with empty food containers) gives elementary students experience in planning meals, reading labels, staying within a budget, and making change. Though simulations require additional planning and work on the part of the teacher, they are an excellent way to increase meaning while being highly motivational and stimulating the transfer of knowledge.

Synapse Strengtheners

1. Select a unit that you normally teach in a traditional manner and create a simulation to address its objectives. At the end of the unit, ask students for written feedback of their reactions and how presentation of the unit compared to the more traditional method.

2. If you are reading this book as part of a study group, ask each member to interview teachers at his or her grade level for simulations they have used successfully. Compile these into a booklet and distribute them to the teachers in the school.

3. Prepare a response to a parent who wants to know why you are "playing games" in the classroom, rather than teaching in the more traditional method by which she was taught.

12

Using the Visual and Auditory Senses to Enhance Learning

Take a moment and think about a particularly memorable event in your life. Perhaps you're recalling a special vacation spent at the beach or backpacking in the mountains, or maybe you're thinking about your wedding day or the day your first child entered kindergarten. Whatever event comes to mind, you remember it not so much in words but more often in images and sounds. When you describe the event to someone else, you use words to describe what you see and hear inside your head.

As we discussed in Chapter 8, Daniel Siegel explains that when you mentally "see" an image or "hear" a sound, you are reactivating or reconstructing the neural pathways that were formed when you first experienced the stimulus. In fact, it is nearly impossible not to recall those sights and sounds. If I say, "Picture an elephant" or "Think about the 'ABC Song,'" you see an elephant or hear the song. If I say, "Do *not* picture an elephant" or "Do *not* hear the 'ABC Song,'" you still see the elephant or hear the song. These sensory abilities are powerful components of brain functioning, and we can use them in the classroom to enhance our students' understanding and retention of information.

A Picture Is Worth at Least 10,000 Words

Humans are intensely visual animals. Our eyes contain nearly 70 percent of the body's sensory receptors, and they send millions of signals per second along optic nerves to the visual processing centers of the brain. It is not surprising, then, that the visual components of a memory are so robust. Although each of us has the ability to process kinesthetic and auditory information, we take in more information visually than through any of the other senses.

"I Never Forget a Face"

Several studies validate how well the mind processes and remembers visual information. One of the most remarkable was a 1973 study conducted by Lionel Standing at Bishop's University in Canada. He presented volunteers with 10,000 photographic slides depicting a variety of subject matter. The volunteers viewed each picture for five seconds over a period of five days. At the end of the fifth day, they were tested with a random sample of 160 out of the full set of 10,000. Researchers paired the pictures they had seen with ones they had not seen; and for each pair, the volunteers had to choose the picture they had seen before. Remarkably, the subjects selected the correct picture about 73 percent of the time (Squire & Kandel, 2000; Standing, 1973).

In a similar study, investigators showed subjects photographs of classmates two months after graduation. Not surprisingly, the subjects were able to recognize 90 percent of those who had been in their class. The amazing fact is that the recognition rate was still close to 90 percent when they were tested 15 years later. The capacity for long-term memory of visual information seems almost unlimited (Bahrick, Bahrick, & Wittlinger, 1976).

The fact that images are memorable is supported not only by the research but by our own observations. When we have difficulty

Our eyes contain nearly 70 percent of the body's sensory receptors, and they send millions of signals per second along optic nerves to the visual processing centers of the brain.

The capacity for long-term memory of visual information seems almost unlimited.

recalling something, we often explain our failure as an inability to "picture" it. You've probably had the experience of taking a test and trying to recall the information that was represented by a chart or drawing. You could "see" the chart and remember where on the page it was located, and with a little luck you might have been able to recall the information it contained. The importance of visualizing is also evident in many common metaphors, such as "I see what you mean" or "He can't see the forest for the trees."

Thinking in Pictures

Not only are visuals powerful retention aids, but they also serve to increase understanding.

Not only are visuals powerful retention aids, but they also serve to increase understanding. Imagine trying to comprehend the structure of an atom without an illustration or trying to understand the operation of an internal combustion engine without a diagram. The ability to transform thoughts into images is often viewed as a test of true understanding, but some people appear to process information the other way around, literally seeming to comprehend information by visualizing it. One such person was Albert Einstein, who appeared to process information primarily in images, rather than in written words or spoken language. He wrote that all of his ideas came to him in more or less clear images and that he had great difficulty putting his ideas into words (Shaw, 2000). Another such person is Temple Grandin, a professor of animal science at Colorado State University and a leading expert in the design of livestock-handling facilities. Grandin is autistic, and, in her autobiography, she explained that her only avenue to understanding abstract concepts is through picturing them (1995).

Physicist Gordon Shaw proposed that spatial-temporal reasoning is critical for comprehending math and science concepts (2000). One of the defining characteristics of this type of reasoning is the ability to transform abstract concepts into visual images. Perhaps this is why 5th grade students have such difficulty multiplying and dividing fractions. It is very difficult for most students to create a mental picture of ¼ × ⅓. It can be done if you understand (and can see a diagram that shows) that ¼ × ⅓ really means ¼ of ⅓ *of a whole.* Shaw and his colleagues collected impressive data showing that piano keyboard training, taught in conjunction with a computer program that uses images to depict math and science concepts, dramatically increases elementary students' math understanding and test scores.

Many studies have shown the facilitating effect of imagery, especially pictures, on learning and memory. One study used two different strategies to examine 6th graders' understanding and recall of vocabulary words. One group of students memorized dictionary definitions of the words, while a second group drew their own pictures to represent the words' meanings. Students in the second group demonstrated much higher retention levels (Bull & Wittrock, 1973). Using a keyword imagery mnemonic process in which subjects linked the sound of a word to an image of a concrete noun in English, researchers increased college students' retention of Spanish vocabulary words from 28 percent to 88 percent (Atkinson & Raugh, 1975; Raugh & Atkinson, 1975).

Classroom Strategies Using Visual Processing

As many of the examples above show, using visuals in the classroom can greatly increase students' understanding and retention of the curriculum. However, a word of caution is merited when designing visuals at different grade levels. Young children in kindergarten or 1st grade sometimes have difficulty drawing visual representations. In these situations, imposed visuals in which students use an image provided by the teacher will often be necessary. For older students, induced visuals in which students generate their own images are generally more effective.

Elementary School

In their 1st grade team, a group of teachers design a "gallon person" to teach and review volumes. The body represents a gallon, the arms and legs are one quart each, the wrists and ankles make up eight pints (two each), and four digits on each hand and foot (ignoring the thumb or big toe) represent cups. Also in 1st grade, a teacher posts pictures of activities students will be doing throughout the day. She then rings a bell and removes a picture as a signal for the children to change activities. Pictures of routines in the order they are to be completed can also be extremely useful for autistic children or other children who have difficulty following verbal directions.

A 2nd grade teacher, looking for a way to help students understand and remember that every word has a vowel in it, creates a bulletin board that contains six houses with doors that students can open. Inside each door "lives" one of the five vowels (plus *y*). Students are reminded that if there is no vowel in a word they are writing, it is just a group of letters and not a word. Beginning writers can draw illustrations of each new word they learn and keep them in individual booklets, relieving the teacher of having to continually spell words for them.

Teachers can help students understand the correct placement of quotation marks in written dialogue by drawing a happy face on the board and placing the quotation marks at the corners of the mouth. (See Figure 12.1.) A 5th grade teacher has students make illustrations of rules and procedures and puts them in book form. For example, they create books titled *What Respect Means* and *This Is the Way We Do Things Here.*

Middle School

A science teacher instructs students to take notes in a "split page" formation. On the left side of the page, students take notes on what

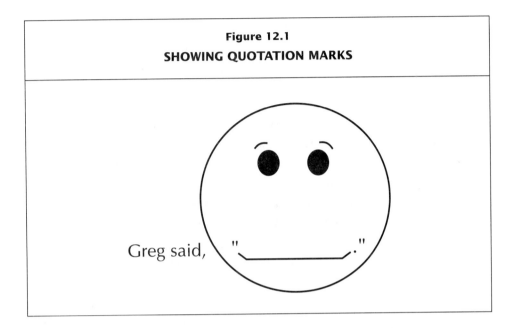

Figure 12.1
SHOWING QUOTATION MARKS

they read, and on the right side, they draw a picture to represent what they have written.

Students in a math class are asked to determine which of the following decimals has the greatest value—.08, .8, .080, or .008000—and to explain their answer. Most students pick the correct answer (.8), but their explanations (".8 is the greatest because it has no zeros before or after it") demonstrate that they lack a concrete understanding of why. The teacher then has the students create a drawing that illustrates these values and has them share their drawings in groups. This results in an animated discussion as the students discover how many different ways this concept can be correctly illustrated.

A middle school English teacher helps students understand the framework for nearly every short story by graphically representing the plot on a diagram. An inverted *V* diagram is drawn, starting with the rising action, rising to the climax of the plot, and ultimately descending with the resolution. Students can use this graphic as a reminder as they write their own stories. (See Figure 12.2.)

Secondary School

A freshman English teacher decides to involve her students more actively in weekly vocabulary lessons by letting partners peer teach their classmates an assigned word. She challenges the partners to present their assigned word in such a way that everyone in the class will remember the word—not just for the test but "for the rest of their lives." She is surprised to discover that their two- to three-minute presentations are extremely creative and that the students thoroughly enjoy this novel way of studying vocabulary. Two girls display a lovely, drooping rose, explaining that it is a sad rose and should be recalled when the word *morose* is read. Another pair creates a giant report card with an *F* in every subject, and they call on their teacher to be the 9th grade recipient of the card. She is then instructed to act *disconsolately* (their assigned word).

The *History Alive!* curriculum suggests that students expand their note-taking and understanding by keeping an interactive notebook.

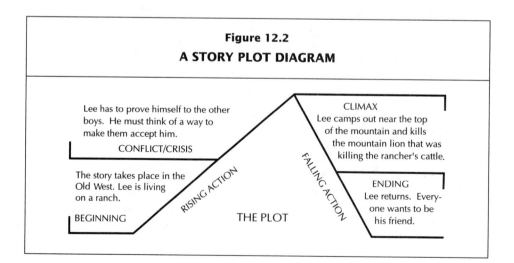

Figure 12.2
A STORY PLOT DIAGRAM

Lee has to prove himself to the other boys. He must think of a way to make them accept him.
CONFLICT/CRISIS

The story takes place in the Old West. Lee is living on a ranch.
BEGINNING

RISING ACTION

THE PLOT

FALLING ACTION

CLIMAX
Lee camps out near the top of the mountain and kills the mountain lion that was killing the rancher's cattle.

ENDING
Lee returns. Everyone wants to be his friend.

(See Figure 12.3.) Periodically during a lecture or during the reading, the teacher asks students to interact with their notes using one of several suggested alternatives. Some options are to create a map or web of the content, draw a cartoon, or sketch a particular scene. Teachers using this technique report that it results in increased retention and understanding of the content studied (Teachers' Curriculum Institute, 1999).

Figure 12.3

AN INTERACTIVE NOTEBOOK

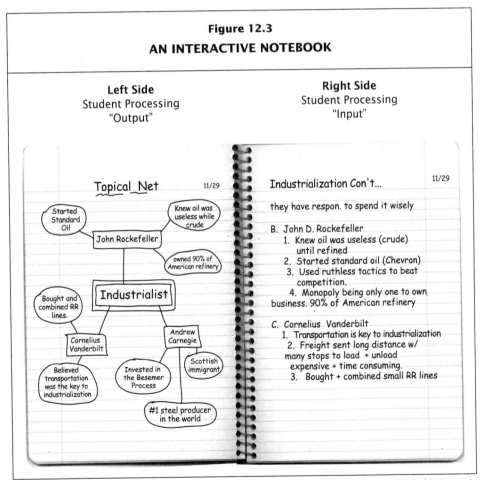

Teachers' Curriculum Institute. (1999). *History alive! Engaging all learners in the diverse classroom* (2nd ed.). Mountain View, CA: Author, p. 127. Reproduced with permission.

All Levels

Many teachers use graphics to help students organize their thinking. Known as mind maps, thinking maps, webs, clusters, network trees, fishbone maps, and graphic organizers, they have proved to be particularly effective at increasing students' understanding and retention of information. Perhaps this is because these visual devices make it possible to see connections between aspects of information that are not obvious in a linear form, such as an outline or narrative. The structure of these frameworks resembles the structure used by the brain to organize information. In other words, the brain does not naturally outline; it organizes information in networks or maps.

The structure of graphic organizers resembles the structure used by the brain to organize information.

Remember that the various aspects of a memory—or of a learned fact—are not stored in a single, specific location in the brain but in networks of networks. Images are stored in the visual cortex, sounds in the auditory cortex, and so forth. This may be why visually mapping information has proved productive for enhancing students' storage and retention of information: It mirrors the structure used by the brain.

Teachers can select from many visual structures, depending on the desired outcome. They can use graphics called advanced organizers to help students organize information in a predetermined format. Figure 12.4 shows an example that helps students focus on essential aspects of a chapter in an environmental science text.

Another visual organizer is the familiar web or bubble map. These organizers have a number of uses. They can be used before writing to help students brainstorm aspects of a topic they might include in their compositions, or they may serve as a way to display and organize what students know about a particular topic before beginning a unit of study. Another application is as a framework for organizing main ideas and subtopics as students read information in a text. Figure 12.5 is an example of a "double bubble" map designed

Figure 12.4
AN ADVANCED ORGANIZER

Biome	Climate	Main Plants	Main Animals	Human Activities	Environmental Problems
Tropical Rain Forest					
Desert					
Temperate Grasslands					

to help students organize information about Julius Caesar's private and public lives. *A Field Guide to Using Visual Tools* (Hyerle, 2000) is an excellent source of information regarding the many forms of graphics and their uses in educational settings.

Music (Rhyme and Rhythm) Hath Many Charms

We tend to think of music only in cultural or artistic terms, but scientists have found that music is a highly complex neural activity. Sound waves enter our ears and are converted into nerve impulses by the organ of Corti in the cochlea. From there, the impulses are transmitted to specialized regions in our left and right temporal lobes for processing. Suppose that the sounds entering our ears are the notes of a symphony. For us to make sense of the music, the signals must travel from the temporal lobes to working memory in the frontal lobes. Sounds unfold over time, and our brain must be able to hold on to a sequence of sounds for several seconds or minutes in order to compare them with new sounds arriving in the brain. This is what working memory does so well. It allows us to hold the musical information over a period of time to decode it. The frontal

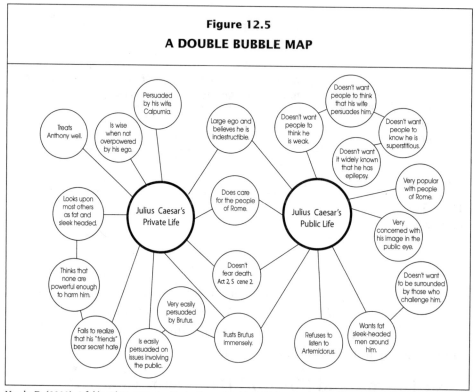

Figure 12.5

A DOUBLE BUBBLE MAP

Hyerle, D. (2000). *A field guide to using visual tools*. Alexandria, VA: ASCD, p. 27. Reprinted with permission from Thinking Maps, Inc.

lobes are where the sounds are recognized as patterns of notes and musical phrases that make up sonatas and symphonies.

Contrary to the popular misconception that music is the property of the right hemisphere, new imaging techniques have shown that music is distributed across specialized regions in both hemispheres. In fact, many musical experiences can activate the cognitive, visual, auditory, affective, and motor systems, depending on whether you are reading music, playing an instrument, composing a song, beating out a rhythm, or just listening to a melody.

The mental mechanisms that process music are deeply entwined with the brain's other basic functions, including emotion, memory, and language. Research shows that the human brain is predisposed to detect patterns in both music and language. It is interesting that we appear to favor certain types of musical patterns over others. Canadian researcher Sandra Trehub has found that infants prefer consonant to dissonant passages. Four-month-old infants demonstrate a preference for hearing Mozart sonatas as originally written, compared to "unnatural" versions (Krumhansl & Jusczyk, 1996).

Music and Emotion

Music's emotional impact is well documented. Robert Zatorre, a neuroscientist at McGill University in Montreal, used PET scans to examine cerebral blood flow changes related to affective responses to music. He found that the parts of the brain involved in processing emotion "light up" with activity when a subject hears music (Blood, Aztorre, Bermudez, & Evans, 1999). It is not surprising that music can incite a broad range of emotions, including passion, serenity, and fear. Most of us can recall instances when music caused changes in our own emotional levels, perhaps when we listened to Handel's Hallelujah Chorus or the background music in a movie thriller. The reason for the emotional arousal appears to be that music affects levels of several brain chemicals, including epinephrine, endorphins, and cortisol, the hormone involved in the "fight-or-flight" response. In Chapter 9, we saw that one of the links between emotion and memory involves these same neurotransmitters and hormones. Perhaps this is why a mere snippet of a song from our past can trigger highly vivid memories.

You Must Remember This . . .

If you are of a certain age, the preceding phrase will result in the automatic response, "a kiss is just a kiss." Regardless of age, if you grew up in an English-speaking environment, you can most likely complete the following phrases: "In fourteen hundred and ninety-two . . ."; "Thirty days hath September . . ."; "M-I-C, K-E-Y . . ."; or

The mental mechanisms that process music are deeply entwined with the brain's other basic functions, including emotion, memory, and language.

There is little doubt that when information is embedded in music or rhyme, its recall is enhanced.

"Humpty Dumpty sat on a wall . . . ." There is little doubt that when information is embedded in music or rhyme, its recall is enhanced. People can typically remember lyrics of tunes and rhymes, but they are much less successful in recalling prose passages.

Although many scientists believe that language and music are closely linked and share some of the same neural circuits, music (or rhyme set to music) clearly has the advantage when it comes to recall. We can use this natural proclivity of the brain to design educational activities that will enhance the retention of certain kinds of information.

Music, Mozart, and Math

By now, almost everyone has heard of the "Mozart Effect." Various news and popular magazines have touted it as a way to enhance relaxation, increase concentration, boost intelligence in babies, and make the listener a math whiz. However, the original study that spawned those stories made no such claims. In 1993, physicist Gordon Shaw and his colleagues at the University of California, Irvine reported that college students who listened to Mozart's Sonata for Two Pianos in D Major performed better on reasoning tasks than they did after listening to a relaxation tape or silence (Shaw, 2000). The results lasted only 10 minutes. The report, however, captured the imagination of people around the world as an effortless way to boost intelligence; and it resulted in countless articles, books, and recordings that all made unsubstantiated claims to increase intelligence.

Although people have widely misinterpreted the Mozart Effect, researchers have found that music does have certain beneficial effects on learning. Shaw believed that music uses many of the same higher brain functions as math and science and that training in music can enhance these functions. He and Frances Rauscher, at the University of Wisconsin, conducted a number of additional studies that examined the link between music training and spatial-temporal reasoning (Shaw, 2000). Spatial-temporal reasoning is the ability to visualize a problem and a solution; it generally results in increased conceptual understanding of the problem. Temple Grandin, mentioned earlier in this chapter, is gifted with this type of reasoning.

Shaw's studies produced amazing results. He and his colleagues developed an interactive math software program called Spatial Temporal Animation Reasoning (STAR), which allows children to solve math puzzles that increase their ability to manipulate shapes mentally. Inner-city 2nd graders who received instruction on piano keyboards alongside STAR training scored 27 percent higher in proportional math and fractions than did children who played a computerized English-language instruction game or those who received only the STAR training. Incredibly, half of these 2nd graders scored as well as 5th graders in a more affluent, neighboring district; and they scored twice as high as children in the 2nd grade without either training (Shaw, 2000).

Using Music, Rhyme, and Rhythm in the Classroom

Teachers can find many ways to use music to enhance both the classroom environment and student learning. Certain types of music affect brain wave patterns, resulting in a slowing down or speeding up of brain activity. Some teachers report that playing music such as Handel's *Water Music Suite* or Vivaldi's *Four Seasons* soothes and calms their students, whereas marches have an opposite, energizing effect. These same selections could also be used to increase an ability to analyze musical sounds and patterns and to develop an understanding of how composers communicate through their music. In the same vein, elementary students enjoy learning to identify the characters portrayed by different instruments in Prokofiev's *Peter and the Wolf.*

Music can be a powerful and effective method to integrate various curricular areas. Musical patterns and symbols are underlying concepts that help to make math more understandable. For example, one natural link is to teach students about fractions as they learn

Music can be a powerful and effective method to integrate various curricular areas.

the values of whole, half, and quarter notes. We can also enhance the study of history by looking at the effects of patriotic songs on people's emotions and actions. Students can gain increased understanding of communication by learning how people have used drum rhythms and songs of traveling minstrels to disseminate information or elements of a culture from one place to another. In a film and drama class, students can experience and document how different types of music affect their mood as they watch a horror film. Environmental science students can map the food chain described in Pete Seeger's folk song "The People Are Scratching." These same students can also demonstrate their understanding of an ecological concept by producing an original music video.

Rhyme and rhythm provide great mechanisms for storing information that would otherwise be difficult to retain. As mentioned earlier, information embedded in music or rhyme is much easier to recall than the same information in prose. Think about very young children who are able to repeat dozens of nursery rhymes and songs. In Chapter 9, we learned that five-year-old children can work consciously with approximately two bits of information at a time, which would seem to put severe limits on the capacity of their memories. Nearly all children in kindergarten, however, can sing the ABC song, which strings together 26 bits of data that have no intrinsic relationship to each other. (It is noteworthy that the tune to this song, "Twinkle, Twinkle, Little Star," was composed by Mozart.)

Rhyme and rhythm are great methods for storing information that would otherwise be difficult to retain.

Piggyback Songs

The ABC song is an example of what is sometimes called a piggyback song—a song in which new words or concepts are set to a familiar melody. Young children often lack the ability to create their own piggyback songs, but they quickly learn to sing songs taught to them by their parents or teachers. One 1st grade teacher helps students remember how to end a sentence by teaching them the "Period Song," sung to the tune of "Row, Row, Row Your Boat":

> *Stop, stop, stop the words*
> *With a little dot.*
> *Use a period at the end,*
> *So they'll know to stop.*

Another example of a piggyback song is "The Continent Song," sung to the tune of "Frere Jacques." This song also uses motion of body parts to show the general locations of the continents:

> *North America (hold up left hand),*
> *Europe (point to nose),*
> *Asia (hold up right hand),*
> *Africa, Africa (make a circle around the waist with both hands),*
> *South America (point to left knee),*
> *Australia (point to right knee)*
> *Antarctica, Antarctica (stomp feet).*

In this example, adding movement provides an extra sensory input to the brain and enhances the learning. Rhymes to teach spelling or punctuation rules, names of planets, parts of the human body, and so forth can all be set to jump-rope jingles or other movements.

Remembering how to spell a word is easier if you sing it to a familiar tune. Five-letter words can be sung to the tune of "You Are My Sunshine," six-letter words fit the tune of "Happy Birthday," and seven-letter words can be sung to the tune of "Twinkle, Twinkle, Little Star." Piggyback songs are also a preferred learning strategy in many foreign language and bilingual classes. I can still remember learning the numerals and months of the year in Spanish by singing *Uno de enero, dos de febrero, tres de marzo, quatro de abril* to the tune of "San Fermin."

Rhythm, Rhyme, and Rap

Learning content by embedding it in music or rhyme is generally more effective if students are involved in creating the product, rather

Adding movement to music and rhymes provides an extra sensory input to the brain and enhances learning.

Learning content by embedding it in music or rhyme is generally more effective if students are involved in creating the product, rather than simply using one composed by someone else.

than simply using one composed by someone else. In a driver's education class in Illinois, I watched students as they demonstrated their knowledge of a car's operating systems with songs set to the tunes of their favorite songs. One group of boys explained the braking system of a car to the tune of "YMCA" (with all the appropriate motions), and a group of girls entertained the class with a rap of the cooling system. In an environmental science class I observed, students wrote riddles about various chemical elements such as, "I'm the lightest of gases; I'm found in all stars. Touch me with matches, and I'll blow things apart. What am I?" (*Hydrogen*).

Upper elementary and middle school teachers often find that many of their students still do not know some of their multiplication tables. The 2s, 5s, and 10s are usually the easiest, perhaps because many teachers have taught students to count in rhythm by these numbers, a process that quickly becomes automatic. All the multiplication tables would likely be learned more quickly if we taught students to count by all numbers, not just by 2, 5, and 10. Even with our best efforts, however, some students still have difficulty. One middle school teacher faced this problem. Knowing that these students probably wouldn't be too excited about singing to the tune of "Three Blind Mice," she suggested that they put the multiplication tables in a rap. They did so, and it wasn't long before they had mastered all the tables and made a recording of their rap called "Tough Times," which they offered to their peers.

An expectation of many 1st grade students is that they will learn to read on the first day of school. One creative teacher fulfills this expectation with a simple song that she has duplicated in a booklet for each child. She has the children sing the song repeatedly throughout the day, color the pictures in their booklet, and practice singing the song to each other. At the end of the day, each child "reads" the words of the song aloud and receives a certificate stating that he or she learned to read on the first day of 1st grade.

Commercial Songs

Many songs, jingles, and raps are commercially available and can be used to teach a variety of concepts to students. Schools can purchase tapes and CDs to teach nouns and verbs, countries of the world, the order of the planets from the sun, the freedoms listed in the Constitution, and addition and subtraction facts. Although these can be beneficial teaching aids, there is probably more value in having students create or compose their own if they are able.

Synapse Strengtheners

1. Select a concept that your students normally have difficulty understanding and design a graphic organizer for it. Give students the major topics and subtopics that are going to be addressed and have them put them into the organizer. At the end of the unit, ask students whether it helped them organize their thoughts and better comprehend the concept.

2. If you are reading this book as part of a study group, start a booklet containing simulations, and add to it by interviewing teachers and gathering examples of visuals, songs, and rhymes that they have used successfully with their students.

3. Prepare a response to a colleague or a parent who has heard that listening to Mozart makes you smarter.

13

A Toolkit of Brain-Compatible Strategies

Recall that, in Chapter 9, we discussed that students need to practice some skills over and over to become proficient. There are no shortcuts to learning how to read or how to play the flute; both require a great deal of rote rehearsal with guidance from a skilled teacher. These skills fall into the category of procedural memory—learning and remembering *how* to do something. For semantic memory—the nature and rules of language and mathematics, and our general knowledge about the world—rote rehearsal is generally much less effective. To store semantic information, a different type of rehearsal, called *elaborative rehearsal,* is needed.

This chapter describes strategies that elaborate on information to increase its meaning, as well as the probability of its retention. For the most part, these strategies are not new or esoteric; some—like mnemonics—have been used for thousands of years. With an increased awareness of how the brain processes information, however, we are beginning to understand why these strategies work, and we can therefore select those that fit the needs of students in particular learning situations.

Enhancing Understanding Through Writing Activities

There is a saying that writing is nature's way of letting us see how sloppy our thinking is. Anyone who has written an article or a book knows just how true this is. Writing and thinking are strongly linked, and writing can serve as a tool for refining thinking. At the same time, complex, cognitive activity produces more articulate and expressive writing. Writing activities fit in the category of elaborative rehearsal because they challenge students to clarify, organize, and express what they learn.

Writing Strategies for Mathematics

At every grade level, students' understanding of mathematical concepts can be enhanced by writing about what they are studying. For example, we can teach children in the primary grades to write simple sentences explaining equations. Figure 13.1 shows one 1st grader's understanding of addition as illustrated in a problem he generated himself.

The purpose of instruction in mathematics is to give students the skills they will need to solve real-life problems involving numbers. Texts typically include word problems to provide practice with problem solving. Too often, however, these problems are abstract and meaningless. When students write their own word problems for their classmates to solve, the problems have more meaning and can be a lot of fun. Consider this problem written by a 4th grade student: "My teacher talks 50 miles an hour. In the first 45 minutes of class, how many miles has she talked?" Another student wrote, "I started out with 37 ants. I put 15 of them in my sister's bed and 16 in my mother's cookie dough. How many ants did I have left?"

Writing is nature's way of letting us see how sloppy our thinking is.

At every grade level, students' understanding of mathematical concepts can be enhanced by writing about what they are studying.

Figure 13.1
A 1ST GRADER'S DRAWING

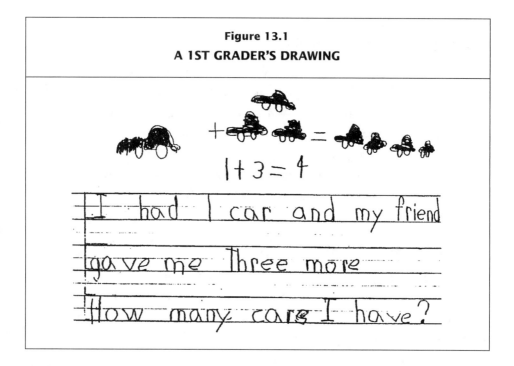

$$1 + 3 = 4$$

I had 1 car and my friend
gave me Three more
How many cars I have?

Middle and secondary school students also can benefit from generating their own mathematical problems. A geometry teacher asks her students to create original theorems to help them understand the underlying structure of the problems in the text. Another secondary teacher has his students brainstorm money problems they face in their own lives, formulate them into a problem-solving format, and present them to the class. These problems center on credit card debt (and the associated interest), expenses involved in purchasing and maintaining a car, and whether a part-time job is really profitable.

Writing about what they learn in math helps students make sense of the information by putting the ideas and methods they use in their own words. Periodically, teachers can ask students to complete sentences such as "I'm really confused about . . . ," "Factoring is easy if . . . ," and "I think calculators . . . ." Another strategy is to ask students to write a note to an absent classmate describing what they learned in class that day. These comments by students greatly facilitate a teacher's diagnosis of students' understanding and skills.

Writing Strategies for History and Social Studies

Writing assignments in social studies or history (at any grade level) typically require students to research a country, an event, or a person and to write a paper. These assignments are often meaningless because they don't relate to the students' lives and result in some creative plagiarism but little learning. Writing can be a motivating learning experience, however, if students have something memorable to write about. Much of the success in writing depends on what has occurred before students start writing. When students see well-designed, motivating slides or films, discuss a controversial issue, or act out a moment in history, they gain information and a motivation for writing.

In the *History Alive!* curriculum mentioned in Chapter 12, students work on many kinds of writing activities, including dialogues, poetry, stories, newspaper eulogies, speeches, and letters. For example, suppose that the assignment is to write a dialogue between Martin Luther King Jr. and Malcolm X. The students first read, view, and discuss primary source material on the Civil Rights Movement. Then, working with partners, they assume the role of either person and engage in a role-play designed to give them ideas for the dialogue. By the time students are ready to write, they are much more likely to really understand the ideas of these two men and are much better prepared and motivated to write the dialogue (Teachers' Curriculum Institute, 1999).

During a study of World War I, *History Alive!* students pretend to be soldiers in trenches writing letters to their families at home. To get a feel for this event, the students write while sitting on the floor between rows of upside-down chairs, which simulate trenches. A slide of a WWI battle projected on the wall in front of them adds to the atmosphere.

Other writing activities might include composing a memorandum to a historical leader that recommends a course of action or

Writing can be a motivating learning experience if students have something memorable to write about.

new policy, writing a newspaper editorial about a historical event, or writing a eulogy extolling the virtues of a prominent historical figure. Although the *History Alive!* curriculum is designed for middle and secondary school use, students at all levels benefit from these types of writing experiences. Elementary students can assume the role of a person living during a particular time period or another part of the country and make entries in a diary that the person might have kept. Students can create a newsletter reporting "current" events that occurred during a period of history they are studying.

In a kindergarten class, students can draw small pictures representing various activities that have taken place in their class that week and then dictate a sentence to the teacher describing each one. The final product is a newsletter to parents of their classroom's "current events." Before taking them home at the end of the week, the students can role-play "reading" the newsletter to their parents. This type of dictated writing is especially important for young children, as it allows them to see that what they say can be written with words.

Dictated writing is especially important for young children, as it allows them to see that what they say can be written with words.

Writing Strategies for Science

Although an understanding of scientific concepts is critical, the larger goal of science instruction is to help students learn to think and act like scientists. Writing plays an important role in the life of scientists because they must describe their hypotheses and experimental designs in a precise manner, carefully document each step of their studies, and accurately communicate their findings and conclusions to readers.

An environmental science teacher teaches the importance of careful observation and accurate description by asking students to observe and write detailed descriptions of simple objects such as leaves. Other students try to identify the objects from their descriptions. In a similar activity, designed to stress the need for accurate written directions, the teacher directs students to make three folds in a note card to create a certain shape and write directions for another student to follow that will result in the same shape.

An earth science teacher asks students to assume the role of a space traveler on a tour of the solar system and accurately describe what they observe for scientists on Earth. A biology teacher combines writing and drawing with an activity called Quick Write/Quick Draw. The example shown in Figure 13.2 is an example of a student diagram that summarizes the process of photosynthesis.

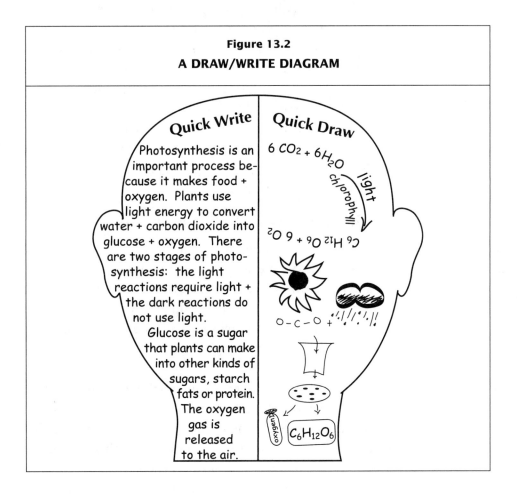

Figure 13.2
A DRAW/WRITE DIAGRAM

Quick Write

Photosynthesis is an important process because it makes food + oxygen. Plants use light energy to convert water + carbon dioxide into glucose + oxygen. There are two stages of photosynthesis: the light reactions require light + the dark reactions do not use light.
Glucose is a sugar that plants can make into other kinds of sugars, starch fats or protein. The oxygen gas is released to the air.

Quick Draw

$6\ CO_2 + 6H_2O$

light

chlorophyll

$C_6\ H_{12}\ O_6 + 6\ O_2$

$O - C - O +$

oxygen

$C_6H_{12}O_6$

At every grade level, students can find many ways to clarify their thinking through writing. An important part of being a scientist is asking questions. Students can find answers to their questions from a variety of sources, but one of the most exciting is by direct communication with actual scientists. The Internet provides convenient access to many scientists. For example, Eric Chudler, a research associate professor at the University of Washington in Seattle, routinely answers students' questions about the brain on a Web site called *Neuroscience for Kids* (Chudler, 2001). Writing to an actual scientist requires careful thought about what questions to ask and how to phrase them. This experience creates a great deal of excitement as students eagerly await and check their e-mail inboxes for a response. Students can also use the Internet to communicate with other students around the world to obtain firsthand information about climate, living conditions, food sources, flora and fauna, and so forth. In addition to collecting data, students can formulate hypotheses about why differences exist among geographic regions and work with their peers to correlate the data.

Writing Strategies Across All Curriculum Areas

Student journals are a rich source of information for the teacher, and they serve as efficient vehicles for reflections as students refine their thinking.

Opportunities for writing exist in all classes and at every grade level. Student journals are a rich source of information for the teacher, and they serve as efficient vehicles for reflections as students refine their thinking. Although free writing is valuable, there are times when the teacher may wish to add structure by asking students to respond to questions or to complete sentences. Figure 13.3 shows some examples.

A secondary school French teacher uses writing in a unique manner in her two advanced classes: She has each class write anonymous love letters in French to students in the other class. She reports that this is one of her students' favorite activities and that their vocabulary increases dramatically, especially for adjectives. Two 5th grade teachers collaborate on a project in which students also exchange letters.

Figure 13.3

QUESTIONS OR SENTENCE STARTERS FOR JOURNAL WRITING

The one thing I'll remember about today's lesson is _____

_____

I'm still confused about _____

What I'm finding hardest right now is_____

How does what I learned today fit with something I already know?_____

_____

_____

What I understood today that I haven't understood before was _____

_____

The problem in this lesson that was most difficult for me was _____

_____

The activity I liked best today was_____

Explain the steps you used to solve a problem today:

1. _____

2. _____

3. _____

4. _____

A new insight or discovery for me was _____

_____

In this activity, however, students in one class write "Dear Abby" letters to students in the other class. Students describe a classroom or playground problem and ask "Abby" how she thinks it should be solved. When the letters are received, students hold class discussions about possible solutions before they write their responses.

Teachers can adapt the well-known K-W-L tool (What I *Know,* What I *Want* to Know, and What I *Learned*) to be a writing strategy by instructing students to start a reflection journal at the beginning of a new unit of study. Students begin by writing what they already know about a topic and then add to this by writing what they would like to know. As they progress through the unit, they can add observations about what they are learning. These journals are excellent sources of discussion when students compare what they have written. In addition, student journals can be an excellent diagnostic tool for monitoring student thinking and adjusting instruction appropriately.

Mnemonics as Tools to Aid Memory

How do you remember the number of days in a month, the order of the colors in the visible spectrum, or the names of the lines on the treble clef? You probably use a mnemonic device or strategy—a method for organizing information in a way that makes it more likely to be remembered. The term *mnemonic* appears to be derived from the Greek word *mnemosyne* (remembrance), the name of the goddess of memory in Greek mythology. Mnemonics have a long, rich history; people in ancient Greece used them extensively and considered mnemonics a rigorous art requiring imagination, effort, and a good mind. They considered the study of mnemonics an essential element of a classical education. (This made sense in a culture where stone or clay tablets were the primary medium used for writing.)

Today, however, the topic of mnemonics is rarely discussed in educational journals or among teachers. The reason for this is that, given the emphasis on learning through relevancy and meaningfulness, many teachers view mnemonics as mere memorization or "memory tricks." Many educators consider mnemonics to be intellectually unrespectable because they do little to enhance meaningful understanding. The truth, however, is that mnemonics can be effective learning strategies. We can use them successfully to help students recall the significance of important terms, dates, and facts; foreign language vocabulary; scientific and mathematical terminology;

The ancient Greeks considered the study of mnemonics an essential element of a classical education.

music notation; the chronology of historical events; and factual information in nearly every subject area. Contrary to what many people believe, mnemonic strategies do not foster simple rote memory at the expense of comprehension and problem solving. In fact, available research evidence suggests that the use of mnemonic strategies to acquire factual information can often improve students' ability to apply that information (Levin & Levin, 1990).

Why Mnemonics Work

Mnemonics are based on the principle that the brain is a pattern-seeking device, always looking for associations between the information it receives and the information it has already stored. If the brain can find no link or association, it is highly unlikely that the information will be stored in long-term memory. Unfortunately, this scenario is relatively commonplace in the classroom. We require students to remember a considerable body of material that has little or no inherent meaning, such as letters of the alphabet or the items that make up a classification system. For this type of information, mnemonic strategies are extremely effective. They create links or associations that give the brain an organizational framework on which to hook new information. The process is relatively simple and consists of three basic steps:

1. The student has—or is given—a framework.
2. New items are associated with the framework.
3. The known cues (the framework) aid in the recall of new information.

For example, suppose a teacher wants her students to remember the order of the colors in the visible spectrum. Since there is no readily apparent reason why the order is red, orange, yellow, green, blue, indigo, and violet, it might be difficult to remember. However, if students are introduced to a fictitious person, Roy G. Biv, and told that the letters of his name each stand for the first letter of the colors

Mnemonics are based on the principle that the brain is a pattern-seeking device, always looking for associations between the information it receives and the information it has already stored.

in the spectrum, they are provided with a framework that makes the information easier to learn and more likely to be recalled. Later, students generate their own frameworks for other pieces of knowledge, which are often more meaningful and powerful as memory tools.

Types of Mnemonic Strategies

Mnemonics encompass a broad range of categories, some more familiar than others. One of the most common is the acrostic sentence. If you took music lessons as a child, you probably learned the notes of the lines on the treble clef by repeating the sentence "Every good boy does fine" (or a slight variation thereof). The first letter of each word is the note on one of the lines, and the order of the sentence is the order of the lines from the bottom to the top of the staff. Other familiar acrostic sentences include "My very eager mother just served us nachos" (for the order of the planets from the sun—Mercury, Venus, Earth, Mars, Jupiter, Saturn, Uranus, and Neptune), "In Persia, men are tall" (for the stages of the cell cycle—interphase, prophase, metaphase, anaphase, telophase), "All hairy men will buy razors" (for the constituents of soil—air, humus, mineral salts, water, bacteria, rock particles), and "Kids prefer cheese over fried green spinach" (for the zoological classifications in descending order—kingdom, phylum, class, order, family, genus, species). Incidentally, if you'd like to remember how to spell *mnemonics*, you might remember that "Mnemonics neatly eliminate man's only nemesis, insufficient cerebral storage."

Acronyms are similar to acrostic sentences, except that they use single words rather than sentences. If students have difficulty remembering when to use *affect* versus *effect*, they will probably benefit from the acronym RAVEN, which stands for "Remember *affect* (is a) verb, *effect* (is a) noun." The name McHale will help students remember the forms of energy: mechanical, chemical, heat, atomic, light, and electrical. An acronym for the names of the great lakes is HOMES: Huron, Ontario, Michigan, Erie, and Superior.

Many mnemonics take the form of rhymes and phrases. The best-known rhymes are probably "*I* before *E* except after *C*, or when rhyming with *A*, as in *neighbor* and *weigh*" and "Thirty days hath September, April, June, and November." Many elementary teachers use the rhyme "When two vowels go walking, the first one does the talking" to help students remember when a vowel is not pronounced. Many chemistry students are familiar with the rhyme "May her rest be long and placid; she added water to acid. The other girl did what she oughta; she added acid to water." Reading Roman numerals is easier if you learn the rhyme "X shall stand for playmates ten; V for five stalwart men; I for one as I'm alive; C for a hundred, D for five (hundred); M for a thousand soldiers true; and L for fifty, I'll tell you."

Mnemonic phrases are used primarily for assistance in remembering which spelling to use for homonyms or other words that are easily confused. To recall, for example, when to use *principle* versus *principal*, students are typically taught to remember that "the principal is your pal." Other phrases help with words often misused or misspelled, such as "Dessert is bigger in the middle, just like you'll be if you eat too much of it," "Miss Pell never misspells," "Stationery goes in envelopes," or "There's a rat in separate."

When you recall how powerful visuals are for storing and recalling information, it isn't surprising that they play a role in many mnemonic strategies. *Keyword mnemonics* make up one of the few mnemonic strategies that have been the subject of numerous research studies. The use of keywords involves associating two items through mental imagery and is often employed in the study of new vocabulary. For example, suppose you are taking a class in Spanish and need to memorize a vocabulary list for the next class. You could say the words over and over (rote rehearsal), hoping that they eventually "stick" in your brain; or perhaps you might make flash cards with the Spanish word on one side and its English equivalent on the other, and use them to try to remember the meanings. If you had learned how to use keyword mnemonics, however, you would

When you recall how powerful visuals are for storing and recalling information, it isn't surprising that they play a role in many mnemonic strategies.

take each Spanish word and select a concrete noun in English that sounds like that word. For the word *carta* (letter), you might imagine a large grocery cart and picture a giant letter in the cart; or for the word *pato* (duck), you could picture a duck with a pot on its head.

Research on the keyword method produced impressive results. Using this strategy, 6th graders recalled twice as many foreign words as children of comparable age and ability who were left to learn the words by different strategies. Further research found that the keyword mnemonic strategy was successful when extended to other areas, such as abstract prose. When the investigators tested students after a period of time, they maintained their gains, suggesting that keyword mnemonic strategies have a lasting effect (Joyce & Showers, 1988; Pressley & Levin, 1978).

Loci mnemonics also use links or associations to create memory hooks, but rather than linking a word to an image, this strategy links words to physical locations that are already firmly established in memory. Cicero and other orators of the classical era used this method to remember the content and order of their speeches. In loci mnemonics, you take a mental walk through a familiar place, such as your house, and visualize the items to be remembered in various locations in your house. As with all imagery, it helps to make the images vivid by exaggerating their size, making them animated, or changing their color. When you need to recall the list, you take another walk through the house and "see" the items in the order you placed them.

Narrative chaining is closely related to loci mnemonics and involves weaving items to be remembered into a story framework. As an example, students in a civics class create a narrative to help them remember the freedoms listed in the Bill of Rights (the freedoms of religion, speech, the press, assembly, and the right to bear arms):

A large group of people marches through a town and eventually assembles in front of a large cathedral. They string cables, set up microphones, and begin giving speeches about their right to have guns to protect themselves. Many members of the press arrive and begin taking photographs and videotaping interviews with members of the group.

The narrative-chaining method has been shown to be far superior to ordinary rote memorization in which subjects try to remember without aids. Researchers Joseph Bower and Gilbert Clark instructed subjects to learn 12 different lists of 10 unrelated words. Some subjects made up a story linking together the words in each list. Students in the control group studied the words without the aid of this technique. Students who used the narrative-chaining mnemonic strategy later recalled more than 90 percent of the 120 words, whereas the control group remembered only 13 percent (McGee & Wilson, 1984).

Teaching Mnemonic Strategies

Research indicates that student performance on memory tasks is related to age. Immature learners (including children with mental and learning disabilities) are most likely to have problems with memory tasks and, therefore, a greater risk of experiencing learning difficulties (Pressley & Levin, 1987). Throughout the elementary school years, students progressively perform better on memory tests, but they do not spontaneously produce memory strategies at times when such strategies would be useful. Around 5th grade, though, students begin to demonstrate a more efficient use of memory strategies (Moely, Olson, Halwes, & Flavell, 1969).

Robert Kail has also shown that higher-achieving students of all ages are more likely to invent effective learning strategies on their own, whereas lower-achieving students or students with learning disabilities are less likely to do so (1984). Immature students, however, and those who generally are not successful learners, can be taught to use efficient strategies through demonstration and numerous

Research indicates that student performance on memory tasks is related to age.

opportunities to practice. Even a common memory technique, such as repeating information, is probably learned by example rather than developed spontaneously. Where do children learn these skills? Evidence indicates that the classroom plays an important role (Moely et al., 1969). Teachers can help students understand how their memories work, demonstrate various mnemonic devices, and provide prompts for when to use these strategies. When students know appropriate strategies and how to use them, they are much more likely to make "informed" judgments about when to use them.

Active Rehearsal Strategies for Long-Term Retention

The discussion of working memory in Chapter 9 distinguished between rote and elaborative rehearsal. We saw that rote rehearsal is a productive method for acquiring certain skills or procedures and for attaining automaticity in them. For example, to become proficient at touch typing or throwing a softball, you have to practice the skills over and over. For semantic information, though, rote rehearsal is not efficient, and elaborative rehearsal is much more effective. Preceding chapters presented many elaborative rehearsal strategies that work well for encoding and retrieving the enormous amount of information we teach in school. You may have noticed that all these strategies actively involve the learner. This chapter examines additional strategies that allow students to actively process information.

Peer Teaching

There is a lot of truth in the saying "The best way to learn something is to teach it."

There is a lot of truth in the saying "The best way to learn something is to teach it." Teaching a concept or skill to someone else requires a fairly high level of understanding. Too often, we check for students' understanding by asking them if they understand or if they have any questions. Though this might work in some situations, students often think they understand when they don't, or they are hesitant to admit that they don't understand something. Instead of asking these questions, a better method might be for students to select partners and decide which of them will be "A" and which will be "B." After teaching a portion of the lesson, the teacher asks "A" to pretend that "B" was out of the room for the last few minutes and missed the instruction. "A" now has the job of teaching "B" the information that was just covered. Later in the lesson, the roles are reversed. While the students teach each other, the teacher carefully monitors their explanations for accuracy.

Peer teaching accomplishes several objectives. First, it allows students an opportunity to rehearse what they have learned, thus strengthening their neural pathways. Students are also likely to pay more attention to the lesson if they know they'll be required to share the information. This approach also teaches mental organization; when "A" takes his or her turn to teach "B," it provides an opportunity to discover what he or she really understands and what is still unclear. Finally, peer teaching provides valuable diagnostic information for the teacher, who finds out how well students comprehend the material and what misconceptions they may have formed. It is much better to discover these misconceptions while you are teaching rather than wait until a test to uncover them.

Peer teaching can be structured in various ways. Students can write a short summary or sketch a quick web of what they've learned before teaching each other; the teacher can instruct students to reflect on what they've learned for one minute before engaging in teaching (often called "Think, Pair, Share"); or student pairs can teach other pairs.

A secondary science teacher uses a modification of peer teaching that he calls "Double Check." He pairs students and gives them three to five minutes to accomplish two tasks. First, each student silently reads a paragraph in the text; then, with the book closed, he or she verbally summarizes the information while the partner checks the text for content accuracy. The partners take turns generating and answering questions.

Active Review

Although a review of previously learned material is essential, it can be boring and unproductive, especially if the teacher takes full responsibility for the review. (Remember that the person doing the work is the one growing the dendrites.) Involving students in the process can increase the effectiveness of the review and is motivating and fun for students as well. After the first six weeks of school, a geometry teacher schedules reviews once a week throughout the school year. She does not conduct the reviews, however—her students do. The students are assigned a date, but they may choose any previous content they wish to review for the class. They complete a form indicating what content they have chosen, why they chose it, and what materials or props they will use. They also write a one-page description of their topic and objectives for approval. The teacher says that her students choose an amazing variety of presentation structures, from puppet shows to cartoons, quizzes, and mini-dramas. Best of all, she reports that her students' interest in and understanding of geometry have increased tremendously.

Games can provide an active, motivating way for students to review what they've learned, but their effectiveness is enhanced if students participate in the design or construction of the game. One 6th grade teacher instructs student teams to design a game to review a social studies unit. They brainstorm qualities of a good game, develop a rubric from their brainstorming, and then create the games. Some teams construct board games, others design game shows. One day is set aside as "Review Day," and teams rotate through each game, providing multiple opportunities for rehearsal of the material.

Vocabulary review is more fun when the meanings of words are tested in a game format. One teacher uses a Pictionary-type game in which students draw pictures to represent words and the other students try to determine the word and its meaning. Another class reviews vocabulary words for an upcoming test by acting them out in teams.

The person doing the work is the one growing the dendrites.

Hands-On Learning Activities

Would you rather go on a cruise to Hawaii or see slides of someone else's trip there? This may sound like a silly question, but we have traditionally structured our students' learning by "showing them slides." We place students at desks, admonish them to be quiet, and limit their study of the curriculum to reading or hearing rather than experiencing. Aristotle supposedly said, "What we have to learn to do, we learn by doing." Concrete experience is one of the best ways to make strong, long-lasting neural connections. These experiences engage more of the senses, and they use multiple pathways to store—and therefore recall—information. This is probably why we remember what we experience much better than what we hear or read. True, it is not possible for students to experience everything we want them to learn, but we invariably miss many opportunities to engage students in more authentic learning.

In selecting or designing hands-on activities, it is important to emphasize that the purpose of these activities is to enhance learning within a rigorous, relevant curriculum. We may be tempted to read or hear about an activity that sounds like a lot of fun and to "insert" it into the day's agenda to add interest or motivation, but, while you might be able to justify the activity as helping students follow directions or work cooperatively in a group, the activity should serve a broader purpose. Remember that hands-on activities are extremely valuable as long as they are also "minds-on."

Lower Elementary School. A study of birds and how they reproduce is enhanced by hatching chicken or duck eggs in an incubator. Additional information that will help young children learn includes time lines for development, required nutrients (both for the unborn bird and after hatching), and how to care for baby birds after they hatch. A follow-up unit could include how human activities affect birds. The activity mentioned in Chapter 11 about the effect of oil spills on birds would fit well with this unit. Students in the early grades can gain a

Hands-on activities are extremely valuable as long as they are also "minds-on."

better understanding of money when the teacher has them "build" a grocery store in the classroom, bring in empty food containers to stock the store, and buy and sell the grocery items using play money. Growing plants from seeds is another favorite activity used by many elementary teachers to teach the growing cycle to young children.

Upper Elementary School. To begin a unit on fractions, students can peel and section an orange, count the sections, and discuss the parts (fractions) of the whole. In a study of the human body, students are much more likely to understand the functions of the heart if they are shown how to measure their pulse while resting and then after running in place. A stethoscope and blood-pressure cuff can be used to further extend the learning. Partially inflating a balloon and squeezing the air from one end of the balloon to the other will help students understand the pressure of air in their lungs and introduce them to Boyle's Law (decreasing a gas's volume increases its pressure).

Middle School. Well-structured, hands-on activities are ideal for high-energy adolescents. These students generally love activities that contain an element of surprise and that engage them in physical activity. For example, in a unit on measurement, students will be fascinated to discover that they are all approximately six "feet" tall (if they use their own feet as the measure). They can prove this by marking their heights on the wall and then measuring this height with tracings of their feet. They can also construct graphs and determine averages as part of this activity.

Many of today's classrooms include students from various backgrounds and cultures. To increase cultural understanding, students can create bags of artifacts that represent elements of their culture. They can then present their "culture sacks" to the class, explaining the significance of the items they contain.

Students will long remember the process of osmosis, which is vital to maintain the water balance of living cells, if they use an egg with a dissolved shell as a model for a living cell membrane. They weigh two fresh eggs and then remove the shells by soaking the eggs overnight in vinegar. Students then place one egg into corn syrup and the other into distilled water for another 24 hours. On the third day, the difference in size, shape, and weight of the two eggs due to loss or uptake of water through the outer membrane (osmosis) is striking and unforgettable. Seeing is believing and understanding.

Secondary School. The concept of forces on structures is made clearer by a classic science activity that has many variations. Students are challenged to build the strongest structures they can with simple materials such as plastic straws, cellophane tape, and popsicle sticks. It is important for students to record the building process they used, what principles they discovered, and how these principles apply equally to real structures. In the same vein, teachers can challenge students to build a brick wall with wooden blocks that is strong enough to withstand a moderate earthquake. Teams of students brainstorm an appropriate design, draw the pattern, build a segment of the wall, and then compare their designs to other teams', noting the number of bricks needed, which walls are most likely to withstand the earthquake, etc.

Many physics teachers believe that their subject is best learned through hands-on activities. In these classrooms, you typically see mini-lectures combined with groups of students involved in activities such as measuring density with self-built hydrometers or testing basic physics concepts of force and friction with small cars on an intricate model of tracks.

Hands-on activities generate energy and enthusiasm about a subject by getting students to interact with and learn from one another. These activities require careful planning, organization, resources, and often a good deal of creativity, but teachers report that the payoff for student learning is well worth it.

Conclusion

We've now reached the end of our journey through the brain, but it might be more accurate to say that we've just begun a much larger

Hands-on activities generate enthusiasm and energy about a subject by getting students to interact with and learn from one another.

journey. During the past three decades, we've learned more about the brain than in all of recorded history, but there is much more to learn. As exciting as new developments in neuroscience are, the dialogue that has begun among neuroscientists, cognitive scientists, and educators is even more exciting. For the first time, we're seeing substantive conversations between those who are conducting the research and educators who are looking for applications of that research. Our challenge is to continue to read, study, and become informed consumers. Information about the brain and how it learns is not merely interesting, it's an essential element in the foundation on which we should base our educational decisions. The brain matters because our children matter.

Synapse Strengtheners

1. Select one of the writing activities to use with your students. Keep a written record that contains a description of the activity, students' reactions, problems encountered, and your assessment of its effectiveness.

2. Prepare a short presentation, to be given at a faculty meeting, explaining what mnemonics are, why they work, and when it would be appropriate to use them. Schedule a follow-up session for teachers to share mnemonics they or their students have created.

3. If your study group has started a booklet of brain-compatible strategies, add examples of writing activities, mnemonics, and other active learning strategies.

14

A Final Note on Brain-Compatible Teaching and Learning

Now that you've finished reading (or skimming) this book, you may be asking yourself, "What do I do tomorrow in my classroom? What does a brain-compatible classroom really look like? Am I already including brain-compatible aspects as I teach and just not aware of them?" To hopefully answer some of these questions, I'm including a final brief chapter to summarize what I feel are the major components of brain-compatible instruction. As you create your day-to-day plans for implementing the curriculum, here are some things to remember. Brain-compatible instruction

- **Provides as much experiential learning as possible.** Remember that we generally learn best from concrete experiences. The more "real-life" problems you give students to solve, the more hands-on activities in which they are involved, and the more modalities involved in the learning, the more likely the information is to be understood, retained, and used in the world outside of school.
- **Builds on prior knowledge.** The brain seeks meaningful patterns. Every new experience causes the brain to search through its existing networks to find a connection. Find out

what students have already experienced in order to tie new learning to what your students already know and understand.

- **Requires the use of appropriate rehearsal strategies.** Before you begin to determine how to have students rehearse, determine whether the information fits into the procedural or declarative memory categories. Remember that simply repeating something over and over (rote rehearsal) works very well to get a habit or a skill (procedural memory) to the point of automaticity but is not the best method for learning spelling words, vocabulary definitions, or concepts (declarative memory). For these, you need elaborative rehearsal strategies in which you elaborate on the information to create meaning.

- **Needs to provide many opportunities for students to revisit information over time.** Recall that information is not "fixed" the moment it is processed. It takes time to become consolidated in long-term memory. Learning occurs best when new information is incorporated gradually rather than being jammed in all at one time. Consolidation (retention) is enhanced by spaced intervals of practice.

- **Emphasizes concepts over individual facts.** Information bombards students at an overwhelming rate in today's world, and the facts are changing rapidly. Knowledge of facts is not necessarily an indication of a well-educated person. Concepts that generalize from one era to the next might be called enduring knowledge—that which was true yesterday, is true today, and will be true tomorrow. Only when we teach information within the context of larger concepts does it become enduring knowledge that can be used throughout the course of our students' lives.

- **Assists students in understanding information and when and how that information is used in the "real world."** Students often do well on tests by memorizing information they do not understand. In all probability, though, they will not be able to use that information when they leave the classroom after the test. Whenever possible, give students real-life problems to solve that use the concepts and skills they are learning.

- **Takes place in a safe psychological environment.** Under perceived threat, the brain does not operate well. Higher-level, rational thinking takes a back seat when the emotional center of the brain is in control. Try to plan lessons that are rigorous but nonthreatening to obtain the best effort and thinking of all students.

- **Takes advantage of the fact that emotional events are remembered longer.** In a sense, emotion is a double-edged sword. Whereas perceived threats impede learning, classroom events and activities that have a positive emotional component enhance learning and retention. Many elaborative rehearsal strategies (e.g., simulations, music, hands-on activities, storytelling) can be categorized as positive emotional experiences.

Glossary

Acetylcholine: A neurotransmitter found in the brain, spinal cord, neuromuscular junction, and autonomic nervous system.

Action Potential: The nerve impulse that is conducted down the axon to transmit information to other neurons.

Adrenalin: A neurotransmitter synthesized from norepinephrin, also called *epinephrin.*

Agnosia: Loss of the ability to name or interpret what is seen.

Agonist: A drug that activates a particular receptor; the opposite of *antagonist.*

Agraphia: Loss or lessened ability to write.

Alexia: The inability to recognize and name written words.

Amygdala: A nucleus of cells located at the base of the temporal lobe (in the basal ganglia) believed to be the source of emotions and emotional memory.

Anomia: The inability to verbalize the names of people, objects, and places.

Anosognosia: The denial of loss of a capacity, such as the denial of paralysis after a stroke.

Antagonist: A drug that blocks a particular receptor; the opposite of *agonist.*

Aphasia: The loss or lessened ability to produce speech.

Apraxia: The inability to make purposeful movements despite normal muscles and coordination.

Astrocytes: Glial cells involved in nutritive support for neurons; also called *astroglia.*

Autism: A condition usually appearing in early childhood and characterized by abnormal social interaction, resistance to physical or eye contact, and lack of communication.

Autonomic Nervous System: Located outside the brain and spinal cord; obtains information from internal organs and provides output to them.

Axon: A long fiber that emerges from a neuron and carries nerve impulses to other neurons.

Axon Terminal: The ending of an axon branch that connects to the neural target; also called the *terminal bouton* or the *presynaptic terminal.*

Blood–Brain Barrier (BBB): A filtering system of glial cells that keeps many substances out of the brain.

Brainstem: A structure just above the spinal cord that allows the brain to communicate with the spinal cord and peripheral nerves and controls; also responsible for other functions, respiration, and heartbeat.

Broca's Area: The central region for the production of speech, typically located in the brain's left hemisphere.

Carotid Artery: Any of the four main arteries located in the neck and head that supply the brain with blood.

Central Nervous System (CNS): The collective term for the brain and spinal cord, which receives information from the body's sensory organs and triggers appropriate motor responses.

Cerebellum: A two-lobed structure overlying the top of the brainstem that helps control coordination, balance, and some aspects of motor learning.

Cerebral Cortex: The deeply folded outer layer of the cerebral hemispheres (the "gray matter") that is responsible for perception, awareness of emotion, planning, and conscious thought; also called the *neocortex.*

Cerebrospinal Fluid (CSF): A clear fluid found in the brain's ventricles, the protective covering (meninges) of the brain, and the spinal cord.

Computerized Axial Tomography (CAT): A technique that uses a computer and X-rays to produce a cross-sectional picture of tissue.

Consolidation: The process by which memories are moved from temporary storage in the hippocampus to more permanent storage in the cortex.

Corpus Callosum: A large bundle of myelinated axons that connects the left and right cerebral hemispheres.

Cortisol: A steroid hormone that mobilizes energy stores, suppresses the immune system, and has direct actions on some central nervous system neurons.

Dendrite: The branched extension from the cell body that receives information from other neurons.

Dendritic Spine: Small extensions on dendrites that are often the site of a synapse.

Dopamine: A neurotransmitter found in many areas of the brain that has multiple functions depending on where it acts. It is important for movement and thought to regulate emotional responses.

Electroconvulsive Therapy (ECT): An electric shock applied to the brain to induce seizures; used in some cases of severe depression.

Electroencephalogram (EEG): A recorded tracing of electrical brain activity (brain waves) obtained through electrodes placed on the skull.

Endorphins: Neurotransmitters (opioid peptides) produced in the brain that generate cellular and behavioral effects like those of morphine.

Epinephrine: A neurotransmitter synthesized from norepinephrine and acting with it to activate the autonomic nervous system; also called *adrenalin.*

Fetal Alcohol Syndrome (FAS): A condition in which a pregnant woman's consumption of alcohol produces a range of physical and mental characteristics in the developing fetus.

Frontal Lobe: One of the four major divisions in each hemisphere of the cerebral cortex; located in the most anterior (front) part of the brain and responsible for higher-level cognition.

Functional Magnetic Resonance Imaging (fMRI): A technique for imaging brain structure and activity by measuring oxygen use in the brain.

Gamma-Amino Butyric Acid (GABA): A neurotransmitter synthesized from glutamate, whose primary function is to inhibit the firing of neurons.

Glial Cell (Neuroglia): The most common cell in the nervous system. It plays various roles in support and protection of neurons.

Glutamate: A neurotransmitter that acts primarily to excite neurons.

Habituation: A process by which a nerve cell adapts to an initially novel stimulus and decreases behavioral responses to repeated stimulation.

Hebb Synapse: A synapse that increases in strength when both the presynaptic and postsynaptic neurons are active at the same time.

Hippocampus: A structure near the center of the brain deep within the temporal lobe in each hemisphere that plays an important role in declarative memory storage and retrieval.

Homeostasis: The balanced functioning of physiological processes and maintenance of the body's constant internal environment.

Hypothalamus: A structure near the center of the brain in each hemisphere that controls body temperature, heart rate, hunger, thirst, sex drive, aggressive behavior, and pleasure and is responsible for responses to the stress response.

Ion: A charged atom, the most common of which in the brain are sodium, potassium, calcium, and chloride.

Ion Channel: A protein that lies in the cell membrane and allows ions to pass from one side of the membrane to the other.

Limbic System: An older term referring to a group of brain structures that regulate emotions.

Long-Term Potentiation (LTP): A persistent strengthening of synaptic strength that occurs with repeated activation of the synapse and may be the analog of the Hebb synapse.

Magnetic Resonance Imaging (MRI): A technique for imaging soft tissue in the brain, using magnets and radio waves.

Medial Temporal Lobe (MTL): An area of the brain that houses the hippocampus and is critical to the formation of memory.

Mitochondria: Small organelles inside the cell body that provide energy for the cell by converting sugar and oxygen into special energy molecules.

Motor Cortex: The lateral part of the frontal lobes that extends from ear to ear across the roof of the brain. It governs movement.

Myelin: A sheath of fatty tissue that forms an insulating cover around some axons. It permits faster conduction of the action potential. The layer is formed by Schwann cells in the peripheral nervous system and oligodendrocytes in the central nervous system.

Neuron: The principal information-carrying cellular unit of the nervous system generally consisting of a cell body (soma), dendrites, and an axon.

Neuropeptides: Peptides (short sequences of amino acids) that serve as neurotransmitters.

Neurotransmitter: A chemical released by neurons that crosses the synapse and allows communication between neurons.

Norepinephrine: A neurotransmitter synthesized from dopamine. It is involved in arousal, reward, and regulation of mood; also known as *noradrenalin*.

Nucleus Accumbens: A structure in the middle of the brain that has a large number of dopamine receptors and is central to the reward system pathway.

Occipital Lobe: One of the four major divisions in each hemisphere of the cerebral cortex; located in the back of the brain and responsible for the processing of visual stimuli.

Oligodendrocyte: A glial cell that provides myelin in the central nervous system.

Parietal Lobe: One of the four major divisions in each hemisphere of the cerebral cortex; located in the upper back part of the brain (between the occipital and frontal lobes), with responsibility for sensory integration.

Peripheral Nervous System (PNS): Located outside the brain and spinal cord, it carries information from the body to the CNS and provides motor output to the muscles that allow the body to move. It includes the autonomic nervous system (ANS).

Pineal Gland: An endocrine organ in the center of the brain responsible for secreting the hormone melatonin, which is responsible for regulating circadian rhythms.

Plasticity: Changes in neural connectivity.

Positron Emission Tomography (PET): A technique for imaging physiological activity in the brain, using radioactive dyes injected into the bloodstream.

Postsynaptic Neuron: The neuron that receives neurotransmitters released by the presynaptic neuron.

Presynaptic Neuron: The neuron that releases neurotransmitters into the synapse.

Prosopagnosia: A neurological condition in which specific faces can't be recognized.

Rapid Eye Movement (REM) Sleep: A type of sleep characterized by decreased muscle tone and an increase in rapid eye movement, electrical activity, and deep dreaming.

Receptor: A site on a cell membrane where a neurotransmitter can bind. Most receptors are highly selective and will only bind with a particular neurotransmitter.

Reticular Activating System (RAS): A system of nerve pathways in the brainstem concerned with levels of arousal from hypervigilance to drowsiness.

Reuptake: A process by which released neurotransmitters are absorbed for subsequent reuse.

Serotonin: A neurotransmitter believed to play a role in temperature regulation, sensory perception, mood, and sleep. A number of antidepressant drugs target the brain's serotonin systems.

Somatosensory Cortex: A part of the cortex just behind the motor cortex that receives information through the sensory organs.

Spinal Cord: A large bundle of fibers in the CNS (beginning at the base of the brainstem and continuing down to the tailbone) that serves motor and sensory functions.

Stimulus: A maneuver that can activate a sensory receptor.

Synapse: The physical structure that makes an electrochemical connection between a sending (presynaptic) neuron and a receiving (postsynaptic) neuron.

Synaptic Cleft: The gap separating two neurons at a synapse.

Temporal Lobe: One of the four major divisions in each hemisphere of the cerebral cortex; located in the lower part of the brain near the ears and responsible for auditory processing and some aspects of memory.

Terminal: The end of an axon branch.

Thalamus: A large collection of cells that relays all sensory information (except smell) to the appropriate part of the cortex for processing.

Ventricles: Four fluid-filled (cerebrospinal fluid) cavities in the brain.

Vesicle: A membrane-enclosed structure (organelle) containing neurotransmitters and found in the axon terminal.

Wernicke's Area: The language center responsible for the syntax and comprehension of speech (typically in the left hemisphere).

References

Aamodt, S., & Wang, S. (2008). *Welcome to your brain*. New York: Bloomsbury USA.

Ackerman, S. (1992). *Discovering the brain*. Washington, DC: National Academy Press.

Amaral, D. (2000, May 6). Memory and the brain: The hippocampus at work [Speech]. At the Spring 2000 Symposium on Brain Research: Implications for Teaching and Learning, San Diego, CA.

Amaral, D., & Soltesz, I. (1997). Hippocampal formation. In *Encyclopedia of human biology* (2nd ed.; Vol. 4, pp. 565–573). New York: Academic Press.

Anderson, C. (2004). An update on the effects of playing violent video games. *Journal of Adolescence, 27*(1), 113–122.

Atkinson, R., & Raugh, M. R. (1975). An application of the mnemonic keyword method to the acquisition of a Russian vocabulary. *Journal of Experimental Psychology (Human Learning and Memory), 104*(2), 126–133.

Azer, S. (2008). *Navigating problem-based learning*. Sydney, Australia: Elsevier Press.

Bahrick, H. P., Bahrick, P. O., & Wittlinger, R. P. (1976). Fifty years of memory for names and faces: A cross-sectional approach. *Journal of Experimental Psychology (General), 104*(1), 54–75.

Bear, M. F., Conners, B. W., & Paradiso, M. A. (1996). *Neuroscience: Exploring the brain*. New York: Lippincott, Williams & Wilkins.

Begley, S. (2008, October). Why we believe. *Newsweek*. Available: http://www.newsweek.com/id/165678

Berger, R. J., Berger, B. A., & Oswald, I. (1962). Effects of sleep deprivation on behaviour, subsequent sleep, and dreaming. *Journal of Mental Science, 108,* 457–465.

Binney, R., & Janson, M. (Eds.). (1990). *Atlas of the mind and body*. London: Mitchell Beazley Publishers.

Blood, A. J., Aztorre, R. J., Bermudez, T., & Evans, A. C. (1999). Emotional responses to pleasant and unpleasant music correlate with activity in para-limbic brain regions. *Nature Neuroscience, 2,* 382–387.

Bloom, B. (1986). Automaticity, the hands and feet of genius. *Educational Leadership, 43*(5), 70–77.

Borne, R. (1994). *Serotonin: The neurotransmitter for the 90s* [Online article]. Available: http://www.ouch-us.org/chgeneral/seratonin/serotonin3.htm

Brandt, R. (1998). *Powerful learning*. Alexandria, VA: ASCD.

Brashers-Krug, T., Shadmehr, R., & Bizzi, E. (1996). Consolidation in human motor memory. *Nature, 382*(6588), 252–255.

Bremner, J. D. (2002). *Does stress damage the brain?* New York: W. W. Norton.

Brown, S. A., Tapert, S. F., Granholm, E., & Delis, D. (2000, February). Neurocognitive functioning of adolescents: Effects of protracted alcohol use. *Clinical and Experimental Research, 24*(2), 164–171.

Buck Institute of Education. (2010). *What is project based learning?* Available: http://www.bie.org/index.php/site/PBL/pbl_handbook_introduction

Bull, B. L., & Wittrock, M. C. (1973). Imagery in the learning of verbal definitions. *British Journal of Educational Psychology, 43,* 289–293.

Burchers, S. (1997). *Vocabutoons: Vocabulary cartoons.* Punta Gorda, FL: New Monic Books.

Bush, R. (2009, July 30). Rates of childhood obesity have tripled. *Medical News Today.* Available: http://www.medicalnewstoday.com/articles/159334.php

Cahill, L. (2000, January 19). *Emotions and memory* [Speech]. At the Learning Brain Expo, San Diego, CA.

Callicott, J. H., Mattay, V. S., Bertolino, A., Finn, K., Coppola, R., Frank, J. A., Goldberg, T. E., & Weinberger, D. R. (1999). Physiological characteristics of capacity constraints in working memory as revealed by functional MRI. *Cerebral Cortex, 9*(1), 20–26.

Cameron, H. A., Woolley, C. S., McEwen, B. S., & Gould, E. (1993). Differentiation of newly born neurons and glia in the dentate gyrus of the adult rat. *Neuroscience, 56*(2), 337–344.

Carskadon, M. (1999). When worlds collide: Adolescent need for sleep versus societal demands. In K. Wahlstom (Ed.), *Adolescent sleep needs and school starting times.* Phi Delta Kappa Educational Foundation.

Carskadon, M. A. (Ed.). (2002). *Adolescent sleep patterns: Biological, social, and psychological influences.* Cambridge, UK: Cambridge University Press.

Carter, R. (1998). *Mapping the mind.* Los Angeles: University of California Press.

Castelli, D. M., Hillman, C. H., Buck, S. M., & Erwin, H. (2007). Physical fitness and academic achievement in third- and fifth-grade students. *Journal of Sport and Exercise Psychology, 29*(2), 239–252.

Center for Problem-Based Learning. (2001). *About the Center for Problem-Based Learning.* Illinois Mathematics and Science Academy. Available: http://pbln.imsa.edu

Central Queensland University. (2002). *Problem based learning online resources.* Available: http://pbl.cqu.edu.au/content/online_resources.htm

Chase, W., & Simon, H. (1973). Perception in chess. *Cognitive Psychology, 4,* 55–81.

Cherry, E. C. (1953). Some experiments on the recognition of speech, with one and two ears. *Journal of the Acoustical Society of America, 25*(5), 975–979.

Chudler, E. (2001). *Neuroscience for kids* [Online resource]. Available: http://faculty.washington.edu/chudler/neurok.html

Chugani, H. (1998). A critical period of brain development: Studies of cerebral glucose utilization with PET. *Preventive Medicine, 27*(2), 184–188.

Countryman, J. (1992). *Writing to learn mathematics: Strategies that work, K–12.* Portsmouth, NH: Heinemann Educational Books.

Cowan, W. M. (1979). The development of the brain. *Scientific American, 241*(3), 106–117.

Cozolino, L. (2008). *The healthy aging brain: Sustaining attachment, attaining wisdom.* New York: W. W. Norton & Company.

Crick, F. (1994). *The astonishing hypothesis: The scientific search for the soul.* New York: Scribner.

Damasio, A. (1994). *Descartes' error: Emotion, reason, and the human brain.* New York: G. P. Putnam's Sons.

Davis, J. (1997). *Mapping the mind: The secrets of the human brain and how it works.* Secaucus, NJ: Carol Publishing Group.

Davis, M. (2008, May 12). PBS revives a show that shines a light on reading. *New York Times.* Available: http://www.nytimes.com/2008/05/12/arts/television/12elec.html?_r=1

De Bellis, M. D., Clark, D. B., Beers, S. R., Soloff, P. H., Boring, A. M., Hall, J., Kersh, A., & Keshavan, M. S. (2000). Hippocampal volume in adolescent-onset alcohol use disorders. *American Journal of Psychiatry, 157*(5), 737–744.

Delisle, R. (1997). *How to use problem-based learning in the classroom.* Alexandria, VA: ASCD.

Dewey, J. (1937). *Experience in education.* New York: Macmillan.

Diamond, M. C. (1988). *Enriching heredity: The impact of the environment on the anatomy of the brain.* New York: Free Press.

Diamond, M., Hopson, J., & Diamond, M. C. (1998). *Magic trees of the mind: How to nurture your child's intelligence, creativity, and healthy emotions from birth through adolescence.* New York: E. P. Dutton.

Dietz, W. H., & Gortmaker, S. L. (1985). Do we fatten our children at the television set? Obesity and television viewing in children and adolescents. *Pediatrics, 75*(5), 807–812.

Eliot, L. (1999). *What's going on in there? How the brain and mind develop in the first five years of life.* New York: Bantam Books.

Erickson, H. L. (2002). *Concept-based curriculum and instruction.* Thousand Oaks, CA: Corwin Press.

Evans, A. (1996). Addressing TV violence in the classroom. *Phi Delta Kappa Research Bulletin, 16,* 1–4.

Fajardo, M., Florido, J., Villaverde, C., Oltras, C., Gonzales-Ramirez, A., & Gonzalez-Gomez, F. (1994). Plasma levels of beta-endorphin and ACTH during labor and immediate puerperium. *European Journal of Obstetrics, Gynecology, and Reproductive Biology, 55*(2), 105–108.

Fischer, K. W., & Immordino-Yang, M. H. (2008). The fundamental importance of the brain and learning for education. In *Jossey-Bass reader on the brain and learning,* pp. 183–198. San Francisco, CA: Jossey-Bass.

Flavell, J., Friedrichs, A., & Hoyt, J. (1970). Developmental changes in memorization processes. *Cognitive Psychology, 1*(4), 324–340.

Gazzaniga, M. (1997). *Conversations in the neurosciences.* Cambridge, MA: Massachusetts Institute of Technology Press.

Gazzaniga, M. (1998). *The mind's past.* Berkeley, CA: University of California Press.

Gazzaniga, M., Bogen, J., & Sperry, R. (1962). Some functional effects of sectioning the cerebral commissures in man. *Proceedings of the National Academy of Sciences of the United States of America, 48*(10), 1765–1769.

Gazzaniga, M., Ivry, R., & Mangun, R. (1998). *Cognitive neuroscience.* New York: W. W. Norton.

Gentile, D. A. (2009, July 23). Video games affect the brain—for better and worse. *The Dana Foundation.* Available: http://www.dana.org/printerfriendly.aspx?id=22800

Gentile, D., Anderson, C., Yukawa, S., Saleem, M., Lim, K., Shibuya, A., Liau, A., Khoo, A., Bushman, B., Huesmann, L., & Sakamoto, A. (2009). The effects of prosocial video games on prosocial behaviors: International evidence from correlational, longitudinal, and experimental studies. *Personality and Social Psychology Bulletin, 35*(6), 752–763.

Gentile, D. A., & Gentile, J. R. (2008). Violent video games as exemplary teachers: A conceptual analysis. *Journal of Youth and Adolescence, 37*(2), 127–141.

Giedd, J. (2007, January). The adolescent [Speech]. At the Brainy Bunch Renewal Conference, Yountville, CA.

Goodlad, J. (1984). *A place called school.* New York: McGraw-Hill.

Goodwyn, S. W., Acredolo, L. P., & Brown, C. A. (2000). Impact of symbolic gesturing on early language development. *Journal of Nonverbal Behavior, 24*(2), 81–103.

Gopnik, A., Meltzoff, A., & Kuhl, P. (1999). *The scientist in the crib: What early learning tells us about the mind.* New York: HarperCollins.

Gould, E., Reeves, A., Graziano, M., & Gross, C. (1999). Neurogenesis in the neocortex of adult primates. *Science, 286*(5439), 548–552.

Grandin, T. (1995). *Thinking in pictures.* New York: Doubleday.

Greenfield, S. A. (1996). *The human mind explained.* New York: Henry Holt.

Greenfield, S. A. (1997). *The human brain: A guided tour.* New York: BasicBooks.

Greenough, W. (2002, January). Enriched environments [Speech]. At the Brainy Bunch Renewal Conference, Yountville, CA.

Gregory, R. (Ed.). (1987). *The Oxford companion to the mind.* New York: Oxford University Press.

Hart, L. (1983). *Human brain, human learning.* New York: Longman.

Healy, J. (1990). *Endangered minds: Why our children don't think.* New York: Simon & Schuster.

Hebb, D. O. (1949). *The organization of behavior: A neuropsychological theory.* New York: Wiley.

Helms, D., & Sawtelle, S. (2007). A study of the effectiveness of cognitive skill therapy delivered in a video-game format. *Optometry & Vision Development, 38*(1), 19–26.

Hilt, P. J. (1995). *Memory's ghost.* New York: Simon & Schuster.

Hobson, J. A. (1989). *Sleep.* New York: Scientific American Library.

Hoetker, K., & Ahlbrand, W. (1964). The persistence of the recitation. *American Educational Research Journal, 6*(2), 145–167.

Hooper, J., & Teresi, D. (1986). *The 3-pound universe.* New York: Dell.

Huber, R., Ghilardi, M., Massimini, M., & Tononi, G. (2004). Local sleep and learning. *Nature, 430*(6995), 78–81.

Hunt, M. (1982). *The universe within: A new science explores the human mind.* New York: Simon & Schuster.

Hunter, M. (1991, January). The new science of teaching and learning [Speech]. At the Brainy Bunch Renewal Conference, Yountville, CA.

Hyerle, D. (2000). *A field guide to using visual tools.* Alexandria, VA: ASCD.

Johnston, L. D., O'Malley, P. M., & Bachman, J. G. (2001). *Monitoring the future: National results on adolescent drug use: 2000, overview of key findings.* Bethesda, MD: National Institute on Drug Abuse.

Joyce, B., & Showers, B. (1988). *Student achievement through staff development.* New York: Longman.

Kail, R. (1984). *The development of memory in children.* New York: W. H. Freeman and Company.

Kain, D. L. (2003). *Problem-based learning for teachers, grades 6–12.* New York: Allyn & Bacon.

Kann, L., Kinchen, S. A., Williams, B. I., Ross, J. G., Lowry, R., Grunbaum, J. A., & Kolbe, L. J. (2000). Youth risk behavior surveillance in the United States, 1999. *Journal of School Health, 70*(7), 271–285.

Kempermann, G., & Gage, F. (1999). New nerve cells for the adult brain. *Scientific American, 280*(6), 48–53.

Kluger, J. (2008). *Simplexity.* New York: Hyperion Press.

Kotulak, R. (1996). *Inside the brain: Revolutionary discoveries of how the mind works.* Kansas City, MO: Andrew McMeel.

Krumhansl, C. L., & Jusczyk, P. W. (1996). Infants' perception of phrase structure in music. *Psychological Science, 1*(1), 70–73.

LeDoux, J. (1996). *The emotional brain.* New York: Simon & Schuster.

LeDoux, J. (2003). *The synaptic self: How our brains become who we are.* New York: Penguin.

Levin, M. E., & Levin, J. R. (1990). Scientific mnemonomies: Methods for maximizing more than memory. *American Educational Research Journal, 27*(2), 301–321.

Levinthal, C. F. (1988). *Messengers of paradise: Opiates and the brain.* New York: Anchor Press/Doubleday.

Lewis, T., Amini, F., & Lannon, R. (2001). *A general theory of love.* New York: Vintage Books.

LiveScience. (2009, August 25). Obese people have "severe brain degeneration" [Online article]. Available: http://www.livescience.com/health/090825-obese-brain.html

Loftus, G. R., & Loftus, E. F. (1975). *Human memory: The processing of information.* New York: Halsted Press.

Maquet, P. (2001). The role of sleep in learning and memory. *Science, 294*(5544), 1048–1052.

Markwiese, B. J., Acheson, S. K., Levin, E. D., Wilson, W. A., & Swartzwelder, H. S. (1998). Differential effects of ethanol on memory in adolescent and adult rats. *Alcoholism: Clinical and Experimental Research, 22*(2), 416–421.

McGaugh, J. L. (2003). *Memory and emotion.* New York: Weidenfield & Nicholson.

McGee, M. G., & Wilson, D. W. (1984). *Psychology: Science and application.* New York: West Publishing Company.

Medina, J. (2008). *Brain rules: 12 principles for surviving and thriving at work, home, and school.* Seattle, WA: Pear Press.

Meyers, F., Sampson, A., Weitzman, M., Rogers, M., & Kayne, H. (1989). School breakfast program and school performance. *American Journal of Diseases of Children, 143*(10), 1234–1239.

Miller, G. A. (1956). The magical number seven, plus or minus two: Some limits on our capacity for processing information. *Psychological Review, 63,* 81–97.

Miller, S., Merzenich, M. M., Saunders, G. H., Jenkins, W. M., & Tallal, P. (1997). Improvements in language abilities with training of children with both attentional and language impairments. *Society for Neuroscience, 23,* 490.

Moely, B. E., Olson, F. A., Halwes, T. G., & Flavell, J. H. (1969). Production deficiency in young children's clustered recall. *Developmental Psychology, 1*(1), 26–34.

Moyers, B. (1993). *Healing and the mind.* New York: Doubleday.

National Research Council. (1999). *How people learn: Brain, mind, experience, and school.* Washington, DC: National Academy Press.

Nelson, C. (2006, January). The impact of the environment on brain development [Speech]. At the Brainy Bunch Renewal Conference, Yountville, CA.

Neville, H. (2008, January). Neuroplasticity [Speech]. At the Brainy Bunch Renewal Conference, Yountville, CA.

OCED/CERI. (2007). *Understanding the brain: The birth of a learning science.* Paris, France: Organization for Economic Co-operation and Development.

Olsen, K. (1995). *Science continuum of concepts for grades K–6.* Kent, WA: Center for the Future of Public Education.

Ornstein, R. (1997). *The right mind.* Orlando, FL: Harcourt Brace.

Ornstein, R. (1998). *Psychology: The study of human experience* (2nd ed.). San Diego, CA: Harcourt Brace Jovanovich.

Pascual-Leon, J. (1970). A maturational model for the transition rule in Piaget's developmental stages. *Acta Psychologica, 32,* 301–345.

Patoine, B. (2007, May 1). Move your feet, grow new neurons?: Exercise-induced neurogenesis shown in humans. *The Dana Foundation.* Available: http://www.dana.org/news/brainwork/detail.aspx?id=7374

Perkins, D. (1992). *Smart schools: From training memories to educating minds.* New York: The Free Press.

Pert, C. (1997). *Molecules of emotion.* New York: Scribner.

Posner, M. I., & Raichle, M. E. (1997). *Images of mind.* New York: Scientific American Library.

Pressley, M., & Levin, J. R. (1978). Developmental constraints associated with children's use of the keyword method of foreign language vocabulary learning. *Journal of Experimental Child Psychology, 26*(2), 359–372.

Pressley, M., & Levin, J. R. (1987). Elaborative learning strategies for the inefficient learner. In S. J. Ceci (Ed.), *Handbook of cognitive, social and neuropsychological aspects of learning disabilities* (Vol. 2, pp. 175–212). Hillsdale, NJ: Erlbaum.

Ratey, J., & Hagerman, E. (2008). *Spark: The revolutionary new science of exercise and the brain.* New York: Little, Brown and Company.

Raugh, M. R., & Atkinson, R. C. (1975). A mnemonic method for learning a second-language vocabulary. *Journal of Educational Psychology, 67*(1), 1–16.

Restak, R. (1994). *Receptors.* New York: Bantam Books.

Rona, R., Li, L., Gulliford, M., & Chinn, S. (1998). Disturbed sleep: Effects of sociocultural factors and illness. *Archives of Disease in Childhood, 78*(1), 20–25.

Sadah, A., Gruber, R., & Rav, A. (2003). The effects of sleep restriction and extension on school-age children: What a difference an hour makes. *Child Development, 74*(2), 444–455.

Sadato, N., Pascual-Leone, A., Grafman, J., Deiber, M. P., Ibanez, V., & Hallett, M. (1998). Neural networks for Braille reading by the blind. *Brain, 121*(7), 1213–1229.

Sapolsky, R. (1994). *Why zebras don't get ulcers.* New York: W. H. Freeman & Company.

Schacter, D. (1996). *Searching for memory: The brain, the mind, and the past.* New York: BasicBooks.

Scheibel, A. (2000, May 6). A journey through the development of the human brain [Speech]. At the Spring 2000 Symposium on Brain Research: Implications for Teaching and Learning, Berkeley, CA.

Shaw, G. (2000). *Keeping Mozart in mind.* San Diego, CA: Academic Press.

Shaywitz, S. (1999). Learning about learning to read: A conversation with Sally Shaywitz. *Educational Leadership, 57*(2), 26–31.

Siegel, D. J. (1999). *The developing mind: Toward a neurobiology of interpersonal experience.* New York: Guilford Press.

Siegel, D. J. (2000, January 18). The developing mind [Speech]. At the Learning Brain Expo, San Diego, CA.

Sirotnik, K. (1983). What you see is what you get: Consistency, persistence, and mediocrity in classrooms. *Harvard Educational Review, 53*(1), 16–31.

Society for Neuroscience. (2003a, March). *Diet and the brain.* Available: http://www.sfn.org/skins/main/pdf/BrainBriefings/BrainBriefings_Mar2003.pdf

Society for Neuroscience. (2003b, April). *Sleep and learning.* Available: http://www.sfn.org/skins/main/pdf/BrainBriefings/BrainBriefings_Apr2003.pdf

Spear, L. P. (2000). The adolescent brain and age-related behavioral manifestations. *Neuroscience and Behavioral Reviews, 24*(4), 417–463.

Squire, L. R., & Kandel, E. R. (2000). *Memory from mind to molecules.* New York: Scientific American Library.

Standing, L. (1973). Learning 10,000 pictures. *Quarterly Journal of Experimental Psychology, 25*(2), 207–222.

Stickgold, R. (2003). Human studies of sleep and off-line memory reprocessing. In T. Maquet, C. Smith, & R. Stickgold (Eds.), *Sleep and Brain Plasticity.* New York: Oxford University Press.

Sylwester, R. (1995). *A celebration of neurons: An educator's guide to the human brain.* Alexandria, VA: ASCD.

Tallal, P. (2000). Experimental studies of language learning impairments: From research to remediation. In D.V.M. Bishop & L. B. Leonard (Eds.), *Speech and language impairments in children: Causes, characteristics, intervention, and outcome.* Hove, UK: Psychology Press.

Teachers' Curriculum Institute. (1999). *History alive! Engaging all learners in the diverse classroom* (2nd ed.). Mountain View, CA: Author.

Thach, W. T. (1996). On the specific role of the cerebellum in motor learning and cognition: Clues from PET activation and lesion studies in man. *Behavioral and Brain Sciences, 19,* 411–431.

Thompson, R. (1985). *The brain: An introduction to neuroscience.* New York: W. H. Freeman.

Torgesen, J. K. (1996). A model of memory from an information processing perspective: The special case of phonological memory. In G. R. Lyon & N. A. Krasnegor (Eds.), *Attention, memory, and executive function* (pp. 157–184). Baltimore, MD: Paul H. Brookes.

Torp, L., & Sage, S. (1998). *Problems as possibilities: Problem-based learning for K–12 education.* Alexandria, VA: ASCD.

Towse, J. N., Hitch, G. J., & Hutton, U. (1998). A reevaluation of working memory capacity in children. *Journal of Memory and Language, 39*(2), 195–217.

Underwood, B. J. (1968). Forgetting. *Scientific American, 5*(228).

Wagner, R. (1996). From simple structure to complex function: Major trends in the development of theories, models, and measurements of memory. In G. R. Lyon & N. A. Krasnegor (Eds.), *Attention, memory, and executive function* (pp. 139–156). Baltimore, MD: Paul H. Brookes.

Walker, M. P., Brakefield, T., Morgan, A., Hobson, J. A., & Stickgold, R. (2002). Practice with sleep makes perfect: Sleep-dependent motor skill learning. *Neuron, 35*(1), 205–211.

Wesnes, K., Pincock., C., Richardson, E., Helm, G., & Hails, S. (2003). Breakfast reduces declines in attention and memory over the morning in schoolchildren. *Appetite, 41*(3), 329–331.

Wolf, M. (2007). *Proust and the squid: The story and science of the reading brain.* New York: HarperCollins.

Wolfson, A. R., & Carskadon, M. A. (1998). Sleep schedules and daytime functioning in adolescents. *Child Development, 69*(4), 875–887.

Zimmerman, F., Christakis, D., & Meltzoff, A. (2007). Associations between media viewing and language development in children under age 2 years. *The Journal of Pediatrics, 151*(4), 364–368.

Index

The letter *f* following a page number denotes a figure, and the letter *g* following a page number denotes a definition found in the glossary.

About the Author

Patricia Wolfe is an independent consultant who speaks to educators and parents in schools across the United States and around the world. Her professional background includes work as a public school teacher at all levels; staff development trainer for the Upland (California) School District; Director of Instruction for the Napa County Office of Education, Napa, California; and lead trainer for the International Principal Training Center in Rome and London. Her staff development experience includes conducting workshops for educators in Madeline Hunter's Elements of Effective Teaching and Clinical Supervision, Anthony Gregorc's Mind Styles, Carolyn Evertson's Classroom Management and Organization, and Peer Coaching. She has been featured in a number of ASCD, National Professional Resources, and National Staff Development Council video productions and satellite broadcasts.

Wolfe's major interest over the past 25 years has centered on the educational implications and applications of current neuroscience, cognitive science, and educational research for teaching and learning. She also conducts workshops on the brain and addiction, reading and the brain, early brain development, and the aging brain. She can be reached at Mind Matters, Inc., 555 Randolph Street, Napa, CA 94559; phone and fax: (707) 226-1777; Web site: www.patwolfe. com; e-mail address: wolfe@napanet.net.

Related ASCD Resources

At the time of publication, the following ASCD resources were available (ASCD stock numbers appear in parentheses). For up-to-date information about ASCD resources, go to www.ascd.org. You can search the complete archives of Educational Leadership at http://www.ascd.org/el.

Print Products
The Brain-Compatible Classroom: Using What We Know About Learning to Improve Teaching by Laura Erlauer (#101269)

Brain Friendly Strategies for the Inclusion Classroom by Judy Willis (#107040)

The Motivated Student: Unlocking the Enthusiasm for Learning by Bob Sullo (#109028)

Multiple Intelligences in the Classroom (3rd Edition) by Thomas Armstrong (#109007)

Teaching to the Brain's Natural Learning Systems by Barbara K. Given (#101075)

Teaching with the Brain in Mind (2nd Edition) by Eric Jensen (#104013)

Videos
Teaching the Adolescent Brain (#606050)

Online Courses
The Brain: Developing Lifelong Learning Habits by Kathy Checkley (#PD090C16)

The Brain: Memory and Learning Strategies by Marcia D'Arcangelo (#PD090C15)

THE WHOLE CHILD The Whole Child Initiative helps schools and communities create learning environments that allow students to be healthy, safe, engaged, supported, and challenged. To learn more about other books and resources that relate to the whole child, visit www.wholechildeducation.org.

For more information: send e-mail to member@ascd.org; call 1-800-933-2723 or 703-578-9600, press 2; send a fax to 703-575-5400; or write to Information Services, ASCD, 1703 N. Beauregard St., Alexandria, VA 22311-1714 USA.